CERTIFICATE IN BOOKKEEPING
(MANUAL)

Institute of Certified Bookkeepers

Level II

British Library Cataloguing-in-Publication Data

A catalogue record for this book is available from the British Library.

Published by:

Kaplan Publishing UK
Unit 2 The Business Centre
Molly Millars Lane
Wokingham
RG41 2QZ

ISBN 978-1-78415-512-4

© Kaplan Financial Limited, 2015

Printed and bound in Great Britain.

CONTENTS

INTRODUCTION

HOW TO USE THESE MATERIALS

These Kaplan Publishing learning materials have been carefully designed to make your learning experience as easy as possible and to give you the best chance of success in your ICB assessments.

They contain a number of features to help you in the study process.

The sections on the Syllabus, the Assessment and Study Skills should be read before you commence your studies.

They are designed to familiarise you with the nature and content of the assessment and to give you tips on how best to approach your studies.

STUDY TEXT

This study text has been specially prepared for the ICB qualification.

It is written in a practical and interactive style:

- key terms and concepts are clearly defined

- all topics are illustrated with practical examples with clearly worked solutions

- frequent activities throughout the chapters ensure that what you have learnt is regularly reinforced

- 'pitfalls' and 'assessment tips' help you avoid commonly made mistakes and help you focus on what is required to perform well in your assessment

- practice workbook activities can be completed at the end of each chapter.

WORKBOOK

The workbook comprises:

Practice activities at the end of each chapter with solutions at the end of the text, to reinforce the work covered in each chapter.

The questions are divided into their relevant chapters and students may either attempt these questions as they work through the textbook, or leave some or all of these until they have completed the textbook as a final revision of what they have studied.

ICONS

The study chapters include the following icons throughout.

They are designed to assist you in your studies by identifying key definitions and the points at which you can test yourself on the knowledge gained.

 Definition

These sections explain important areas of Knowledge which must be understood and reproduced in an assessment.

 Example

The illustrative examples can be used to help develop an understanding of topics before attempting the activity exercises.

 Activity

These are exercises which give the opportunity to assess your understanding of all the assessment areas.

Quality and accuracy are of the utmost importance to us so if you spot an error in any of our products, please send an email to mykaplanreporting@kaplan.com with full details, or follow the link to the feedback form in MyKaplan.

Our Quality Co-ordinator will work with our technical team to verify the error and take action to ensure it is corrected in future editions.

THE SYLLABUS

Purpose of the Level II Certificate in Bookkeeping

The Level II Certificate in Bookkeeping covers the basic principles of single and double entry bookkeeping and its application to business in both a manual and a computerised system.

The ICB has stated that the Level II Certificate in Bookkeeping unit is designed to equip students with the knowledge and skills they need for the role of an assistant bookkeeper under supervision. Students should be able to make postings from the books of prime entry and from source documents to the ledger accounts and produce an initial trial balance.

They will also be able to set up a computerised bookkeeping system, enter details of all transactions and produce reports.

This study text covers all the aspects of manual bookkeeping included in the syllabus.

Computerised Bookkeeping for Level II is covered in a separate study text.

Learning objectives

On completion of the Level II Certificate in Bookkeeping, the student will be able to:

- Understand the following areas of underpinning knowledge:
  - The importance of adhering to a code of professional ethics
  - The differences between the structure of different types of businesses
  - The importance of legislation that applies to bookkeepers
  - The basic elements of a contract
  - The accounting equation
  - The concept of reporting on a cash basis for income tax purposes
  - The concept of business entity, duality and historical cost
- Understand banking procedures including the need for security
- Understand the purpose and range of business documents, and accurately prepare them

- Understand the purpose of, and make entries into, the ledgers and books of prime entry including the use of control accounts
- Understand the process of dealing with and accounting for VAT in the ledgers
- Understand the purpose and use of the two and three-column cash book, the analysed cash book and the petty cash book
- Understand the purpose and use of the trial balance
- Understand when to open a suspense account
- Set up a business in a computerised system
- Process entries into nominal and subsidiary ledger accounts
- Print out reports as follows:
  - Trial balance
  - Audit trail
  - Nominal account transactions
  - Sales and purchase ledger transactions

Learning outcomes and Assessment criteria

The unit consists of eight Learning Outcomes which are further broken down into Assessment criteria.

Learning Outcomes 1 – 7 are covered in this study text and Learning Outcome 8 is covered in the study text for Computerised Bookkeeping at Level II.

Learning Outcomes 1 – 7 and their Assessment criteria are listed below:

Topic 1 – Underpinning knowledge	
Learning outcome	**Assessment criteria**

1.1 Understand the importance of adhering to a code of Professional Ethics	Be able to:
	• explain why each of the following professional values is important to bookkeepers and why they should adhere to a code of ethics
	
	  – Confidentiality
	  – Security of data
	  – Competency
	  – Duty of care
	  – Integrity

1.2	Understand the basic differences between the structures of different types of businesses	Be able to:
		• explain the basic structure and reasons for operating as one of the following types of businesses:
		  – Sole Trader
		  – Partnership
		  – Limited Company
		  – Limited Liability Partnership
		  – Not-for-Profit Organisation
		• understand and explain the basic principles behind the Construction Industry Scheme (CIS)
		  – Understand the duties of a contractor to verify sub-contractors
		  – Explain the criteria under which some sub-contractors are paid gross
		  – Understand the different levels of tax that might be deducted at source from a CIS invoice

1.3	Understand the importance of legislation that applies to bookkeepers	Be able to:
		• understand the basics of current legislation such as:
		  – Money Laundering
		  – Data Protection Act
		  – The Bribery Act
		  – Health and Safety at Work

1.4	Understand the basic elements of a contract	Be able to: • understand the basic elements of a contract (e.g. offer, acceptance and consideration) • given certain circumstances, decide whether a contract exists
1.5	Understand the Accounting Equation	Be able to: • show an understanding of the terms Assets, Liabilities, Capital • state the Accounting Equation • explain how the Accounting Equation relates to a double-entry bookkeeping system

1.6	Understand the concept of reporting on a cash basis for income tax purposes	Be able to: • explain when the use of a cash based system is sufficient for the smallest of businesses to enable them to correctly report income and expenditure for taxation purposes

1.7	Identify the various methods of payments and receipts to and from a bank account	Be able to:
		
		• identify the different types of receipts and payments available through banks and building societies including:
		   – cash
		   – cheques
		   – direct debits
		   – standing orders
		   – BACS
		   – CHAPS
		   – credit and debit cards
		   – Paypal and other online methods

1.8	Understand the need for bank security	Be able to:
		
		• describe the various forms of security that relate to the different forms of payments including:
		   – PIN numbers
		   – online passwords
		   – telephone banking passwords
		   – dual signatures
		   – payment value restriction

1.9	Understand the basic accounting concepts	Be able to
		
		• explain the concepts of:
		   – business entity
		   – duality
		   – historic cost

Topic 2 – Business documents	
Learning outcome	**Assessment criteria**
2.1 Understand the purpose and range of business documents	Be able to: • explain the purpose and flow of documents between seller and buyer for both cash and credit transactions including: – quotation – purchase order – delivery note – invoice – credit note – returns note – remittance note – statement – cash receipts • Understand the importance of source documents • Explain the action to be taken where no source document exists
2.2 Understand the need to accurately prepare business documents for goods supplied	Be able to: • accurately prepare invoices and credit notes including the treatment of VAT and cash discount allowed • ensure that these are correctly authorised • where applicable, ensure that they are correctly coded • prepare statements for despatch to debtors
2.3 Understand the need to check business documents received	Be able to: • check supplier invoices and credit notes with relevant documents • check calculations on supplier invoices and credit notes including treatment of VAT and discount received • correctly code invoices and credit notes • identify and resolve discrepancies • identify when and why authorisation may be required to process such documents

Topic 3 – Ledger accounts and the division of the ledger	
Learning outcome	**Assessment criteria**

3.1 Understand the purpose of, and make entries into, the ledger accounts	Be able to:
	• understand the divisions of the ledger
	• enter invoices and credit notes into the appropriate ledger accounts including the treatment of VAT:
	   – sales ledger
	   – purchase ledger
	   – main/nominal/general ledger
	• enter relevant CIS invoices, credit notes, receipts and payments showing how to deal with any tax deducted at source for sole traders, partnerships and limited companies
	• record income into the ledgers including:
	   – income from trading and supply of services
	   – income from capital invested
	   – loans
	   – sale of capital items
	   – donations
	   – subscriptions
	• record expenditure into the ledgers including
	   – both capital and revenue expenditure
	   – the treatment of wages and salaries
	   – the drawings of a sole trader or partner via drawings accounts
	   – withdrawal of funds by a director of a company (salary, dividends, loans) via a director's loan account
	• balance off accounts at the end of an accounting period
	• post relevant figures from the books of prime entry into the ledgers
	• post opening entries
	• write off of a bad debt including the treatment of VAT

3.2	Use a set of control accounts in the ledgers	Be able to: • understand the use of control accounts in a double entry system • understand the role of supplier and customer accounts as memorandum accounts when using control accounts • enter transactions into control accounts from the relevant books of prime entry

Topic 4 – Books of prime entry

Learning outcome	Assessment criteria

4.1 Understand the purpose of, and make entries into, the books of prime entry	Be able to:
	
	• explain how the books of prime entry integrate with the ledgers
	
	• enter invoices and credit notes into books of prime entry and prepare:
	
	   – sales day book
	
	   – sales returns day book
	
	   – purchases day book
	
	   – purchase returns day book
	
	• prepare an opening journal entry for a business
	
	• prepare a journal entry to record purchase of a fixed asset

Topic 5 – Accounting for VAT

Learning outcome	Assessment criteria

5.1 Understand the process of dealing with and accounting for VAT in the ledgers	Be able to:
	
	• explain the difference between the following levels of VAT:
	
	   – standard rate
	
	   – reduced rate
	
	   – zero rate
	
	   – exempt of VAT
	
	   – outside the scope of VAT
	
	• extract the VAT from a VAT inclusive amount
	
	• correctly account for input and output tax in the ledgers including amounts that are VAT inclusive

xiv	
	• explain the significance of debit and credit balances in the VAT accounts
	• understand how VAT is calculated and entered into the books of account for the following types of invoices:
	– invoices to customers and from suppliers outside the EU that are zero rated
	– invoices to customers and from suppliers outside the UK but within the EU that
	(a) are not registered for VAT in their own country
	(b) are registered for VAT in their own country

Topic 6 – Making and receiving payments

Learning outcome	Assessment criteria
6.1 Understand the use of an analysed cash book	Be able to: • understand when an analysed cash book is suitable as the sole record of income and expenditure for the smallest of businesses • record income and expenditure into an analysed cash book
6.2 Understand the purpose and need to record petty cash	Be able to: • explain the purpose of the imprest system • prepare petty cash vouchers • seek authorisation for a petty cash payment • code the expenditure • record the transactions in the petty cash book • balance off and restore the imprest • post to ledger accounts

KAPLAN PUBLISHING

6.3 Understand the purpose and use of the two and three column cash books	Be able to: • accurately record receipts and payments in a two column cashbook • accurately records receipts and payments in a three column cash book including the treatment of cash discount allowed and received • balance off cash and bank columns and bring down balances • complete the double entry to main and subsidiary ledgers
Topic 7 – Trial Balance	
Learning outcome	**Assessment criteria**
7.1 Understand the purpose and use of the trial balance	Be able to: • prepare a trial balance from the ledger accounts • understand what to do if the trial balance does not balance • open a suspense account where applicable to account for any imbalance

THE ASSESSMENT

The format of the assessment

The assessment for the qualification will comprise three online tests, all of which are taken in the candidate's home or place of work. The first two will test manual knowledge of double entry bookkeeping to trial balance for a variety of types of businesses; the third will test the set up and data entry to trial balance using a computerised system. The content of each paper is listed below, together with the relevant weighting of each section within each paper.

Paper B1 – Home/place of work based test to include:

Underpinning knowledge (10% weighting)

- terms in bookkeeping (assets, liabilities etc)

- banking procedures

- Understanding the different categories of VAT (standard, reduced, zero, exempt, outside the scope)

Preparation of business documents including calculation of VAT (20% weighting)

- entering transactions into the ledgers including the analysed cash book, cash transactions, credit transactions, discounts, petty cash book, two column cash book and VAT (40% weighting)

Making and receiving payments (20% weighting)

Production and explanation of a trial balance (10% weighting)

Paper B2 – Home/place of work based test to include:

Underpinning knowledge (10% weighting)

- ethics

- legislation

- types of businesses including simple cash based businesses

- identifying sections of the ledger

- accounting concepts

Day books and control accounts in a double entry system (30% weighting)

Further double entry including the following (40% weighting)

- Topics from paper 1
- Bad debts
- Construction Industry Scheme
- Non-sole trader entries (subscriptions, donations, drawings of partners etc)

Making and receiving payments (10% weighting)

- Three column cash book
- The analysed cash book
- Production and explanation of a trial balance (10% weighting)

Paper B3 – Home/place of work based test to include the use of a computerised accounting package to include:

- opening entries
- entering cash and credit transactions
- producing a trial balance
- producing reports for debtors, creditors, bank and the audit trail

The three tests should be taken in the order listed above.

Each test will generate a unit accreditation notification. Successful candidates will need to pass all three tests to gain the full qualification.

STUDY SKILLS

Preparing to study

Devise a study plan

Determine which times of the week you will study.

Split these times into sessions of at least one hour for study of new material. Any shorter periods could be used for revision or practice.

Put the times you plan to study onto a study plan for the weeks from now until the assessment and set yourself targets for each period of study – in your sessions make sure you cover the whole course, activities and the associated questions in the study text and revision kit.

When working through your course, compare your progress with your plan and, if necessary, re-plan your work (perhaps including extra sessions) or, if you are ahead, do some extra revision/practice questions.

Effective studying

Active reading

You are not expected to learn the text by rote, rather, you must understand what you are reading and be able to use it to pass the assessment and develop good practice.

A good technique is to use SQ3Rs – Survey, Question, Read, Recall, Review:

1   **Survey the chapter**

    Look at the headings and read the introduction, knowledge, skills and content, so as to get an overview of what the chapter deals with.

2   **Question**

    Whilst undertaking the survey, ask yourself the questions you hope the chapter will answer for you.

3 Read

Read through the chapter thoroughly working through the activities and, at the end, making sure that you can meet the learning objectives shown within the summary.

4 Recall

At the end of each section and at the end of the chapter, try to recall the main ideas of the section/chapter without referring to the text. This is best done after short break of a couple of minutes after the reading stage.

5 Review

Check that your recall notes are correct.

You may also find it helpful to re-read the chapter to try and see the topic(s) it deals with as a whole.

Note taking

Taking notes is a useful way of learning, but do not simply copy out the text.

The notes must:

- be in your own words
- be concise
- cover the key points
- be well organised
- be modified as you study further chapters in this text or in related **ones.**

Trying to summarise a chapter without referring to the text can be a useful way of determining which areas you know and which you don't.

Three ways of taking notes

1 Summarise the key points of a chapter

2 Make linear notes

A list of headings, subdivided with sub-headings listing the key points.

If you use linear notes, you can use different colours to highlight key points and keep topic areas together.

Use plenty of space to make your notes easy to use.

3   **Try a diagrammatic form**

The most common of these is a mind map.

To make a mind map, put the main heading in the centre of the paper and put a circle around it.

Draw lines radiating from this to the main sub-headings which again have circles around them.

Continue the process from the sub-headings to sub-sub-headings.

Highlighting and underlining

You may find it useful to underline or highlight key points in your study text – but do be selective.

You may also wish to make notes in the margins.

Revision phase

Kaplan has produced material specifically designed for your final assessment preparation for this unit.

These include a bank of revision questions that both test your knowledge and allow you to practise questions similar to those you will face in the exam.

Further guidance on how to approach the final stage of your studies is given in these materials.

Types of business units

1

Introduction

In your studies of bookkeeping and accounting with the ICB you will encounter various types of business unit. At this initial stage of your studies you need an awareness of the structure of the following:

- Sole Trader
- Partnership
- Limited company
- Limited liability partnership
- Not-for-profit organisation

You will also need an understanding of the factors that influence the choice of how a business and its owners operate.

CONTENTS

1 Sole Trader
2 Partnership
3 Limited company
4 Limited liability partnerships
5 Not-for-profit organisations

---

1 Sole Trader

Within the UK this is the most common form of business unit. It has been defined as 'A sole trader is an individual trading in his or her own name or under a trading name'.

1.1 Examples

Examples of individuals trading as a sole trader would include:

- Hairdresser
- Plumber
- Joiner
- Window cleaner.

These have in the past been those engaged in the 'trades', usually providing a service in their own locality, but it is often the case that they may trade with others as a partnership or as a private limited company.

1.2 Advantages to trading as a sole proprietor (sole trader)

- Administrative set up costs are minimal.
- The independence of working alone.
- If profitable, benefits from all the profit.
- Personal interest and job satisfaction.
- Accountancy and administration fees are relatively low.

1.3 Disadvantages to trading as a sole proprietor (sole trader)

- Must provide their own capital and capital is usually in short supply.
- Must take all the responsibility of running the business, with no cover for holidays and sickness.
- Is liable to all debts incurred by the business as the business is not a separate entity from the person running the business.
- It may be difficult in the current economic climate to borrow money for expansion from the bank.

2 Partnership

The Partnership Act of 1890, defines a partnership as: 'The relationship that subsists between persons carrying on a business in common with a view to profit'.

2.1 Formation of a partnership

A contract of partnership may be formed by consent. There are no legal formalities, as a contract may be created orally.

However it is common practice to prepare a deed of partnership to prevent disagreements arising in the future.

Such a deed usually states the following:

- Name of the partners
- Name of the business
- The amount of capital contributed by each
- The rate of interest, if any, payable on the capital
- The ratio in which the partners are to share profits and losses
- The amount of drawings each partner may draw for private use
- The rate of interest, if any, payable on the drawings.

If the partners do not draw up an agreement, the Act of 1890 states that all partners are entitled to share profits and losses equally.

2.2 Liability of partners

The partners are jointly and severally liable for all the debts incurred by the partnership.

2.3 Benefits of trading as a partnership

Often, solicitors, accountants, dentists, doctors, vets and skilled tradesmen trade as partnerships.

- Additional capital, over that of a sole trader, is made available.
- Specialisation: partners may have differing skills and specialisms.
- There is a shared responsibility of running the business.
- If a partner or partners are unable to work, say through illness, then the business may be able to continue as a going concern, as the responsibility would fall on one or more of the other partners.
- With specialisation an increased market share may be possible.
- Business growth may result in greater profitability.

3 Limited company

At this level of your studies you need an awareness of the two main types of Limited Company.

- Private Limited Companies (Ltd)
- Public Limited Companies (plc)

Unlike sole traders and partnerships, Limited Companies are incorporated businesses: they are established as legal entities in their own right and exist independently from their owners.

The owners of a Limited Company are referred to as shareholders, each owning a share of the business. Company shareholders have limited liability for the debts of the company.

3.1 Private limited companies

These are usually smaller, owner-managed companies.

A private limited company must have at least one director, although it is often the case there are two or more directors, one of whom is the company secretary.

Shares in a private limited company are often held by its directors and private limited companies cannot raise capital by issuing shares to the public.

Private limited companies are the most common type of company in the UK, with over one million being registered with Companies House.

3.2 Public limited companies

Public limited companies are by nature much larger businesses than private companies. The name must end with "plc". They may raise capital by issuing shares to the public and often issue debentures that are a form of fixed interest loan, this being done via the Stock Market or The Alternative Investment Market.

To form a public company, there must be a minimum amount of allotted shares of £50,000. A Public company must obtain a trading certificate from the Registrar before it can commence trading.

KAPLAN PUBLISHING

3.3   Company formation

In order for either a private or public company to be formed, it must be registered with the Registrar of Companies. It must also prepare a Memorandum of Association and Articles of Association and submit these to the Registrar, and it must comply with the requirements of the Companies Act 2006.

The documents submitted to Companies House to form a company will set out: the name of the company, its registered office, its purpose and its objectives of business. They will set out the number of shares issued, their aggregate nominal value and how much of this has been paid up. They will also state that the shareholders have limited liability and give names and addresses of the company directors. The Articles of Association will set out the way in which the company is to be governed and its responsibility to report its activities on an annual basis to Companies House.

3.4   Advantages and disadvantages of trading as a limited company

- Shareholders have limited liability.

- There will be access to a wider pool of available capital.

- Borrowing from banks and other institutions may be easier.

- The business is a separate legal entity so it can own property and form contracts in its own name.

There are also some disadvantages to trading as a limited company:

- Legal formalities on formation.

- Costly administrative procedures.

- Audit fees may be payable, depending on the size of the company.

4   Limited liability partnerships

A limited liability partnership (LLP) is a form of legal entity with limited liability for its members.

Two or more persons carrying on business with a view to profit can incorporate an LLP. An application to register an LLP needs to be lodged with Companies House. The difference between an LLP and a private company is that an LLP has the flexibility of a partnership.

4.1 Registration

The application to register an LLP must include:

- The LLP's name.

- The address of the registered office.

- Details of each proposed member and whether the member is a designated member.

- Statement of compliance.

4.2   Members

An LLP must have at least two designated members.

Such members are responsible for:

- Appointing an auditor if required.

- Signing accounts on behalf of the members.

- Filing the accounts with Companies House.

- Notifying Companies House of changes.

- Filing the Annual Return.

The decision as to which members will be appointed as designated members is made by the other members.

5 Not-for-profit organisations

These include Charities and, more common for your ICB studies, Clubs and Societies.

5.1 Charities

A charity is simply an organisation established for charitable purposes. Charities are subject to the provisions of the Charities Act 2011.

A charity must be registered with the Charity Commission where it has an income of over £5,000 per year, unless it is an exempt charity such as a national museum.

There are over 160,000 registered charities in the UK and many more with an income less than £5,000 per annum.

Where a registered charity has income over £10,000 per annum it must file an annual return to the Charity Commission.

5.2 Clubs and societies

Many of you reading this text are no doubt members of a club or society. Although these are classified as not-for-profit organisations it is desirable that, as with a charity, they achieve surpluses that are used for the benefit of members.

Each organisation will have their own constitution which sets out its rules and will normally appoint three officials to run the club affairs. These include a Chairman, a Treasurer and a Secretary, whose responsibilities are to conduct the activities of the organisation in accordance with club rules.

N.B. We must also acknowledge that some organisations are Central Government funded and are those in the Public Sector, examples of which are the NHS and Local Authorities. However these are outside the scope of this syllabus and your studies at this level.

6 Summary

For your assessment, you will need to know the differences between the various types of business units covered in this chapter, and also the advantages and disadvantages of each.

7 Test your knowledge

 ## Workbook Activity 1

What is the main requirement of the Companies Act 2006 relating to a private company?

A   The allotted capital must not exceed £50,000

B   It must not have more than 50 members

C   It must have two directors

D   It must not invite the public to subscribe for its shares

 ## Workbook Activity 2

Fill in the gap, delete as appropriate and complete the sentence

The term 'partnership' is defined in ……………………….. People can form such organisations informally or formally and they need/do not need written agreements.
The definition of a partnership is ……………

(Your answer must not exceed 20 words.)

 ## Workbook Activity 3

Two brothers, Spencer and Trevor, have set up a software consultancy service and may wish to become a public company. What are the main characteristics of this business entity?

Double entry bookkeeping – introduction

2

Introduction

This chapter introduces the basic concepts and rules of bookkeeping. In particular we study:

- the dual effect principle
- the separate entity principle; and
- the accounting equation.

Together these will show how the assets of a business will always equal its liabilities and pave the way for studying double entry bookkeeping in the next chapter.

CONTENTS
1   Types of accounting
2   Double entry bookkeeping
3   The accounting equation: examples

1 Types of accounting

1.1 Management accounting and financial accounting

Depending on what purposes the statements are being produced for, the accounts can be referred to as being either **management accounts** or **financial accounts.**

Management accounts

These are usually prepared on a monthly basis to present the financial information in a way that enables the managers to run the business more effectively.

Financial accounts

These are prepared annually, mainly for the benefit of people outside the management of the business, such as the owners of the business (for example, shareholders who have appointed directors to run the business on their behalf), HM Revenue and Customs, banks, customers, suppliers and government.

In this text we focus on financial accounting principles, though the majority of concepts also apply to management accounting.

1.2 The two main financial statements

The objective of financial accounting is to provide financial information about a business. This information is given in a set of financial statements (or accounts), which consists of two principal statements:

- The **profit and loss account**. This is a summary of the business's transactions (income and expense) for a given period.

- The **balance sheet**. This is a statement of the financial position (assets and liabilities) of the business at a given date. This date is the end of the period covered by the profit and loss account.

These financial statements are the final product of the accounting system of a business and it is useful to be aware of where all of the double entry bookkeeping that you will study in this chapter is leading. However, you do not need to know anything about the format or rules governing the preparation of the financial statements for Level II.

The following definitions will be used throughout your studies.

🔍 Definitions

- An **asset** is something owned by a business, available for use in the business.

- **Fixed asset** – an asset which is to be used for the long term in the business and not resold as part of the trading activities, for example the purchase of a delivery van.

- **Current asset** – a short-term asset of the business which is to be used in the business in the near future.

- A **debtor** is an example of a current asset. A debtor is someone who owes the business money.

- A **liability** is an amount **owed** by the business, i.e. an obligation to pay money at some future date.

- A **creditor** is an example of a liability. A creditor is someone to whom the business owes money.

- **Capital** is the amount which the owner has invested in the business; this is owed back to the owner and is therefore a special liability of the business.

- **Capital expenditure** is the purchase of, or improvement of, fixed assets.

- **Revenue expenditure** includes the day to day operating costs of the business.

1.3   The difference between 'cash' and 'bank'

A possible confusion in terminology is caused by the apparent interchangeable use of the words 'cash' and 'bank'.

The normal use of the words suggests that a bank account operates by paying money out of the account with a cheque and paying either cash or cheques directly into the account. In practice you cannot pay 'cash' out of a bank account.

However, accounting terminology does not stick to this distinction, and the terms cash and bank are for the most part, interchangeable. Thus the bank account is often referred to as the 'cash book'. Similarly we will often refer to someone 'taking cash out of the bank' or we will say things like 'John bought a car for £5,000 cash', whereas in reality John would have paid for the car using a cheque.

For the early part of your studies all movements of cash/cheques shall be made through the bank account and references to 'cash' or 'cheques' effectively mean the same thing.

2 Double entry bookkeeping

2.1 Introduction

Double entry bookkeeping is based upon three basic principles:

- the dual effect principle
- the separate entity principle
- the accounting equation.

2.2 The dual effect principle

This states that every transaction has two financial effects.

(a) If, for example, you spend £2,000 on a car and pay for it by a cheque, you will have £2,000 less money in the bank, but you will also have acquired an asset worth £2,000.

(b) Again, if you owe a creditor £100 and send him a cheque for that amount, you will owe £100 less than before, but you will have £100 less money in the bank.

2.3 The separate entity principle

This states that the owner of a business is, for accounting purposes, a completely separate entity from the business itself. Therefore the money that the owner pays into the business as initial capital has to be accounted for as an amount that the business owes back to the owner. In just the same way, any money that the owner takes out of the business, known as drawings, is treated as a reduction of the initial capital that is owed back to the owner.

The dual effect principle works here as well. If the owner of the business pays £5,000 into his business, one effect is that the business has £5,000 more cash and the second effect is that the business has a £5,000 liability (called 'capital').

Note that we look at this from the **point of view of the business**, not from the owner's point of view. This is because when studying bookkeeping we are only interested in the business – we are not considering the owner's personal finances.

2.4   The accounting equation

At its simplest, the accounting equation simply says that:

Assets = Liabilities

If we treat the owner's capital as a special form of liability then the accounting equation is:

Assets = Liabilities + Capital

Or, rearranging:

Assets – Liabilities = Capital

Profit will increase the proprietor's capital and drawings will reduce it, so that we can write the equation as:

Assets – Liabilities = Capital + Profit – Drawings

3   The accounting equation: examples

Example 1

John starts his business on 1 July and pays £2,000 into his business bank account.

(a)   What is the dual effect of this transaction?

(b)   What is the accounting equation after this transaction?

Solution

(a)   The dual effect

The business bank account has increased by £2,000 (an asset). The business capital has increased by £2,000 (a liability).

(b)   The accounting equation

Assets – Liabilities   = Capital

£2,000 – £0   = £2,000

Example 2

Percy started business on 1 January by paying £20,000 into a business bank account. He then spent £500 on a second-hand van by cheque, £1,000 on purchases of stock for cash, took £500 cash for his own use and bought goods on credit costing £400.

What are the two effects of each of these transactions?

What would the accounting equation look like after each of these transactions?

Solution

(a) **Percy pays £20,000 into a business bank account**

The bank balance increases from zero to £20,000 (an asset) and the business now has capital of £20,000 (a liability); capital is the amount that is owed back to the owner of the business, Percy.

Accounting equation:

Assets – Liabilities = Capital

£20,000 – £0   = £20,000

(b) **Percy buys a second-hand van for £500 by cheque**

The bank balance decreases by £500 (a reduction of assets) but the business has acquired a new £500 asset, the van.

The van is a specific type of asset known as a fixed asset as it is for long-term use in the business rather than an asset that is likely to be sold in the trading activities of the business.

The assets of the business are now:

	£
Van	500
Bank (20,000 – 500)	19,500
	———
	20,000
	———

The liabilities and capital are unchanged.

Accounting equation:

Assets – Liabilities   = Capital

£20,000 – £0   = £20,000

(c) **Percy spends £1,000 on purchases of goods for cash**

The bank balance goes down by £1,000 but the business has another asset, stock of £1,000.

Stock is a short-term asset as it is due to be sold to customers in the near future and is known as a current asset.

The assets of the business are now:

	£
Van	500
Stock	1,000
Bank (19,500 – 1,000)	18,500
	———
	20,000
	———

Accounting equation:

Assets – Liabilities = Capital

£20,000 – £0   = £20,000

(d) **Percy took £500 of cash out of the business**

The bank balance has decreased by £500 and capital has also decreased as the owner has taken money out of the business – this is known as drawings.

Remember that the owner is a completely separate entity from the business itself and if he takes money out of the business in the form of drawings then this means that the business owes him less.

The assets of the business are now:

	£
Van	500
Stock	1,000
Bank (18,500 – 500)	18,000
	———
	19,500
	———

The capital of the business is now £(20,000 – 500) = £19,500.

Accounting equation:

Assets – Liabilities = Capital

£19,500 – £0   = £19,500

(e) Purchased goods on credit for £400

The asset of stock increases by £400 and the business now has a liability of £400, the amount that is owed to the credit supplier. A liability is an amount that is owed by the business.

The assets of the business are now:

	£
Van	500
Stock (1,000 + 400)	1,400
Bank	18,000
	19,900

The liability of the business is £400. The capital is unchanged.

Accounting equation:

Assets – Liabilities = Capital

£19,900 – £400   = £19,500

General notes:

1   Each and every transaction that a business undertakes has two effects. The accounting equation reflects the two effects of each transaction and the accounting equation should always balance.

2   The owner is a completely separate entity from the business, any money the owner puts into the business is known as capital and any amounts taken out by the owner are known as drawings.

4   Summary

You must understand the basic definitions covered in this chapter. You must also understand the principles of dual effect and separate entity. The accounting equation underlies the whole of bookkeeping and it is imperative that you fully understand these foundations which will be built on further. Rework the examples in this chapter if necessary.

5 Test your knowledge

Workbook Activity 1

(a) State whether each of the following are an asset or a liability:

    (i) Money in the business bank account

    (ii) A creditor

    (iii) Stock of goods for resale

    (iv) A computer used in the accounts department

    (v) A debtor

    (vi) A salesman's car.

(b) Name 3 different parties who would be interested in financial statements.

(c) Name the 3 basic principles of double entry bookkeeping and briefly describe each.

Workbook Activity 2

Required:

Show the two effects of each of these transactions and what the accounting equation would look like after each of these transactions.

1   Introduce capital

Example 1

You win £10,000 and use it to create a retail business (called TLC) selling hearts and roses. What is the effect?

Answer 1

Dual effect

TLC has cash of	£10,000	(asset)
TLC owes owner (you)	£10,000	(capital)

TLC's position is:

Assets	Capital
£	£

(In this first example, we recorded the dual effect for you just to get you started. In later examples you will need to enter the dual effect yourself, as well as TLC's position after the transaction.)

2   Buy stock with cash

Example 2

TLC buys 500 chocolate hearts. The cost of each heart is £5. What is the effect?

Answer 2

Dual effect

TLC's position is:

Assets	Capital
£	£

3   Buy stock on credit

In reality a business will not always pay for its purchases with cash but is more likely to buy items on credit.

Example 3

TLC buys stock of 200 red roses on credit. Each red rose costs £10. What is the effect?

Answer 3

Dual effect

TLC's position is:

Net assets	Capital
£	£

4   Buy a delivery van

The delivery van is bought for ongoing use within the business rather than for resale. Such assets are known as **fixed assets.**

Example 4

TLC buys a delivery van for £1,000 cash. What is the effect?

Answer 4

Dual effect

TLC's position is:

Net assets	Capital
£	£

5   Sell stock for profit

Example 5

TLC sells 200 red roses for £15 cash each. What is the effect?

Answer 5

Dual effect

TLC's position is:

| Net assets | Capital |
| £ | £ |

6   Sell stock (on credit) for profit

It is equally likely that a business will sell goods on credit. When goods are sold on credit, an asset of the business called a debtor is generated.

Example 6

TLC sells 400 chocolate hearts to Valentino for £12.50 each on credit. What is the effect?

Answer 6

Dual effect

TLC's position is:

| Net assets | Capital |
| £ | £ |

KAPLAN PUBLISHING

7   Pay expenses

Example 7

In reality, TLC will have been incurring expenses from its commencement. TLC received and paid a gas bill for £500. What is the effect?

Answer 7

Dual effect

TLC's position is:

Net assets	*Capital*
£	£

8   Take out a loan

In order to fund your future expansion plans for TLC, you persuade your Aunt to lend TLC £2,000.

Example 8

TLC is lent £2,000 cash by your Aunt. She expects to be repaid in two years' time. What is the effect?

Answer 8

Dual effect

TLC's position is:

Net assets	*Capital*
£	£

9   Payment to creditors for purchases

Example 9

TLC pays cash of £1,500 towards the £2,000 owed to the supplier. What is the effect?

Answer 9

Dual effect

TLC's position is:

Net assets £	Capital £

10   Receive cash from debtors

Example 10

TLC's debtor sends a cheque for £3,000. What is the effect?

Answer 10

Dual effect

TLC's position is:

Net assets £	Capital £

11   Drawings

Example 11

You withdraw £750 from the business. Such a withdrawal is merely a repayment of the capital you introduced. Your withdrawal is called **drawings.** What is the effect?

Answer 11

Dual effect

TLC's position is:

Net assets £	Capital £

Workbook Activity 3

Bertie Wooster started a business as an antique dealer on 1 July 20X9.

Required:

Show the accounting equation which results from each of the following transactions made during Bertie's first two weeks of trading.

(a)   Started the business with £5,000 in cash as opening capital.

(b)   Bought an Edwardian desk for £500 cash.

(c)   Bought five art deco table lamps for £200 each, on credit from Roderick Spode.

(d)   Sold the desk for £750 cash.

(e)   Sold four of the table lamps for £300 each on credit to his Uncle Tom.

(f)   Paid rent of £250 cash.

(g)   Drew £100 in cash out of the business for living expenses.

(h)   Earned £50 for writing a magazine article, but had not yet been paid for it.

(i)   Paid Roderick Spode £500 on account.

(j)   Received £1,200 from Uncle Tom in full settlement of the amount due.

(k)   Bought a van for use in the business for £4,000 cash.

(l)   Received a telephone bill for £150 but did not pay it yet.

Note: Each transaction follows on from the one before.

KAPLAN PUBLISHING

Ledger accounting

3

Introduction

Now that we have looked at the basic theory of bookkeeping, it is time to learn and practise how to make the correct double entries for the sorts of transactions that are relevant for your ICB studies.

We shall start with accounting for cash transactions, and will study a series of the different sorts of things that a business can buy or sell (or pay for or receive) in cash.

We shall then study how to deal with purchases and sales made on credit.

> **CONTENTS**
>
> 1 Ledger accounting
> 2 Worked examples
> 3 Additional example
> 4 Credit purchases
> 5 Credit sales

1 Ledger accounting

1.1 Introduction

The accounting equation does have limitations. In Activity 2 in Chapter 2, we were able to calculate a profit figure for TLC. We were, however, unable to determine which part of the profit related sales and which part related to expenses. To be able to make this determination, we will now account for the movement in sales and purchases, rather than simply the movement of stock.

Another limitation of the accounting equation is that in practice it would be far too time consuming to write up the accounting equation each time that the business undertakes a transaction. Instead the two effects of each transaction are recorded in ledger accounts.

1.2 The ledger account

A typical ledger account is shown below:

Title of account							
DEBIT				**CREDIT**			
Date	Details	Folio	Amount £	Date	Details	Folio	Amount £

The important point to note is that it has two sides. The left hand side is known as the **debit** side **(DR)** and the right hand side is known as the **credit** side **(CR).**

- The date column contains the date of the transaction.

- The details column (can also be referred to as the narrative column) contains the title of the other account that holds the second part of the dual effect. It may also have a brief description of the nature of the entry (e.g. 'rent 1.1.X3 to 31.3.X3').

- The folio column contains a reference to the source of the information. We shall see some of these sources later on but it could be, for example, 'sales day book p17' or 'payroll month 6'.

- The amount column simply contains the monetary value of the transaction.

- The title of the account is a name that reflects the nature of the transaction ('van account', 'bank account', 'electricity account', etc).

The importance of completing the ledger account correctly, in terms of the presentation, should not be underestimated. Vital marks can be gained in the exam by ensuring all details, including the date and narrative are completed accurately.

1.3   Simplified account

The ledger account in 1.2 is very detailed and in much of this book we use a simpler form of the account. Part of the reason for this is that it is easier to 'see' the entries being made if there is less detail in the accounts. Thus, we sometimes do without the date or the full description or folio to keep things clear and simple.

For example, we will often use accounts which look like this:

Bank account			
	£	Van	£
			500

Van account			
	£		£
Bank	500		

1.4 The golden rule for making entries in the ledger accounts

The golden rule for making entries in ledger accounts is:

'Every debit entry must have an equal and opposite credit entry.'

This reflects the dual effect of each transaction and ensures the accounting equation always balances.

It is also why we refer to the process as "double entry bookkeeping".

1.5 Which accounts to debit and credit

The mnemonic DEAD/CLIC is a good way to help determine if an entry should be made on the debit side or on the credit side of a ledger account.

Ledger account	
DEBITs increase	**CREDITs increase**
Debtors	**C**reditors
Expenses	**L**iabilities
Assets	**I**ncome
Drawings	**C**apital

We need to appreciate the effect a debit or a credit entry will have.

Ledger account	
A **debit entry** represents:	A **credit entry** represents:
• An increase in the value of an asset	• A decrease in the value of an asset
• A decrease in the value of a liability; or	• An increase in the value of a liability; or
• An increase to an item of expenditure	• An increase to an item of income (revenue)
• A decrease to an item of income	• A decrease to an item of expense

1.6 What goes on the debit or credit side?

> ### 💡 Example (part 1)
>
> If John pays £2,000 into his business bank account as capital, we need to ask a number of questions to determine the double entry required.
>
> (a) **Which** accounts are affected?
>
> (b) What **type** of accounts are they i.e. asset/liability/income/ expense?
>
> (c) Is the transaction **increasing or decreasing** the account?
>
> So let's consider these questions for John's investment of capital into his business.
>
> (a) The accounts that are affected are the bank account and the capital account.
>
> (b) The bank account is an asset whereas the capital is a special kind of liability.
>
> (c) As we have paid money into the bank account, the asset is increasing – therefore a debit entry is required.
>
> As John (the owner) has invested £2,000 into the business, the business owes him this amount back. This is an increase to a liability – therefore a credit entry is required.
>
> **To summarise:**
>
> Debit Bank account
>
> Credit Capital account
>
> **Bank account**
>
> | | £ | | £ |
> |---|---|---|---|
> | Capital | 2,000 | | |
>
> **Capital account**
>
> | | £ | | £ |
> |---|---|---|---|
> | | | Bank | 2,000 |

Example (part 2)

If John's business now pays £1,000 out of the bank to buy a van, considering the questions again:

(a)   The accounts that are affected are the bank account and the van account.

(b)   The bank account is an asset and the van account is also an asset (a fixed asset).

(c)   As we have paid money out of the bank account, the asset is decreasing – therefore a credit entry is required.

The business has acquired a van, which is a fixed asset, this is an increase to an asset – therefore a debit entry is required.

To summarise:

Debit Van account

Credit Bank account

Bank account

	£		£
Capital	2,000	Van	1,000

Capital account

	£		£
		Bank	2,000

Van account

	£		£
Bank	1,000		

2 Worked examples

2.1 Introducing capital into the business – explanation

The owner of a business starts the business by paying money into the business bank account. This is the capital of the business. The business will need this money to 'get going'. It may need to pay rent, buy stock for sale or pay wages to its staff before it has actually generated money itself through sales.

 Example

Frankie starts a business and pays £5,000 into the business bank account. What is the double entry for this transaction?

Solution

- £5,000 has been paid into the bank account.

  It represents an asset of the business.

  This is therefore a debit in the bank account.

- The business has a liability because it owes Frankie (the owner) £5,000.

  This liability will be a credit in the capital account.

Bank (or cash book)		Capital	
Capital £5,000		Bank £5,000	

2.2 Purchasing goods for resale

A business buys goods for resale to customers – that is how most businesses (e.g. shops) make their money. These goods (known as "stock") are assets which the business owns.

Example

Frankie buys £300 of chocolate bars for resale. He pays with a cheque to his supplier.

What is the double entry for this transaction?

Solution

- The business has paid £300 out of its bank account.

  Therefore, the £300 will be credited to the bank account.

- Buying the chocolate bars (stock) is known as making a purchase (a type of expense).

  This expense will be debited to the purchases account.

Purchases			Bank		
Bank	£300			Purchases	£300

2.3 Paying office rent

A business will typically rent premises in order to carry out its operations. It will pay rent to the landlord of the premises. Rent is an expense of the business.

 Example

Frankie pays £1,000 per quarter for the rent of his offices. He pays with a cheque to the landlord.

What is the double entry for this transaction?

Solution

- The business has paid £1,000 out of its bank account.

  Therefore, the £1,000 will be credited to the bank account.

- The rent is an expense.

  This expense will be debited to the rent account.

Rent			Bank		
Bank	£1,000			Rent	£1,000

2.4   Buying stationery

A business will buy stationery in order to be able to operate. The items of stationery (pens, paper, etc) are not for resale to customers but they tend to be used quickly after they are purchased. Therefore, stationery tends to be classified as an expense of the business, as opposed to an asset.

:phi:	**Example**

Frankie pays £200 for items of stationery. He pays with a cheque to the supplier.

What is the double entry for this transaction?

Solution

- The business has paid £200 out of its bank account.

  Therefore, the £200 will be credited to the bank account.

- The stationery is an expense.

  This expense will be debited to the stationery account.

Stationery		Bank	
Bank £200			Stationery £200

2.5   Buying a computer

A business will buy computers in order to streamline its operations. These computers are not bought with a view to re-sale and are to be used in the business for the long term. They are therefore a fixed asset of the business.

Example

Frankie pays £900 to purchase a computer. He pays with a cheque to the supplier.

What is the double entry for this transaction?

Solution

- Once again start with the bank account.

  The business has paid £900 out of its bank account.

  Therefore, the £900 will be credited to the bank account.

- The computer is a fixed asset.

  The £900 will be debited to the fixed asset computer account.

Computer			Bank		
Bank	£900			Computer	£900

2.6 Receiving income from sales of goods

A business will sell the goods it has purchased for re-sale. This is income for the business and is referred to as 'sales'. You may also hear the terms "revenue" or "sales revenue".

 Example

Frankie sells goods for £1,500. The customer pays cash.

What is the double entry for this transaction?

Solution

- Once again start with the bank account.

  The business has received £1,500 into its bank account.

  Therefore, the £1,500 will be debited to the bank account.

- The cash received is income.

  This income will be credited to the sales account.

Sales			Bank		
	Bank	£1,500	Sales	£1,500	

2.7 Receiving income for services provided

A business may provide services to its customers, e.g.it may provide consultancy advice. This is income for the business and will usually be referred to as 'sales'.

 Example

Frankie provides consultancy services to a client who pays £2,000 in cash. What is the double entry for this transaction?

Solution

- Once again start with the bank account.

  The business has received £2,000 into its bank account.

  Therefore, the £2,000 will be debited to the bank account.

- The cash received is income.

  This income will be credited to the sales account.

Sales				Bank	
	Bank	£2,000	Sales	£2,000	

2.8 Recording a business loan

A business may borrow money from the bank in the form of a loan. The loan will be a liability of the business which it will have to repay by a set date.

 Example

Kathryn is in business and secures a loan from the bank £5,000.

What is the double entry for this transaction.

Solution

- The business has received £5,000 from the bank making the loan, therefore the bank account in Kathryn's books will be debited with £5,000.

- As the bank is owed the funds, the bank is one of Kathryn's creditors and a Loan Account will be opened in Kathryn's books: this will be credited with £5,000.

Bank		Loan A/c	
Loan A/c £5,000		Bank £5,000	

2.9 Receiving income for the sale of an asset

When a business sells an asset, the money it receives is not recognised as sales income: instead, the sales proceeds received are recognised in a separate fixed asset disposals account (also known as sale of asset account).

 Example

Kathryn has office equipment with a total cost of £3,100 and she decides to dispose of one item recently purchased at a cost of £500. She receives a cheque for £500 that she banks immediately.

What is the double entry for this transaction?

Solution

- As a cheque has been received and banked, the bank account in Kathryn's books will be debited with £500.

- The disposal of the asset will represent income for the business and so £500 will be credited to the disposals account.

Bank		Disposals A/c	
Disposals a/c £500		Bank £500	

2.10   Receipt of donations

When a club, society or charity receives a donation, this is a form of income for the organisation and will be recorded in the donations account.

 Example

Julie is a Certified Bookkeeper working for a County Cricket Club Foundation.

For the week ended 3rd May, total cheque donations of £175 had been received and banked.

What is the double entry for this transaction?

Solution

- As the cheques have been received and banked, the bank account in the foundation's books will be debited with £175.

- The donations are a source of income and sources of income are represented by credit entries: the donations account will be credited with £175.

Bank		Donations	
Donations £175			Bank £175

2.11   Recording private drawings

When a sole trader withdraws amounts from the business bank account at the end of each month for private living expenses, such amounts are referred to as the Proprietor's Drawings: a sole trader takes money out of the business as drawings whereas employed persons are paid a wage or salary.

Example

Kathryn is in business as a sole trader: in January she transfers £1,050 from the business bank account to her own personal account.

What is the double entry for this transaction?

Solution

- The drawings account will be debited with £1,050, as drawings are always a debit entry in the accounts (as per the DEADCLIC mnemonic at the start of this chapter).

- As the funds have been paid and withdrawn from the bank account, we will credit the bank account with £1,050.

Drawings		Bank	
Bank £1,050			Drawings £1,050

Note that the same procedure will also be followed if the person withdrawing the funds is a partner withdrawing funds from a business trading as a partnership.

2.12 Recording the withdrawal of funds by a company director

You will be involved with the accounts of a limited company much later in your studies but will need an awareness of how funds withdrawn by a company director are recorded in the accounts for your Level II exam.

Each director in a limited company has a Director's current account (sometimes called a Director's Loan Account) which is used to record any transactions between the director and the company, other than increases or decreases in the Share Capital.

The payment of a dividend to a company director of a private company will also be dealt with through the director's current account.

Example

Julie is a director of Cheerleaders Ltd and withdraws some funds for private purposes from the business bank account £520.

What is the double entry for this transaction?

Solution

- The director's current account will be debited with £520, as drawings are always a debit entry in the accounts (as per the DEADCLIC mnemonic at the start of this chapter).

- The bank account in the company's books will be credited with £520 as the funds have been withdrawn.

Director's current A/c		Bank	
Bank £520			Director's £520 current A/c

3 Additional example

 Example

Percy started business on 1 January and made the following transactions.

1   Paid £20,000 into a business bank account.

2   Spent £500 on a second-hand van.

3   Paid £1,000 on purchases of stock.

4   Took £50 cash for his own personal use.

5   On 5 January bought goods for cash costing £500.

6   Made sales for cash of £2,000.

7   On 15 January paid £200 of rent.

Task 1

Show how the debit and credit entries for each transaction are determined.

Task 2

Enter the transactions into the relevant ledger accounts.

Solution

Task 1

(1) Capital invested

Percy has paid £20,000 into the bank account – therefore the bank account is debited.

Debit (Dr)   Bank   £20,000

The business now owes the owner £20,000. Capital is the amount owed by the business to its owner – this is a liability, therefore a credit entry is required in the capital account.

Credit (Cr)   Capital   £20,000

(2) Purchase of van

The business has paid £500 out of the bank account – therefore a credit entry in the bank account.

Cr   Bank   £500

The business now has a van costing £500 – this is an asset therefore a debit entry in the van account. This is a fixed asset of the business.

Dr   Van   £500

(3) Purchase of stock for cash

The business has paid out £1,000 out of the bank account – therefore a credit to the bank account.

Cr   Bank   £1,000

The business has made purchases of stock costing £1,000 – this is an item of expenditure therefore a debit entry in the purchases account. Note that the debit entry is to a purchases account not a stock account. The stock account is a different account altogether and stock movements will be considered later.

Dr   Purchases   £1,000

(4)   Drawings

The business has paid £50 out of the bank account – therefore credit the bank account.

Cr   Bank   £50

The proprietor has made drawings of £50 – this is a reduction of capital and therefore a debit entry to the drawings account.

Dr   Drawings   £50

Drawings should not be directly debited to the capital account. A separate drawings account should be used.

(5)   Purchase of goods for cash

The business has paid out £500 – therefore credit the bank account.

Cr   Bank   £500

The business has made purchases of stock costing £500 – an expense therefore debit the purchases account.

Dr   Purchases   £500

(6)   Sale for cash

The business has paid £2,000 into the bank account – therefore a debit to the bank account.

Dr   Bank   £2,000

The business has made sales of £2,000 – this is income therefore a credit to the sales account.

Cr   Sales   £2,000

(7)   Payment of rent

The business now paid £200 out of the bank account – therefore a credit to the bank account.

Cr   Bank   £200

The business has incurred an expense of rent – as an expense item the rent account must be debited.

Dr   Rent   £200

Task 2

Bank

Date			£	Date			£
1 Jan	Capital	(1)	20,000	1 Jan	Van	(2)	500
5 Jan	Sales	(6)	2,000		Purchases	(3)	1,000
					Drawings	(4)	50
				5 Jan	Purchases	(5)	500
				15 Jan	Rent	(7)	200

Capital

Date			£	Date			£
				1 Jan	Bank	(1)	20,000

Van

Date			£	Date			£
1 Jan	Bank	(2)	500				

Purchases

Date			£	Date			£
1 Jan	Bank	(3)	1,000				
5 Jan	Bank	(5)	500				

Drawings

Date			£	Date			£
1 Jan	Bank	(4)	50				

Sales

Date			£	Date			£
				5 Jan	Bank	(6)	2,000

Rent

Date			£	Date			£
15 Jan	Bank	(7)	200				

Activity 1

Write up the following cash transactions in the ledger accounts.

Transaction	Details
1	Set up the business by introducing £150,000 in cash.
2	Purchase property costing £140,000. Pay in cash.
3	Purchase goods costing £5,000. Pay in cash.
4	Sell goods for £7,000. All cash sales.
5	Purchase goods costing £8,000. Pay in cash.
6	Pay a sundry expense of £100, by cheque.
7	Sell goods for £15,000. All cash sales.
8	Pay wages of £2,000 to an employee.
9	Pay postage costs of £100, by cheque.

 Credit purchases

 Definitions

A cash purchase occurs when goods are bought (or a service received) and the customer pays immediately using cash, cheques or credit cards. A receipt is issued for the amount of cash paid.

A credit purchase occurs when goods are bought (or a service received) and the customer does not have to pay immediately but can pay after a specified number of days. An invoice is then issued to request that payment is made.

Example

We have already seen the double entry for a cash purchase and we shall now contrast this with the double entry for a credit purchase by means of an illustration.

John buys goods from Sam for £2,000.

(a) Record the double entry in John's books if John pays for the goods immediately with a cheque.

(b) Record the double entry in John's books if John buys the goods on credit and pays some time later.

Solution

(a) Cash purchase

The double entry is simply to:

Credit the bank account with £2,000 because £2,000 has been paid out.

Debit the purchases account with £2,000 because goods have been purchased with £2,000.

Bank

	£		£
		Purchases	2,000

Purchases

	£		£
Bank	2,000		

(b) Credit purchase

We have to record two transactions separately:

(i) *At the time the purchase is made*

At the time the purchase is made we debit £2,000 to the purchases account because a purchase has been made, but we do not make any entry in the bank account yet, because at that point, no cash has been paid. The other effect is that John has a liability, he owes £2,000 to the supplier, Sam, who we can refer to as a creditor.

The double entry is:

Debit the purchases account with £2,000 because expenses have increased by £2,000.

Credit creditors account with £2,000 (this is a liability of the business).

Purchases

	£		£
Creditor	2,000		

Creditors

	£		£
		Purchases	2,000

(ii) *When John pays the £2,000*

The double entry now will be:

Credit the bank account with £2,000 because £2,000 has been paid out.

Debit the creditor account because John has paid and the creditor has been reduced by £2,000.

Creditors

	£		£
Bank	2,000	Purchases	2,000

Purchases

	£		£
Creditor	2,000		

Bank

	£		£
		Creditor	2,000

4.1 Summary

The net effect of the above credit purchase is that the creditor has a nil balance because John has paid, and we are left with a debit in the purchases account and a credit in the cash book. This is exactly as for a cash purchase – we just had to go through the intermediate step of the creditors account to get there.

5 Credit sales

Definitions

A cash sale occurs when goods are sold (or a service provided) and the customer pays immediately with cash, cheque or credit card. A receipt is issued for the amount of cash received.

A credit sale occurs when goods are sold (or a service provided) and the customer does not have to pay immediately but can pay after a specified number of days. An invoice is issued to request that the balance owed is then paid.

Example

We have already seen the double entry for a cash sale and we shall now contrast this with the double entry for a credit sale by means of an illustration.

George sells goods to Harry for £1,000.

(a) Record the double entry in George's books if Harry pays for the goods immediately with a cheque.

(b) Record the double entry in George's books if Harry buys the goods on credit and pays some time later.

Solution

(a) Cash sale

The double entry is simply to:

Debit the bank account with £1,000 because £1,000 has been paid in.

Credit the sales account with £1,000 because income has increased by £1,000.

Bank			
	£		£
Sales	1,000		

Sales			
	£		£
		Bank	1,000

(b) Credit sale

The double entry will be made at two separate times.

(i) *At the time the sale is made*

At the time the sale is made we credit £1,000 to the sales account because a sale has been made, but we cannot make any entry in the bank account at the time of the sale because no cash is received. However, the dual effect principle means that there must be another effect to this transaction, and in this case it is that the business has acquired a debtor.

The double entry is:

Debit debtors account with £1,000 (this is an asset of the business).

Credit the sales account with £1,000 because income has increased by £1,000.

Debtors			
	£		£
Sales	1,000		

Sales

	£		£
		Debtor	1,000

(ii)   *When Harry pays the £1,000*

The double entry now will be:

Debit the bank account with £1,000 because £1,000 has been paid in.

Credit the debtors account because Harry has paid and the debtor has been reduced by £1,000.

Debtors

	£		£
Sales	1,000	Bank	1,000

Sales

	£		£
		Debtor	1,000

Bank

	£		£
Debtor	1,000		

5.1   Summary

The net effect of the above credit sale is that the debtor has a nil balance because Harry has paid and we are left with a credit in the sales account and a debit in the cash book. This is exactly as for a cash sale – we just had to go through the intermediate step of the debtor account to get there.

📝 Activity 2

We shall now revisit our worked example from Chapter 1 and record the transactions with debits and credits to ledger accounts.

Date	Detail
1.1.X5	TLC commenced business with £10,000 cash introduced by you, the proprietor
2.1.X5	TLC bought stock of 500 chocolate hearts for £2,500 cash
3.1.X5	TLC bought stock of 200 red roses on credit for £2,000
4.1.X5	TLC bought a delivery van for £1,000 cash
5.1.X5	TLC sold all the red roses for £3,000 cash
6.1.X5	TLC sold 400 chocolate hearts for £5,000 on credit
7.1.X5	TLC paid a gas bill for £500 cash
8.1.X5	TLC took out a loan of £2,000
9.1.X5	TLC paid £1,500 cash to trade creditors
10.1.X5	TLC received £3,000 cash from debtors
11.1.X5	The proprietor withdrew £750 cash

Required:

Record these transactions in the relevant ledger accounts. Make your entries in the ledger accounts below.

Cash

	£		£

Capital

	£		£

Purchases

	£		£

Creditors

	£		£

Delivery van

	£		£

Sales

	£		£

Debtors

	£		£

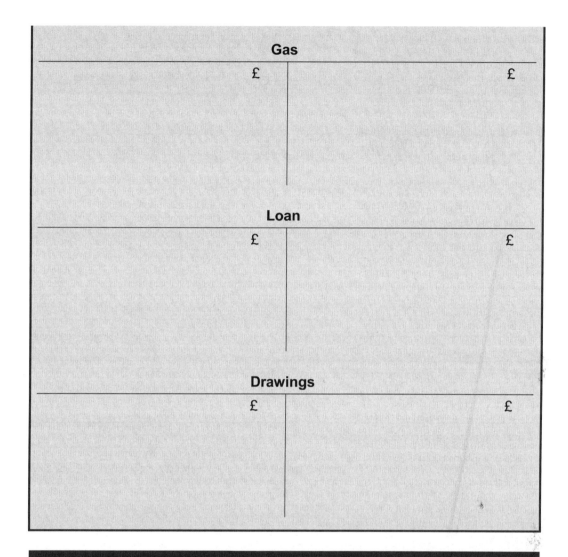

Gas

£		£

Loan

£		£

Drawings

£		£

6 Summary

In this chapter we have studied cash and credit transactions. It is important to always start with the bank account and remember that cash received is a debit in the bank account and cash paid out is a credit in the bank account. If you get that right then the rest really does fall into place.

You should also be aware of the definitions of assets, expenses and income and the normal entries that you would make in the accounts for these.

Answers to chapter activities

Activity 1

The figures in brackets are used here to indicate the transaction number in the activity. They can be used to match the debit entry for the transaction with the corresponding credit entry.

Capital

	£		£
		Cash at bank (1)	150,000

Property

	£		£
Cash at bank (2)	140,000		

Purchases

	£		£
Cash at bank (3)	5,000		
Cash at bank (5)	8,000		

Sales

	£		£
		Cash at bank (4)	7,000
		Cash at bank (7)	15,000

Sundry expenses

	£		£
Cash at bank (6)	100		

Wages payable

	£		£
Cash at bank (8)	2,000		

Postage

	£		£
Cash at bank (9)	100		

Cash at bank

	£		£
Capital (1)	150,000	Property (2)	140,000
Sales (4)	7,000	Purchases (3)	5,000
Sales (7)	15,000	Purchases (5)	8,000
		Sundry expenses (6)	100
		Wages payable (8)	2,000
		Postage (9)	100

Activity 2

Cash

Date	Narrative	£	Date	Narrative	£
1.1.X5	Capital	10,000	2.1.X5	Purchases	2,500
5.1.X5	Sales	3,000	4.1.X5	Delivery van	1,000
8.1.X5	Loan	2,000	7.1.X5	Gas	500
10.1.X5	Debtors	3,000	9.1.X5	Creditors	1,500
			11.1.X5	Drawings	750

Capital

Date	Narrative	£	Date	Narrative	£
			1.1.X5	Cash	10,000

Purchases

Date	Narrative	£	Date	Narrative	£
2.1.X5	Cash	2,500			
3.1.X5	Creditors	2,000			

Creditors

Date	Narrative	£	Date	Narrative	£
9.1.X5	Cash	1,500	3.1.X5	Purchases	2,000

Delivery van

Date	Narrative	£	Date	Narrative	£
4.1.X5	Cash	1,000			

Sales

Date	Narrative	£	Date	Narrative	£
			5.1.X5	Cash	3,000
			6.1.X5	Debtors	5,000

Debtors

Date	Narrative	£	Date	Narrative	£
6.1.X5	Sales	5,000	10.1.X5	Cash	3,000

Gas

Date	Narrative	£	Date	Narrative	£
7.1.X5	Cash	500			

Loan

Date	Narrative	£	Date	Narrative	£
			8.1.X5	Cash	2,000

Drawings

Date	Narrative	£	Date	Narrative	£
11.1.X5	Cash	750			

7 Test your knowledge

 Workbook Activity 3

Z, the owner of a consultancy firm, has the following transactions:

(a) Pays £4,000 into the bank as capital. ✓

(b) Buys a computer for £1,000. ✓

(c) Pays rent of £400. ✓

(d) Earns £800 for consultancy services. ✓

Write up the ledger accounts for the above.

 Workbook Activity 4

B makes the following cash transactions:

(a) Pays £4,000 into the bank as capital. ✓

(b) Buys goods for £700. ✓

(c) Buys champagne to entertain the staff for £300. ✓

(d) Purchases three computers for £3,000. ✓

(e) Sells goods for £1,500. ✓

(f) Draws £500 cash. ✓

(g) Purchases goods for £1,200. ✓

(h) Pays telephone bill of £600. ✓

(i) Receives telephone bill rebate of £200. ✓

(j) Buys stationery for £157. ✓

Write up the ledger accounts for the above.

Workbook Activity 5

A sells books to B for £1,000 on credit.

A also sells books to C for £90 credit.

B pays £500 and C pays £90.

Write up these transactions in the sales ledger accounts of A, using individual debtor accounts for each customer.

Drafting an initial trial balance

Introduction

At the end of a period of time, for example a month of trading, the owner of the business might wish to know some details about the performance of the business in the period. For example how much sales revenue was earned, how much does the business owe to its creditors, how much money is left in the bank?

These figures can be found by balancing the ledger accounts. So in this chapter we will look at the procedure for balancing a ledger account as the first step to drafting an initial trial balance.

CONTENTS
1   Procedure for balancing a ledger account
2   The trial balance

1 Procedure for balancing a ledger account

1.1 Steps to follow

Step 1 Total both the debit and the credit side of the ledger account and make a note of each total.

Step 2 Insert the higher of the two totals as the total on both sides of the ledger account leaving a line beneath the final entry on each side of the account.

Step 3 On the side with the smaller total insert the figure needed to make this column add up to the total. Call this figure the balance carried down (or 'Bal c/d' as an abbreviation).

Step 4 On the opposite side of the ledger account, below the total insert this same figure and call it the balance brought down (or 'Bal b/d' as an abbreviation).

Example

The bank account of a business has the following entries:

Bank

	£		£
Capital	1,000	Purchases	200
Sales	300	Drawings	100
Sales	400	Rent	400
Capital	500	Stationery	300
Sales	800	Purchases	400

Calculate the balance on the account and bring the balance down as a single amount.

Solution

Step 1 Total both sides of the account and make a note of the totals. (Note that these totals that are asterisked below would not normally be written into the ledger account itself. They are only shown here to explain the process more clearly.)

Bank

	£		£
Capital	1,000	Purchases	200
Sales	300	Drawings	100
Sales	400	Rent	400
Capital	500	Stationery	300
Sales	800	Purchases	400
	———		———
Sub-total debits*	3,000	Sub-total credits*	1,400

Step 2   Insert the higher total as the total of both sides.

Bank

	£		£
Capital	1,000	Purchases	200
Sales	300	Drawings	100
Sales	400	Rent	400
Capital	500	Stationery	300
Sales	800	Purchases	400
	———		———
Sub-total debits*	3,000	Sub-total credits*	1,400
	———		———
Total	3,000	Total	3,000
	———		———

Step 3   Insert a balancing figure on the side of the account with the lower sub-total. This is referred to as the 'balance carried down' or 'bal c/d' for short.

Bank

	£		£
Capital	1,000	Purchases	200
Sales	300	Drawings	100
Sales	400	Rent	400
Capital	500	Stationery	300
Sales	800	Purchases	400
	___		___
*Sub-total debits**	*3,000*	*Sub-total credits**	*1,400*
		Bal c/d	1,600
	___		___
Total	3,000	Total	3,000
	___		___

Step 4 Insert the balance carried down figure beneath the total on the other side of the account. This is referred to as 'bal b/d' for short.

Bank

	£		£
Capital	1,000	Purchases	200
Sales	300	Drawings	100
Sales	400	Rent	400
Capital	500	Stationery	300
Sales	800	Purchases	400
	___		___
*Sub-total debits**	*3,000*	*Sub-total credits**	*1,400*
		Bal c/d	1,600
	___		___
Total	3,000	Total	3,000
	___		___
Bal b/d	1,600		

The closing balance carried down at the end of the period is also the opening balance brought down at the start of the next period. This opening balance remains in the account as the starting position and any further transactions are then added into the account. In this case the balance brought down is a debit balance as there is money in the bank account making it an asset.

:Ö: Example

Consider again the ledger accounts from the example Percy in the previous chapter which are reproduced below and balance them.

Bank

Date			£	Date			£
1 Jan	Capital	(1)	20,000	1 Jan	Van	(2)	500
5 Jan	Sales	(6)	2,000		Purchases	(3)	1,000
					Drawings	(4)	50
				5 Jan	Purchases	(5)	500
				15 Jan	Rent	(7)	200

Capital

Date			£	Date			£
				1 Jan	Bank	(1)	20,000

Van

Date			£	Date			£
1 Jan	Bank	(2)	500				

Purchases

Date			£	Date			£
1 Jan	Bank	(3)	1,000				
5 Jan	Bank	(5)	500				

Drawings

Date			£	Date			£
1 Jan	Bank	(4)	50				

Sales

Date			£	Date			£
				5 Jan	Bank	(6)	2,000

Rent

Date			£	Date		£
15 Jan	Bank	(7)	200			

Solution

(a)   The bank account

Bank

Date		£	Date		£
1 Jan	Capital	20,000	1 Jan	Van	500
5 Jan	Sales	2,000		Purchases	1,000
				Drawings	50
			5 Jan	Purchases	500
			15 Jan	Rent	200

Step 1   Total both the debit and the credit side of the ledger account and make a note of each total – debit side £22,000, credit side £2,250.

Step 2   Insert the higher of the two totals, £22,000, as the total on both sides of the ledger account leaving a line beneath the final entry on each side of the account.

Bank

Date		£	Date		£
1 Jan	Capital	20,000	1 Jan	Van	500
5 Jan	Sales	2,000		Purchases	1,000
				Drawings	50
			5 Jan	Purchases	500
			15 Jan	Rent	200
		22,000			22,000

Step 3   On the side with the smaller total insert the figure needed to make this column add up to the total. Call this figure the balance carried down (or Bal c/d as an abbreviation).

Step 4   On the opposite side of the ledger account, below the total insert this same figure and call it the balance brought down (or Bal b/d as an abbreviation).

Bank

Date		£	Date		£
1 Jan	Capital	20,000	1 Jan	Van	500
5 Jan	Sales	2,000		Purchases	1,000
				Drawings	50
			5 Jan	Purchases	500
			15 Jan	Rent	200
			31 Jan	Balance c/d	19,750
		22,000			22,000
1 Feb	Balance b/d	19,750			

This shows that the business has £19,750 left in the bank account at the end of January and therefore also on the first day of February. As the balance that is brought down to start the next period is on the debit side of the account this is known as a debit balance and indicates that this is an asset – money in the bank account.

(b) Capital

Capital

Date		£	Date		£
			1 Jan	Bank	20,000

As there is only one entry in this account there is no need to balance the account. The entry is on the credit side and is known as a credit balance. A credit balance is a liability of the business and this account shows that the business owes the owner £20,000 of capital.

(c) Van

Van

Date		£	Date		£
1 Jan	Bank	500			

Again, there is no need to balance this account as there is only one entry. This is a debit balance as it is an asset – the fixed asset, the van, which cost £500.

(d) Purchases

Purchases

Date		£	Date		£
1 Jan	Bank	1,000			
5 Jan	Bank	500	31 Jan	Balance c/d	1,500
		1,500			1,500
1 Feb	Balance b/d	1,500			

This now shows that during the month £1,500 of purchases were made. This is a debit balance as purchases are an expense of the business.

(e) Drawings

Drawings

Date		£	Date		£
1 Jan	Bank	50			

This is a debit balance as drawings are a reduction of the capital owed to the owner which is a credit balance.

(f) Sales

Sales

Date		£	Date		£
			5 Jan	Bank	2,000

There is no need to balance the account as there is only one entry – a £2,000 credit balance representing income.

(g) Rent

Rent

Date		£	Date		£
15 Jan	Bank	200			

As there is only one entry there is no need to balance the account. This is a debit balance indicating that there has been an expense of £200 of rent incurred during the month.

Activity 1

Given below is a bank account ledger for the month of March. Show the balance b/d at 31st March.

Bank

Date		£	Date		£
1 Mar	Capital	12,000	3 Mar	Purchases	3,000
7 Mar	Sales	5,000	15 Mar	Fixed asset	2,400
19 Mar	Sales	2,000	20 Mar	Purchases	5,300
22 Mar	Sales	3,000	24 Mar	Rent	1,000
			28 Mar	Drawings	2,000

2 The trial balance

2.1 List of balances

The trial balance is a list showing the balances brought down on each ledger account. An example of a simple trial balance is given below:

	Debit £	Credit £
Sales		5,000
Opening stock	100	
Purchases	3,000	
Rent	200	
Car	3,000	
Debtors	100	
Creditors		1,400
	6,400	6,400

The trial balance is produced immediately after the double entry has been completed and balances extracted on the accounts. If the double entry has been done correctly, the total of the debits will equal the total of the credits.

2.2 Reasons for extracting a trial balance

Drafting a trial balance is a way of ensuring that double entries have been correctly completed. It is possible to detect other errors with a trial balance, but this will be discussed in a later chapter.

Example

The following are the balances on the accounts of Ernest at 31 December 20X8.

	£
Sales	47,140
Purchases	26,500
Debtors	7,640
Creditors	4,320
General expenses	9,430
Loan	5,000
Plant and machinery at cost	7,300
Motor van at cost	2,650
Drawings	7,500
Rent and rates	6,450
Insurance	1,560
Bank overdraft	2,570
Capital	10,000

Required:

Prepare Ernest's trial balance as at 31 December 20X8.

Solution

Step 1   Set up a blank trial balance.

Step 2   Work down the list of balances one by one using what you have learned so far about debits and credits. Assets and expenses are debit balances and liabilities and income are credit balances.

The mnemonic DEAD CLIC may help.

Drs increase:	**Crs increase:**
Debtors	Creditors
Expenses	Liabilities
Assets	Income
Drawings	Capital

Trial balance at 31 December 20X8

	Dr £	Cr £
Sales		47,140
Purchases	26,500	
Debtors	7,640	
Creditors		4,320
General expenses	9,430	
Loan		5,000
Plant and machinery at cost	7,300	
Motor van at cost	2,650	
Drawings	7,500	
Rent and rates	6,450	
Insurance	1,560	
Bank overdraft		2,570
Capital		10,000
	———	———
	69,030	69,030
	———	———

Take care with drawings. These are a reduction of the capital owed back to the owner therefore as a reduction of a liability they must be a debit balance.

The bank overdraft is an amount owed to the bank therefore it must be a credit balance.

 Activity 2

Continuing with the example of Percy, complete the trial balance.

3 Summary

Balancing an account is a very important technique which you must be able to master. You must understand how to bring the balance down onto the correct side.

Answers to chapter activities

Activity 1

Bank

Date		£	Date		£
1 Mar	Capital	12,000	3 Mar	Purchases	3,000
7 Mar	Sales	5,000	15 Mar	Fixed asset	2,400
19 Mar	Sales	2,000	20 Mar	Purchases	5,300
22 Mar	Sales	3,000	24 Mar	Rent	1,000
			28 Mar	Drawings	2,000
			31 Mar	Balance c/d	8,300
		22,000			22,000
1 Apr	Balance b/d	8,300			

Activity 2

Trial balance

	Dr £	Cr £
Bank	19,750	
Capital		20,000
Van	500	
Purchases	1,500	
Drawings	50	
Sales		2,000
Rent	200	
	22,000	22,000

4 Test your knowledge

Workbook Activity 3

The following cash book has been written up for the month of May 20X9. There was no opening balance.

Bank

	£		£
Capital	10,000	Computer	1,000
Sales	2,000	Telephone	567
Sales	3,000	Rent	1,500
Sales	2,000	Rates	125
		Stationery	247
		Petrol	49
		Purchases	2,500
		Drawings	500
		Petrol	42

Bring down the balance on the account.

Workbook Activity 4

The following bank account has been written up during May 20X9. There was no brought forward balance.

Bank

	£		£
Capital	5,000	Purchases	850
Sales	1,000	Fixtures	560
Sales	876	Van	1,500
Rent rebate	560	Rent	1,300
Sales	1,370	Rates	360
		Telephone	220
		Stationery	120
		Petrol	48
		Car repairs	167

Bring down the balance on the account.

Workbook Activity 5

The following bank account has been written up during June 20X9.

Bank

	£		£
Balance b/f	23,700	Drawings	4,000
Sales	2,300	Rent	570
Sales	1,700	Purchases	6,000
Debtors	4,700	Rates	500
		Salaries	3,600
		Car expenses	460
		Petrol	49
		Petrol	38
		Electricity	210
		Stationery	89

Bring down the balance on the account.

Workbook Activity 6

The following are the balances on the accounts of XYZ at 31 August 20X9:

	£
Sales	41,770
Purchases	34,680
Debtors	6,790
Creditors	5,650
General expenses	12,760
Loan	10,000
Plant and machinery at cost	5,000
Motor van at cost	6,000
Drawings	2,000
Rent and rates	6,700
Insurance	4,000
Bank overdraft	510
Capital	20,000

Prepare XYZ's Trial Balance as at 31 August 20X9.

Workbook Activity 7

Tony makes the following transactions during the month of July 20X9:

(a)   Purchases goods on credit for £1,000.

(b)   Pays cash for rent of £500.

(c)   Makes sales on credit for £1,500.

(d)   Buys a computer for £900 cash.

(e)   Pays cash for wages of £1,000.

(f)   Receives cash from a credit customer of £400.

(g)   Pays £300 cash to a credit supplier.

(h)   Pays £200 cash for a telephone bill.

(i)   Receives £50 cash refund for overcharge on telephone bill.

(j)   Makes cash purchases of £400.

(k)   Makes cash sales of £2,000.

Write up the ledger accounts for these transactions, balance the accounts off and extract Tony's Trial Balance at 31 July 20X9.

Business documents

5

Introduction

This chapter will take an outline look at the purpose and range of business documents in order that you are able to explain the purpose and flow of documents between seller and buyer.

1 Cash vs credit

1.1 Introduction

Cash sales and purchases are relatively straightforward but credit sales and purchases are more involved. Dependent on whether we are the seller or the buyer dictates whether we view the transaction as a sale or purchase. The details of all of the aspects covered here will be dealt with in greater depth in later chapters.

1.2 Cash sales and purchases

A cash sale or purchase will normally be made in a retail environment. A customer will enter the shop, choose the goods they wish to buy then come to the till in order to pay for them. The seller will tell the customer the price of the goods and the customer then offers payment for them, in the form of notes and coins. Alternatively, the customer may offer to pay for the goods by cheque or credit or debit card. The detailed procedures for accepting payment by these methods will be considered later.

Finally, once the customer has paid for the goods, a receipt of some sort will be given to the customer. This may be printed automatically by the till or may be a handwritten receipt in some businesses. The transaction is now complete.

1.3 Credit sales and purchases

The procedure for a sale or purchase on credit can be rather more involved. The sale or purchase process will normally be initiated by a seller receiving an order from a customer. This order may be in writing, by fax, over the telephone or by email. When your business receives the order, the first decision that must be made is whether or not to allow the customer credit for this sale; a period of time they can take before paying the invoice.

1.4 Offering credit

Selling goods on credit always involves an element of risk. The goods are being taken away or delivered to the customer now with the promise of payment in the future. Therefore your business must be confident that the payment will be received. The decision process as to whether or not to make the sale on credit will be different depending upon whether this is a sale to an existing credit customer or a new customer.

1.5 Existing customers

If an existing credit customer wishes to make a further purchase on credit, it would be normal practice to carry out some basic checks. When the customer was originally taken on as a credit customer, a credit limit will have been set which should not be exceeded. Checks should be made to ensure that the new sale, when added to the amount currently owing, do not take the customer over their credit limit.

It would also be sensible to check that there have been no problems recently with receiving payment from this customer. If the checks are satisfactory then the credit sale can go ahead.

1.6 New customer

If a new customer asks for credit from your business then it would be normal practice to ask the customer to supply some trade references – names of other businesses that they trade with on credit who can vouch for their creditworthiness. Your business may also wish to check the customer's creditworthiness through an agency such as Dun and Bradstreet, or by asking for references from the customer's bank.

If the references and checks are satisfactory then a credit limit will be set for this customer and the sale can go ahead.

2 Summary of the flow of documents

The main document flows for a credit transaction are illustrated below. The various documents are described in the paragraphs that follow.

3 Quotation

3.1 Price enquiry

The first stage of the process of a credit sale may be the receipt of a price enquiry from a customer.

The price enquiry may be a formal written document or more likely a telephone call. When responding to a price enquiry it is important that you make sure that the price you quote is the correct one as if it is incorrect you may find that you are contracted to sell the goods at that price under contract law (see later chapter in this Study Text).

3.2 Price quotation

In some organisations it is common practice to quote prices to customers over the telephone particularly if there is a catalogue or price list from which there are no deviations in price. However, some businesses will be prepared to offer certain customers goods at different prices. Therefore it is often the case that a price quotation is sent out to a customer showing the price at which the goods that they want can be bought.

There may also be discounts offered and/or given to customers which we will consider later.

A typical price quotation is shown on the next page.

City Woods Suppliers

192 Old Kent Road
London
SE1 8QT

*Name and address of
business quoting price*

Tel: 020 7248 7009 – Fax: 020 728 7890

QUOTATION

TO: Alpha Limited
        Mountjoy Street   *Name and address of
        London W12 6RS   customer*

Date: 14 Sept 20X3

Today's date

Thank you for your telephone enquiry of 10 September. We are pleased to quote the following price:

Chipboard sheeting 6' × 4' Code CB0351 £23.00 per unit, excluding VAT

*Details of
goods*

J Kramer   *Authorisation
                    signature*

*Price being
quoted*

Sales Manager

The price quotation is an important document as this is the price that your organisation is now contracted to sell the goods at. Therefore it is important that it is authorised by the appropriate person in the organisation.

4 Purchase order

4.1   The purchase order

If the customer is happy with the price quotation that they have received from your business then they will place a firm order with you. The order may be by telephone or it may be in writing. Whatever method is used for the purchase order, it is important to check all of the details carefully.

- Is the price that which was quoted to the customer?

- Are the delivery terms acceptable?

- Are any discounts applicable?

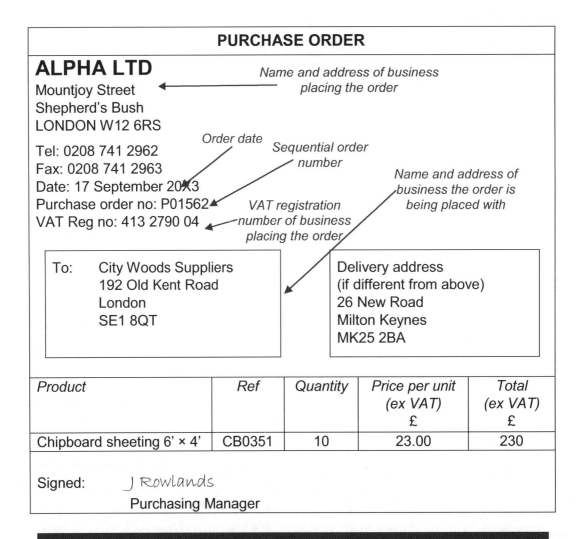

PURCHASE ORDER

ALPHA LTD

Name and address of business placing the order

Mountjoy Street
Shepherd's Bush
LONDON W12 6RS

Tel: 0208 741 2962
Fax: 0208 741 2963

Order date

Sequential order number

Date: 17 September 2013
Purchase order no: P01562
VAT Reg no: 413 2790 04

Name and address of business the order is being placed with

VAT registration number of business placing the order

To: City Woods Suppliers
      192 Old Kent Road
      London
      SE1 8QT

Delivery address
(if different from above)
26 New Road
Milton Keynes
MK25 2BA

Product	Ref	Quantity	Price per unit (ex VAT) £	Total (ex VAT) £
Chipboard sheeting 6' × 4'	CB0351	10	23.00	230

Signed: *J Rowlands*
            Purchasing Manager

5   Sales order

5.1   Confirming sales orders

To avoid misunderstandings, a supplier will normally confirm a customer's order by completing a **sales order**, even if the customer has already sent a written purchase order.

A **sales order** is a document confirming:

- quantity/type of goods or service
- date of supply
- location of supply
- price and terms.

City Woods Suppliers

192 Old Kent Road ◄───── *Name and address*
London   *of business making*
SE1 8QT   *the sale*

Delivery address
and date

Tel: 020 7248 7009 – Fax: 020 7248 7890

SALES ORDER

To: **Delivery:**   **Delivery date:**

Alpha Limited   26 New Road   25 September 20X3
Mountjoy St   ◄─ *Name and*   Milton Keynes
London W12 6RS   *address of* MK25 2BA   *Sales order*
              customer   *number*

Date: 20 September 20X3   **Sales order number:** 41161

We confirm the following order to be delivered as above.
Please note our credit terms are strictly 30 days net.

Code	Quantity	Description	Unit price (excl VAT)	Discount
CB0351	10	Chipboard sheeting 6' × 4'	£23.00	NIL

Details of goods   *Price of goods*

                          Authorised
                           signature
Authorised: *P. Anders* ◄─   Date: 20 September 20X3

---

6 Delivery note

6.1 Introduction

Once all of the negotiations over the price and terms of the credit sale
have been completed, then the goods themselves must be delivered.

6.2 Delivery notes

Delivery note – a document accompanying goods despatched to a
customer.

Delivery notes should have **sequential numbers** that are either pre-
printed for a manual system or computer generated in a computer system,
and should be used in order. Spoiled delivery notes should be cancelled
and kept.

There will normally be three parts to a delivery note:

Part one   – This is kept by the **customer** in order to compare to the purchase order and then to the sales invoice.

Part two   – This is signed and returned to the **supplier** of the goods as evidence that they have been received by the customer in good condition.

Part three – This is signed and kept by the **delivery organisation** as evidence that they have delivered the goods and that the customer has received them.

City Woods Suppliers
192 Old Kent Road
London
SE1 8QT

Tel: 020 7248 7009 – Fax: 020 7248 7890   DN 005673

DELIVERY NOTE

To:	Delivery:	Delivery date:
Alpha Limited	26 New Road	25 September 20X3
Mountjoy St	Milton Keynes	
London W12 6RS	MK25 2BA	
Date: 25 September 20X3	**Sales order number:** 41161	

We confirm the following order to be delivered as above.

Product	Code	Quantity
Chipboard 6' × 4'	CB0351	10

Received in good condition: *A Patel*

---

7   Invoice

7.1   The sales invoice

Once the goods have been delivered the seller must prepare and send out the sales invoice.

In a manual system, sales invoices must be prepared from the details shown on delivery notes. Delivery notes do not normally show details of prices, discounts or VAT. (This is because the customer might mistake the delivery note for a sales invoice.) Price, discounts and VAT are shown on the sales invoice. Discounts and VAT are considered in a later chapter.

                      KAPLAN PUBLISHING

Sales invoices should have pre-printed sequential numbers and should be used in order. Spoiled sales invoices should be cancelled and kept.

In a computer system, the sales invoice will generally be produced at the same time as the delivery note and will be identical except that the delivery note may not have details of price, etc.

City Woods Suppliers

192 Old Kent Road
London
SE1 8QT

Tel: 020 7248 7009 – Fax: 020 7248 7890

Invoice no: 1005673
Tax point: 25 September 20X3
VAT reg no: 618 2201 63
Delivery note: DN005673
Account no: AL6215

INVOICE

To:

Alpha Limited
Mountjoy St
London W12 6RS

Delivery:

26 New Road
Milton Keynes
MK25 2BA

Delivery date:

25 September 20X3

Date: 25 September 20X3   **Sales order number:** 41161

We confirm the following order to be delivered as above.

Product	Code	Quantity	Price per unit £	Total £
Chipboard 6' × 4'	CB0351	10	23.00	230.00
			VAT	46.00
			Total	276.00

7.2   Pricing goods and services

Unit prices for goods or services are kept in master files which must be updated regularly. If a price quotation has been sent to a customer then this must be used to determine the price to use on the invoice.

Prices will normally be quoted exclusive of value added tax (VAT), as this is the true selling price to the business.

7.3 Trade discounts

Trade discounts are a definite amount that is deducted from the list price of the goods for the supplies to some customers, with the intention of encouraging and rewarding customer loyalty. As well as checking the actual calculation of the trade discount on the face of the invoice, the supplier's file or the price quotation should be checked to ensure that the correct percentage of trade discount has been deducted.

Even if no trade discount appears on the purchase invoice, the supplier's file or price quotation must still be checked as it may be that a trade discount should have been deducted but has been inadvertently forgotten by the supplier.

7.4 Bulk discounts

A bulk discount is similar to a trade discount in that it is deducted from the list price on the invoice. However, a bulk discount is given by a supplier for orders above a certain size. As with a trade discount the calculation of any bulk discount must be checked to the supplier's file to ensure that the correct discount has been given.

7.5 Settlement or cash discounts

Settlement or cash discounts (also known as prompt payment discounts) are offered to customers in order to encourage early payment of invoices. The details of the settlement discount will be shown at the bottom of the purchase invoice and it is up to the customer to decide whether to pay the invoice early enough to benefit from the settlement discount or whether to delay payment and ignore the settlement discount.

Again the supplier's file should be checked to ensure that the correct percentage of settlement discount according to the correct terms has been offered.

If there is no settlement discount offered the supplier's details must still be checked to ensure that the settlement discount has not been forgotten by the supplier.

A trade discount or a bulk discount is a definite reduction in price from the list price whereas a cash or settlement discount is only a reduction in price if the organisation decides to take advantage of it by paying earlier.

7.6 VAT calculations and discounts

We will consider the impact on VAT calculations when discounts are offered in a later chapter.

7.7 Customer details

In order to prepare the sales invoice the customer master file must be found. This will show the details of any discounts, etc offered to this customer.

7.8 The effect of value added tax

If the selling business is registered for VAT, VAT must be charged on taxable supplies.

Most goods and services are standard-rated (i.e. 20% rate of VAT must be charged). This will be considered in more detail later.

 Example

Preparing a sales invoice

Thelma Goody is the sales invoicing clerk for a VAT registered clothing wholesaler. Thelma prepares the sales invoices to be sent to the customer from the price list and a copy of the delivery note sent up to her by the sales department.

Today she has received the following delivery note from the sales department.

Delivery note: 2685

To: Kids Clothes Ltd
9 Port Street
MANCHESTER
M1 5EX

A B Fashions Ltd
3 Park Road
Parkway
Bristol
BR6 6SJ
Tel: 01272 695221
Fax: 01272 695222

Delivery date: 20 August 20X6

Quantity	Code	DESCRIPTION	Colour
90	SSB 330	Shawls (babies)	Assorted
30	CJA 991	Cashmere jumpers (adult)	Cream
30	GGC 442	Gloves (children)	Assorted

Received by: ....

Signature: .... Date: ....

Code	Description	Colour	Unit price £	VAT rate
SSG 001	Skirt (girls)	Black	13.50	Zero
SSW 002	Skirt (women)	Navy	15.90	Standard
TTW 037	Trousers (women)	Black	21.00	Standard
TTW 038	Trousers (women)	Navy	15.60	Standard
TTW 039	Trousers (women)	Red	15.60	Standard
SSB 330	Shawl (babies)	Assorted	11.50	Zero
SSB 331	Shawl (babies)	White	11.50	Zero
CJA 991	Cashmere jumper (adult)	Cream	65.00	Standard
CJA 992	Cashmere jumper (adult)	Pink	65.00	Standard
CJA 993	Cashmere jumper (adult)	Blue	65.00	Standard
CJA 994	Cashmere jumper (adult)	Camel	65.00	Standard
HHB 665	Hat (babies)	White	3.50	Zero
HHB 666	Hat (babies)	Blue	3.50	Zero
GGC 442	Gloves (children)	Assorted	6.20	Zero
GGC 443	Gloves (children)	White	6.50	Zero
GGC 444	Gloves (children)	Black	6.50	Zero

The customer file shows that Kids Clothes Ltd's account number is KC 0055 and that a trade discount of 10% is offered to this customer.

Thelma must now prepare the sales invoice. Today's date is 22 August 20X6.

Solution

INVOICE

Invoice to:
Kids Clothes Ltd
9 Port Street
MANCHESTER
M1 5EX

A B Fashions Ltd
3 Park Road
Parkway
Bristol
BR6 6SJ
Tel: 01272 695221
Fax: 01272 695222

Deliver to:

As above

Invoice no:	95124
Tax point:	22 August 20X6
VAT reg no:	488 7922 26
Delivery note no:	2685
Account no:	KC 0055

Code	Description	Quantity	VAT rate	Unit price	Amount excl of VAT
			%	£	£
SSB 330	Shawls (babies) assorted	90	0	11.50	1,035.00
CJA 991	Cashmere jumper (adult) cream	30	20	65.00	1,950.00
GGC 442	Gloves (children) assorted	30	0	6.20	186.00
					3,171.00
Trade discount 10%					(317.10)
					2,853.90
VAT					351.00
Total amount payable					3,204.90

Step 1 Enter today's date on the invoice and the invoice number which should be the next number after the last sales invoice number.

Step 2 Enter the customer details – name, address and account number.

Step 3 Refer now to the delivery note copy and enter the delivery note number and the quantities, codes and descriptions of the goods.

Step 4   Refer to the price list and enter the unit prices of the goods and the rate of VAT (note that the VAT rate for children's clothes is zero).

Step 5   Now for the calculations – firstly multiply the number of each item by the unit price to find the VAT exclusive price – then total these total prices – finally calculate the trade discount as 10% of this total, £3,171 × 10% = £317.10 and deduct it.

Step 6   Calculate the VAT – in this case there is only standard rate VAT on the cashmere jumpers but you must remember to deduct the trade discount (£1,950 – £195) before calculating the VAT amount £1,755 × 20% = £351 – add the VAT to the invoice total after deducting the trade discount.

7.9   The purchase invoice

Now considering the perspective of the customer, what we previously have viewed as a sales invoice, to the customer is a purchase invoice. Once the customer receives their purchase invoice from the seller, a number of checks need to be made on it before it can be passed for payment.

7.10   Order and receipt of goods

Firstly the purchase invoice must be checked to the purchase order and to the delivery note. This is to ensure that not only is this an invoice for goods that were ordered but also for goods that were received. In particular check the description and the quantity of the goods.

For example suppose that the purchase order for goods shows that 100 packs were ordered and the delivery note shows that 100 packs were received. If when the invoice arrives it is for 120 packs then the supplier should be politely informed of the error and a credit note requested.

7.11   Calculations

All of the calculations on the invoice should also be checked to ensure that they are correct. This will include the following:

- all pricing calculations

- any trade discount or bulk discount calculations

- the VAT calculations

- the total addition of the invoice

- any settlement discount calculations.

7.12 Other terms found on invoices

You may also find other terms and conditions shown on invoices or other documents. Here are some of the more common:

E & OE – Errors and omissions excepted. The seller is claiming the right to correct any genuine errors on the invoice (e.g. prices) at a later date.

Carriage paid – The invoice value includes delivery of the goods to the customer's premises.

Ex works – Prices quoted do not include delivery to the customer's premises. The customer must organise and pay for the delivery of the goods.

Cash on delivery – The customer is expected to pay for the goods when they are delivered.

8 Credit note

8.1 Introduction

Credit notes are issued as documentary evidence that goods have been returned and that all or part of a previous sales invoice is cancelled. Therefore a business must keep strict control over the credit notes it issues. Credit notes may also be issued where a customer takes advantage of a settlement discount: this is covered in a later chapter.

Credit note – Document issued by a supplier to a customer cancelling part or all of a sales invoice. Business normally issues a credit note:

- when a customer has returned faulty or damaged goods
- when a customer has returned perfect goods by agreement with the supplier
- to make a refund for short deliveries
- to settle a dispute with a customer.

A credit note is the reversal of a previous invoice or part of the invoice value.

8.2   Return of goods

When a supplier receives returned goods they must be inspected, counted and recorded on receipt. They would normally be recorded on a returns inwards note.

In the perspective of a customer who is returning goods and consequently receives a credit note exactly the same checks should be made on credit notes as on invoices. The reason for the credit note and the amount that has been credited should be checked, so should all of the calculations and the VAT.

8.3   Authorising credit notes

All credit notes must be authorised by a supervisor prior to being issued to the customer.

Some credit notes may be issued without a returns inwards note. For example, an error may have been made in pricing on an invoice but the customer is satisfied with the goods and does not need to return them.

These credit notes must be issued only after written authorisation has been received and must be reviewed and approved before being sent to the customer or recorded.

8.4   Preparing credit notes

A credit note is effectively the reverse of an invoice and therefore will tend to include all the details that would normally appear on a sales invoice.

If Alpha Ltd (as seen earlier in the chapter) returned two of the chipboard panels, the credit note would be as follows.

City Woods Suppliers

192 Old Kent Road   *Name and address*   *Sequential credit*
London   *of issuer of credit*   *note number*
SE1 8QT   *note*

Tel: 020 7248 7009 – Fax: 020 7248 7890   Credit note no: CN 02542
                                            Tax point: 30 September 20X3
                    VAT registration   VAT reg no: 618 2201 63
                    number of supplier   Return inwards note no: 01531
                                            Invoice no: 1005673
                    Returns inwards   Account no: AL 6215
                    note reference

CREDIT NOTE   *Date of credit note*

Credit to: *Name and address*
Alpha Limited   *of customer*   *Customer's account*
Mountjoy St   *code*
London W12 6RS

Date: 30 September 20X3

Description	Code	Quantity	VAT rate %	Unit price £	Amount exclusive of VAT £
Chipboard 6' × 4'	CB0351	2	20	23.00	46.00
			Goods returned total		46.00
					46.00
VAT				*VAT charged*	9.20
				Total amount of credit	55.20

Rate of VAT on goods returned

9 Coding

9.1 Introduction

Invoices should be coded to show:

- product group/type for analysis of sales/purchases

- customer/supplier account number.

There are several different systems of coding which can be used by a business and the main ones are outlined below.

9.2   Sequence codes

Allocate a number, or a letter, to items in a simple list.

For example:

Code	Name
01	ADAMS, Joan
02	AITKEN, James
03	ALCOCK, Freda
04	BROWN, Joe

9.3   Block codes

These allocate bands of numbers to particular categories.

For example, consider a tobacco manufacturer who produces several types of cigarettes, cigars and pipe tobaccos. He could assign a code to each particular brand as follows:

Product type	Block code
Cigarette	01 – 19
Cigar	20 – 29
Pipe tobacco	30 – 39

9.4   Significant digit codes

These are a particular type of group classification code where individual digits and letters are used to represent features of the coded item. The example given is one used to describe different kinds of vehicle tyres.

Code	Item
TT67015B	Tube Tyre 670 × 15 Blackwall
LT67015W	Tubeless Tyre 670 × 15 Whitewall

9.5   Faceted codes

Faceted codes are another type of group classification code by which the digits of the code are divided into facets of several digits and each facet represents some attribute of the item being coded. These codes are similar to significant digit codes but are purely numerical.

Example: faceted code for types of carpet

Facet 1	=	type of weave (1 digit)	1	=	Cord
			2	=	Twist
			3	=	Short tufted, etc
Facet 2	=	material (1 digit)	1	=	All wool
			2	=	80% wool, 20% nylon
			3	=	50% wool, 50% nylon, etc
Facet 3	=	pattern (2 digits)	01	=	Self colour (plain)
			02	=	Self colour (embossed)
			03	=	Fig leaf, etc
Facet 4	=	colour (2 digits)	01	=	Off white
			02	=	Bright yellow
			03	=	Scarlet, etc

A typical code would be 220302 representing a twist carpet in 80% wool, 20% nylon, pattern fig leaf and colour bright yellow.

Note that a two-digit facet allows up to 100 different codings (00 to 99).

9.6 Decimal codes (or hierarchical codes)

These are yet another form of a group classification code. The most obvious example of a decimal code is the Universal Decimal Code (UDC) devised by Dewey and widely used for the classification of books in libraries. UDC divides all human knowledge into more and more detailed categories as shown.

Code	Item
3	Social science
37	Education
372	Elementary
372.2	Kindergarten
372.21	Methods
372.215	Songs and games

Whatever the coding system that is used it is important for further accounting purposes that the invoices and credit notes are coded according to type of sales and the particular customer.

You may be expected to code items included on sales invoices or credit notes according to a coding system that is given to you in an assessment.

Activity 1

Is the cheque number used in a cheque book an example of a sequential code or a hierarchical code?

10 Summary

In this chapter we have concentrated on the purpose and flow of a range of business documents. Before preparing an invoice it is necessary to ensure that this is for a valid sale by checking the order and delivery details. It is important that we understand the need to check business documents that are received and sent to ensure they agree to relating documents, the calculations are correct in accordance with discounts and the treatment of VAT.

Answers to chapter activities

 Activity 1

A sequential code (the numbers run in sequential order).

11 Test your knowledge

 Workbook Activity 2

The purchase order has been received from a customer, M.P. Katz & Co Ltd. M Krupps Cardboard has raised an invoice to send to the customer and both the purchase order and the invoice are shown below.

PURCHASE ORDER

Purchase order to:
M Krupps Cardboard
Hayward Lane
Manor Estate
Stockport
SK7 4AD

M.P. Katz & Company Limited
64 Royce Road
Manchester
M15 5XA
Tel: 0161 560 3392
Fax: 0161 560 5322

Purchase order no: PO02543

Please supply 400 cardboard boxes product code CB1354.
Purchase price: £40 per 100, plus VAT at 20%
Discount: less 10% trade discount, as agreed

INVOICE

Invoice to:
M.P. Katz & Company Ltd
64 Royce Road
Manchester
M15 5XA

M Krupps Cardboard
Hayward Lane
Manor Estate
Stockport
SK7 4AD
Tel: 0161 946 4321
Fax: 0161 946 4322

Deliver to:
As above

Invoice no:	69472
Tax point:	29 January 20X9
VAT reg no:	625 9911 58
Order no:	PO02543
Delivery note no:	68553
Account no:	SL07

Code	Description	Quantity	VAT rate	Unit price	Amount excl of VAT
			%	£	£
CB1354	Cardboard boxes	400	20	0.40	160.00
Trade discount 20%					32.00
					128.00
VAT at 20%					25.60
Total amount payable					153.60

You have been asked to determine whether the invoice has been correctly prepared.

(i) Has the correct pricing been used on the invoice?

(ii) Has the correct discount been applied?

(iii) What should the correct amount of VAT charged be?

(iv) What should the correct total amount payable be?

 Workbook Activity 3

ABC Ltd uses codes within the accounting system. An extract from the general ledger coding list is given below:

General Ledger Account	Code number
Equipment	10
Debtors	20
Electricity	30
Purchases	40
Sales	50

Required:

(a) Why are the general ledger codes numbered in steps of 10, rather than 1,2,3,4?

(b) Give 3 examples of the use of code numbers in an accounting system, other than general ledger accounts codes.

(c)   Are the following statements true or false?

	TRUE/FALSE
General ledger codes help when barcoding an item of stock	
General ledger codes help when filing a financial document	
General ledger codes help trace relevant accounts quickly and easily	
General ledger codes help find the total amount owing to a supplier	

 Workbook Activity 4

Nethan Builders have just received the following credit note. You are required to check that the credit note is clerically accurate and note the details of any problems. Trade discount is 15%.

CREDIT NOTE

Credit note to:
Nethan Builders
Brecon House
Stamford Road
Manchester
M16 4PL

J M Bond & Co
North Park Industrial Estate
Manchester
M12 4TU
Tel: 0161 561 3214
Fax: 0161 561 3060

Credit note no: 06192
Tax point: 22 April 20X1
VAT reg no: 461 4367 91
Invoice no: 331624

Code	Description	Quantity	VAT rate %	Unit price £	Amount excl of VAT £
DGSS4163	Structural softwood untreated	6 m	20	6.85	41.10
					41.10
Trade discount 15%					8.22
					32.88
VAT at 20%					6.57
Total amount of credit					39.45

Workbook Activity 5

You work in the accounts department of Nethan Builders and given below are three purchase invoices together with the related purchase orders and delivery note. You are to check each invoice carefully and note any problems or discrepancies that you find. You may assume that the rates of trade and settlement discounts are correct. All VAT is at 20%.

INVOICE

Invoice to:
Nethan Builders
Brecon House
Stamford Road
Manchester
M16 4PL

A J Broom & Company Limited
59 Parkway
Manchester
M2 6EG
Tel: 0161 560 3392
Fax: 0161 560 5322

Deliver to:
As above

Invoice no: 046123
Tax point: 22 April 20X1
VAT reg no: 661 2359 07
Purchase order no: 7164

Code	Description	Quantity	VAT rate %	Unit price £	Amount excl of VAT £
DGS472	SDG Softwood	9.6 m	20	8.44	81.02 ✓
CIBF653	Joist hanger	7	20	12.30	86.10 ✓
					167.12 ✓
Trade discount 10%					16.71 ✓
					150.41 ✓
VAT					30.08 ✓
Total amount payable					180.49 ✓

INVOICE
Jenson Ltd

Invoice to:
Nethan Builders
Brecon House
Stamford Road
Manchester
M16 4PL

30 Longfield Park
Kingsway
M45 2TP

Deliver to:
As above

Invoice no:	47792
Tax point:	22 April 20X1
VAT reg no:	641 3229 45
Purchase order no:	7162

Code	Description	Quantity	VAT rate %	Unit price £	Amount excl of VAT £
PL432115	Door lining set 32 × 115 mm	14	20	30.25	423.50
PL432140	Door lining set 32 × 138 mm	8	20	33.15	265.20
					688.70
Trade discount 15%					103.30
					585.40
VAT					117.08
Total amount payable					702.48

A discount of 3% of the full price applies if payment is made within 14 days. No credit note will be issued. Following payment you must ensure you have only recovered the VAT actually paid.

If you pay within 14 days the discounted price is:

567.84

Net	*113.56*	561.98
VAT		112.39
Gross		674.37

681.40

INVOICE
Haddow Bros

Invoice to:
Nethan Builders
Brecon House
Stamford Road
Manchester
M16 4PL

The White House
Standing Way
Manchester
M13 6FH
Tel: 0161 560 3140
Fax: 0161 560 5140

Deliver to:
As above

Invoice no: 033912
Tax point: 22 April 20X1
VAT reg no: 460 3559 71
Purchase order no: 7166

Code	Description	Quantity	VAT rate %	Unit price £	Amount excl of VAT £
PLY8FE1	Plywood Hardwood 2440 × 1220 mm	12 sheets	20	17.80	213.60

	213.60
VAT	42.72
Total amount payable	256.32

ONLY 10 DELIVERED

A discount of 2% of the full price applies if payment is made within 10 days. No credit note will be issued. Following payment you must ensure you have only recovered the VAT actually paid.

If you pay within 10 days the discounted price is:

Net	209.33
VAT	41.86
Gross	251.19

PURCHASE ORDER				

Nethan Builders
Brecon House
Stamford Road
Manchester
M16 4PL
Tel: 0161 521 6411
Fax: 0161 521 6
Date: 14 April 20X1
Purchase order no: 7162

To: Jenson Ltd
        30 Longfield Park
        Kingsway
        M45 2TP

Delivery address
(If different from above)

Invoice address
(If different from above)

Code	Quantity	Description	Unit price (exclusive of VAT)
			£
PL432140	8	Door lining set 32 × 138 mm	33.15
PL432115	14	Door lining set 32 × 115 mm	30.25

PURCHASE ORDER

Nethan Builders
Brecon House
Stamford Road
Manchester
M16 4PL
Tel: 0161 521 6411
Fax: 0161 521 6
Date: 14 April 20X1
Purchase order no: 7164

To: A J Broom & Co Ltd
        59 Parkway
        Manchester
        M2 6EG

Delivery address (If different from above)	**Invoice address** (If different from above)

Code	Quantity	Description	Unit price (exclusive of VAT)
			£
DGS472	9.6 m	SDG Softwood	8.44
CIBF653	5	Joist hanger	12.30

7 on invoice

PURCHASE ORDER

Nethan Builders
Brecon House
Stamford Road
Manchester
M16 4PL
Tel: 0161 521 6411
Fax: 0161 521 6
Date: 14 April 20X1
Purchase order no: 7165

To: Haddow Bros
        The White House
        Standing Way
        Manchester
        M13 6FH

Delivery address (If different from above)	**Invoice address** (If different from above)

Code	Quantity	Description	Unit price (exclusive of VAT)
			£
PLY8FE1	12 sheets	Plywood Hardwood 2440 × 1220 mm	17.80

DELIVERY NOTE

Jenson Ltd

Deliver to:
Nethan Builders
Brecon House
Stamford Road
Manchester
M16 4PL

30 Longfield Park
Kingsway
M45 2TP
Tel: 0161 511 4666
Fax: 0161 511 4777

Delivery note no: 47823
Tax point: 19 April 20X1
VAT reg: 641 3229 45

Code	Description	Quantity	VAT rate %	Unit price £	Amount excl of VAT £
PL432115	Door lining set 32 × 115 mm	14			
PL432140	Door lining set 32 × 138 mm	8			

Goods received in good condition

Print name   C JULIAN
Signature   C JULIAN
Date   19/4/X1

DELIVERY NOTE

A.J. Broom & Company Limited

Deliver to:
Nethan Builders
Brecon House
Stamford Road
Manchester
M16 4PL

59 Parkway
Manchester
M2 6EG
Tel: 0161 560 3392
Fax: 0161 560 5322

Delivery note no: 076429
Tax point: 20 April 20X1
VAT reg: 661 2359 07
Purchase order no: 7164

Code	Description	Quantity	VAT rate %	Unit price £	Amount excl of VAT £
CIBF653	Joist hanger	7			
DGS472	SDG Softwood	9.6 m			

Goods received in good condition

Print name   C JULIAN
Signature   C JULIAN
Date   19/4/X1

DELIVERY NOTE

Haddow Bros

Deliver to:
Nethan Builders
Brecon House
Stamford Road
Manchester
M16 4PL

The White House
Standing Way
Manchester
M13 6FH
Tel: 0161 560 3140
Fax: 0161 560 6140

Delivery note no:	667713
Tax point:	17 April 20X1
VAT reg no:	460 3559 71

Code	Description	Quantity	VAT rate %	Unit price £	Amount excl of VAT £
PLY8FE1	Plywood Hardwood 2440 × 1220 mm	10			

Goods received in good condition

Print name	C JULIAN
Signature	C JULIAN
Date	17/4/X1

📝 Workbook Activity 6

Nethan Builders codes all purchase invoices and credit notes with a supplier code and a general ledger code:

Supplier	Supplier account code
Haddow Bros	HAD29
AJ Broom & Company Ltd	AJB14
Jenson Ltd	JEN32
JM Bond & Co	JMB33

Item	General ledger code
Softwood	GL110
Hardwood	GL112
Sand	GL130
Steel	GL140
Brick	GL145

Required:

For each of the invoices and credit notes shown below select the appropriate supplier account code and general ledger code to be used to code them.

	INVOICE				
	Haddow Bros				

Invoice to:
Nethan Builders
Brecon House
Stamford Road
Manchester
M16 4PL

The White House
Standing Way
Manchester
M13 6FH
Tel: 0161 560 3140
Fax: 0161 560 5140

Deliver to:
As above

Invoice no: 033912
Tax point: 22 April 20X1
VAT reg no: 460 3559 71
Purchase order no: 7166

Code	Description	Quantity	VAT rate %	Unit price £	Amount excl of VAT £
PLY8FE1	Plywood Hardwood 2440 × 1220 mm	12 sheets	20	17.80	213.60
					213.60
VAT					42.72
Total amount payable					256.32

A discount of 2% of the full price applies if payment is made within 10 days. No credit note will be issued. Following payment you must ensure you have only recovered the VAT actually paid.

If you pay within 10 days the discounted price is:

Net	209.33
VAT	41.86
Gross	251.19

[Handwritten notes: Supplier code HAD29 General ledger GL112]

INVOICE

Jenson Ltd

Invoice to:
Nethan Builders
Brecon House
Stamford Road
Manchester
M16 4PL

Deliver to:
As above

30 Longfield Park
Kingsway
M45 2TP

Invoice no:	47792
Tax point:	22 April 20X1
VAT reg no:	641 3229 45
Purchase order no:	7162

Code	Description	Quantity	VAT rate %	Unit price £	Amount excl of VAT £
PL432115	Steel door lining set 32 × 115 mm	14	20	30.25	423.50
PL432140	Steel door lining set 32 × 138 mm	8	20	33.15	265.20

	688.70
Trade discount 15%	103.30
	585.40
VAT	117.08
Total amount payable	702.48

A discount of 3% of the full price applies if payment is made within 14 days. No credit note will be issued. Following payment you must ensure you have only recovered the VAT actually paid.

If you pay within 14 days the discounted price is:

Net	567.84
VAT	113.56
Gross	681.40

INVOICE

A J Broom & Company Limited

Invoice to:
Nethan Builders
Brecon House
Stamford Road
Manchester
M16 4PL

59 Parkway, Manchester, M2 6EG
Tel: 0161 560 3392
Fax: 0161 560 5322

Invoice no: 046123
Tax point: 22 April 20X1
VAT reg no: 661 2359 07
Purchase order no: 7164

Deliver to:
As above

Code	Description	Quantity	VAT rate %	Unit price £	Amount excl of VAT £
DGS472	SDG Softwood	9.6 m	20	8.44	81.02
CIBF653	BIC Softwood	7	20	12.30	86.10
					167.12
Trade discount 10%					16.71
					150.41
VAT at 20%					30.08
Total amount payable					180.49

CREDIT NOTE

J M Bond & Co

Credit note to:
Nethan Builders
Brecon House
Stamford Road
Manchester
M16 4PL

North Park Industrial Estate, Manchester, M12 4TU
Tel: 0161 561 3214
Fax: 0161 561 3060

Credit note no: 06192
Tax point: 22 April 20X1
VAT no: 461 4367 91
Invoice no: 331624

Code	Description	Quantity	VAT rate %	Unit price £	Amount excl of VAT £
DGSS4163	Structural softwood untreated	6m	20	6.85	41.10
					41.10
Trade discount 20%					8.22
					32.88
VAT at 20%					6.57
Total amount of credit					39.45

Credit sales – discounts and VAT

Introduction

In this chapter we will consider value added tax, its calculation, the impact of discounts on the calculation and the accounting for credit sales with discounts and VAT.

CONTENTS
1 Value added tax
2 Calculation of VAT
3 Discounts
4 Discounts and VAT
5 Accounting for credit sales and VAT

1 Value added tax

1.1 The operation of VAT

VAT is a tax levied on **consumer** expenditure.

It is suffered by the final consumer, but is collected by businesses on behalf of HM Revenue and Customs (HMRC).

The procedure is that VAT is collected at each stage in the production and distribution process of supplying goods and services as follows:

- Most businesses (being **taxable persons,** as defined later) account to HMRC for the tax (known as output VAT) on sales.

- If the customer is registered for VAT and uses the goods or services for business purposes, they can recover the tax they have paid on the purchase of the item or service (known as input VAT).

- Accordingly, businesses actually account to HMRC for the difference between the output VAT and input VAT (i.e. the tax on the 'value added' to the product at that stage of the process).

Note that businesses are merely acting as collectors of VAT on behalf of HMRC and they do not suffer any tax and it is not charged as an expense in their accounts. It is only the final consumer who cannot recover the input VAT that suffers the tax.

1.2 How VAT works

Let us examine a simple illustration. We will assume a standard rate of 20%, and follow one article, a wooden table, through the production and distribution chain.

- A private individual cuts down a tree and sells it to a timber mill for £10.

  Tax effect – none. The individual is not a 'taxable person' in this case.

  Cash effect – cash paid to the supplier would be £10 and purchases would be recognised at £10.

- The timber mill saws the log and sells the timber to a furniture manufacturer for £100 + VAT.

  Tax effect – Being a taxable person, the mill is obliged to charge its customers VAT at 20% on the selling price (output tax). There is no input tax available for offset.

Cash effect – The mill collected £120 from the customer (or has a debtor for this sum).

Of this, £20 has to be paid to HM Revenue and Customs, and therefore only £100 would be recognised as sales.

- The manufacturer makes a table from the wood, and sells this to a retailer for £400 + VAT (output tax).

   Tax effect – The manufacturer is obliged to charge VAT at 20% on the selling price (i.e. £400 x 20% = £80), but in this instance would be allowed to reduce this amount by setting off the input tax of £20 charged on the purchase of wood from the mill (input tax).

   Cash effect – Net tax of £60 is paid to HM Revenue and Customs (output less input tax = £80 less £20).

   £400 is recognised as sales and £100 as purchases in the accounts

- The retailer sells the table to a private customer for £1,000 plus VAT of £200.

   Tax effect – The retailer charges £200 of VAT to the customer but against this output tax may be set off the input tax of £80 charged on the purchase from the manufacturer.

   Cash effect – £120 (£200 – £80) is paid to HM Revenue and Customs.

   Purchases would be shown in the books at £400 and sales at £1,000.

- The private customer – VAT is a tax levied on consumer expenditure and the chain ends here.

   The customer is not a taxable person, and cannot recover the tax paid.

You will note that everybody else has passed the VAT on and, though the customer has paid his £200 VAT to the retailer, HM Revenue and Customs has received the VAT piecemeal via contributions from each link in the production and distribution chain, as shown below:

	£
Timber mill	20.00
Manufacturer	60.00
Retailer	120.00
	200.00

Definitions

VAT is charged on the **taxable supply of goods and services** in the United Kingdom by a **taxable person** in the course of a business carried on by him.

Output tax is the tax charged on the sale of goods and services.

Input tax is the tax paid on the purchase of goods and services.

1.3 Taxable supply of goods and services

Taxable supply is the supply of all items except those which are **exempt.**

Examples of exempt items are as follows:

- certain land and buildings, where sold, leased or hired
- insurance
- Post Office postal services
- betting, gaming and lotteries.

Input tax cannot be reclaimed where the trader's supplies are all exempt.

1.4 Rates of VAT

There are three rates of VAT on taxable supplies.

Some items are:

- 'zero-rated'
  (similar to exempt except that input tax can be reclaimed)
- charged at a special rate of 5% (for example, domestic fuel and power and some other less important items).

Other items not included in the above definitions are charged at the standard rate of 20%.

Examples of 'zero-rated' supplies include:

- water and most types of non-luxury food
- books and newspapers
- drugs and medicines
- children's clothing and footwear.

However, for our purposes, unless stated otherwise, you will normally be dealing with taxable supplies at the standard rate of 20%.

1.5   Non-deductible VAT

The input VAT on some items is non-deductible from output VAT (also referred to as 'irrecoverable input VAT' or 'blocked VAT').

This means that VAT on any purchases of these items cannot be deducted from the amount of tax payable to HM Revenue and Customs.

The business has to bear the VAT as an expense in their accounts as they are treated as the final consumer of those goods or services.

Non-deductible VAT items include:

- motor cars (unless used 100% used for business purposes)

- business entertaining (except entertaining staff and overseas customers)

- personal expenses (drawings).

1.6   Taxable person

A taxable person is any individual, partnership or company who:

- makes or intends to make taxable supplies, and

- is liable to register for VAT.

A person is liable to register if the value of his taxable supplies exceeds a specified amount in a 12-month period.

Most companies and partnerships and many sole traders are liable to register.

2   Calculation of VAT

2.1   VAT exclusive amounts

If you are given the net price of goods, the price excluding VAT, then the amount of VAT (at a standard rate of 20%) is 20/100 of this price.

Note: VAT is always rounded down to the nearest penny.

Example

A sale is made for £360.48 plus VAT. What is the amount of VAT to be charged on this sale?

Solution

VAT = £360.48 × 20/100 = £72.09

Remember to round down to the nearest penny.

Say we were considering VAT at a reduced rate of 5% and a net sale was made for £150. What is the amount of VAT to charge on this sale?

Solution

VAT = £150 × 5/100 = £7.50

Although a rounding hasn't been necessary for this calculation, remember to always round down to the nearest penny when necessary.

2.2 VAT inclusive amounts

If a price is given that already includes the VAT then calculating the VAT requires an understanding of the price structure where VAT is concerned.

	%
Selling price excluding VAT (net)	100
VAT	20
	___
Selling price including VAT (gross)	120
	___

 Example

Goods have a selling price of £3,000 inclusive of VAT. What is the VAT on the goods and the net price of these goods?

Solution

	£
Net price (£3,000 × 100/120)	2,500
VAT (£3,000 × 20/120)	500
	___
Gross price	3,000
	___

Activity 1

What is the amount of VAT on each of the following transactions?

(i)   £100 net of VAT

(ii) £250 excluding VAT

(iii) £480 including VAT

(iv) £960 including VAT

3 Discounts

3.1 Introduction

Within Chapter 5 we reviewed the three main types of discount that a business might offer to its credit customers; a bulk discount, a trade discount and a settlement (cash) discount. We shall briefly revise each discount now.

3.2 Bulk discounts

A bulk discount is a percentage reduction in the sale or list price of goods when a large quantity is purchased.

3.3 Trade discounts

A trade discount is a percentage of the list price of the goods being sold that is deducted from the list price for certain customers.

This discount may be offered due to the fact that the customer is a frequent and valued customer or because the customer is another business rather than an individual.

A trade discount is a definite amount deducted from the list price total of the invoice.

3.4 Settlement (cash) discounts

A settlement discount is offered to customers if they settle the invoice within a certain time period.

It is up to the customer whether or not to take advantage of it (i.e. whether or not to pay early and therefore take the settlement discount).

The discount is expressed as a percentage of the invoice total but is not deducted from the invoice total as it is not certain when the invoice is sent out whether or not it will be accepted. Instead the details of the settlement discount will be noted at the bottom of the invoice.

A settlement discount is sometimes referred to as a "prompt payment discount" or "cash discount". However, the term "cash discount" may also specifically refer to a discount being offered as an incentive for the customer to pay cash immediately.

4 Discounts and VAT

4.1 Introduction

Bulk discounts and trade discounts are straightforward in that VAT is calculated and charged on the discounted amount on the invoice.

However, settlement discounts are more complicated as the supplier will not know whether the settlement discount will be taken up by the customer until they have either been paid in accordance with the terms of the settlement discount offer, or the time limit for the settlement discount has elapsed.

A two stage process for dealing with VAT is therefore required as follows:

* When issuing a sales invoice on which a settlement discount is offered, suppliers will enter the invoice into their accounts and record the VAT on the full invoice price in the normal way (i.e. ignoring the settlement discount).

* When the supplier receives payment within the settlement period, they can choose between two methods of adjusting their accounts to reflect a settlement discount which is taken up by a customer.

   (i)   The supplier will issue a credit note as evidence of the reduction in the sales value.

         A copy of this credit note must be kept as evidence.

         This method will however be time-consuming for the business.

   (ii) Alternatively, the supplier can include the following information on the sales invoice (in addition to the usual invoicing requirements) and it will not then need to issue a credit note:

         –   The terms of the settlement discount (this must include the time by which the discounted price must be paid).

         –   A statement that the customer can only recover as input VAT the VAT paid to the supplier (see below).

It is also helpful if the invoice shows:

- the discounted price

- the VAT on the discounted price, and

- the total amount due if the settlement discount is taken up.

The supplier must retain the VAT invoice together with proof of receipt of the discounted amount as evidence of the reduction both in the value of the sale and the output VAT.

HMRC recommends that businesses use the following wording on the sales invoice:

> "A discount of X% of the full price applies if payment is made within Y days of the invoice date.
>
> No credit note will be issued.
>
> Following payment you must ensure you have only recovered the VAT actually paid."

The amount paid by the customer is:

(a) if taking the discount

= discounted amount of goods

plus VAT on the discounted amount

(b) if not taking the discount

= full amount of the goods

plus VAT on the full amount.

If the customer pays the discounted price, the supplier must then adjust their records to record the output VAT on the amount actually received.

If the customer does not take up the discount, no adjustment will be necessary.

In some cases, the customer may pay the discounted price in accordance with the terms of the settlement discount before the sales invoice is issued. In that case, the sales invoice should show the discounted price paid only.

Example

A purchase is made for 20 items costing £15 each. This totals £300.

A 2% discount is offered for settlement within 30 days.

(a) Calculate the VAT on the full sales invoice price.

(b) Calculate the VAT on the discounted price.

Solution

(a) The VAT is calculated as:

£300 × 20% = £60.00

(b) The discounted price of the goods is (£300 × 98%) = £294

The VAT on the discounted price is (£294 × 20%) = £58.80

 Example

A sales invoice is to be prepared for two adult Fair Isle sweaters at a cost of £50.00 each.

A settlement discount of 5% for payment within 30 days is offered.

The company's policy is to include the terms of the settlement discount on the sales invoice rather than to issue a credit note to reflect any settlement discount taken.

VAT is charged at 20%.

What would the sales invoice look like?

Solution

INVOICE

Creative Clothing

3 The Mall, Wanstead, London, E11 3AY,
Tel: 0208 491 3200, Fax: 0208 491 3220

Invoice to: VAT Registration: 487 3921 12
Smith & Isaacs   Date/tax point: 14 February 20X0
23 Sloane Street   Invoice number: 149
London   Delivery note no: 41682
SW3   Account no: SL43

Code	Description	Quantity	VAT rate %	Unit price (£)	Amount (£)
FW168	Fair Isle Sweater (adult)	2	20.00	50.00	100.00

Total net amount	100.00
VAT	20.00
Total amount payable	120.00

A discount of 5% of the full price applies if payment is made within 30 days.

No credit note will be issued. Following payment you must ensure you have only recovered the VAT actually paid.

If you pay within 30 days, the discounted price is:

Net	95.00
VAT	19.00
Gross	114.00

 Activity 2

A customer orders 10 Sansui radios priced at £25 each.

The customer is given a 20% trade discount and a 10% settlement discount for prompt payment.

Calculate the VAT charged on the sale and show the figures to be included on the invoice.

5 Accounting for credit sales and VAT

5.1 Accounting entries

We have already seen in this chapter that a business merely acts as a collector of taxes on behalf of HM Revenue and Customs and therefore makes no profit out of any VAT charged on its sales.

Any output tax collected in excess of input tax suffered is paid over to HM Revenue and Customs. Accounting for VAT therefore does not affect the value of the sales or purchases actually made by the business, nor the profits recorded on the sales.

Accordingly, when a credit sale is recorded in the sales account, or a credit purchase in the purchases account it must be at the net of VAT amount.

However, when a customer eventually pays the supplier, they will pay the full amount due (i.e. the gross amount including VAT).

Consequently, when a debtor or creditor is recorded in the ledger accounts it must be at the full gross amount of the invoice.

The difference between the gross and net amounts (i.e. the VAT) is then recorded in the VAT control account.

5.2 Summary of entries

In summary the accounting entries for a credit sale with VAT are:

Debit   Debtors account with the gross amount

Credit   Sales account with the net amount

Credit   VAT account with the VAT.

The accounting entries for a credit purchase with VAT are:

Debit   Purchases account with the net amount

Debit   VAT account with the VAT

Credit   Creditors account with the gross amount.

Work through the following examples to practise the double entry for credit sales.

Example 1

C sells £2,000 of goods net of VAT (at 20%) to Z on credit.

He offers Z a 5% settlement discount if Z pays within 30 days.

Z does not pay his account within 30 days and so does not take the settlement discount. Z pays after 40 days.

Enter these transactions in the accounts.

Solution

Step 1   Calculate the VAT on the sale.

	£
Sales value net of VAT	2,000.00
VAT	400.00
Invoice value	2400.00

Step 2   Enter the invoice in the accounts.

Debtors

	£		£
Sales and VAT	2,400.00		

Sales

	£		£
		Debtors	2,000.00

VAT

	£		£
		Debtors	400.00

Step 3   Enter the payment by Z in the accounts.

Debtors

	£		£
Sales and VAT	2,400.00	Bank	2,400.00

Sales

	£			£
		Debtors		2,000.00

VAT

	£			£
		Debtors		400.00

Bank

	£		£
Debtors	2,400.00		

Note:

As Z does not take the settlement discount, there is no entry for the settlement discount at all in the accounts.

 Example 2

Two months later C sells another £2,000 of goods net of VAT at 20% to Z on credit.

He offers Z a 5% settlement discount if Z pays within 30 days.

This time Z does pay his account within 30 days and takes the settlement discount.

Enter these transactions in the accounts.

Solution

Step 1   Calculate the VAT on the sale.

Note: This is exactly the same as the previous example because the invoice is initially recorded at its full price until it is known whether the customer takes up the settlement discount.

	£
Sales value net of VAT	2,000.00
VAT	400.00
Invoice value	2,400.00

Step 2   Enter the invoice in the accounts.

> **Note:** This is exactly the same as the previous example because the value of the invoice is exactly the same as the previous example.

Debtors

	£		£
Sales and VAT	2,400.00		

Sales

	£		£
		Debtors	2,000.00

VAT

	£		£
		Debtors	400.00

Step 3   Calculate the amount paid by Z.

> **Note:** The amount paid by Z will be different from the previous example because Z does take the 5% discount.

	£
Sales value net of VAT	2,000.00
Less: Settlement discount (5% × £2,000)	(100.00)
Sales value net of settlement discount	1,900.00
VAT	380.00
Amount paid by Z	2,280.00

Step 4   Enter this amount in the accounts.

Because Z takes the settlement discount, he pays C £120 less than the invoice value.

In order to clear the debtors account we have to credit that account with the £120, debit the discount allowed account with £100 and debit the VAT account with £20 to reflect the reduction in Output VAT.

This £100 is an expense of the business as we have allowed our customer to pay less than the invoice value in order to have the benefit of receiving the money earlier.

Sales

	£		£
		Debtors	2,000.00

VAT

	£		£
Debtors	20.00	Debtors	400.00

Debtors

	£		£
Sales and VAT	2,400.00	Bank	2,280.00
		Discount allowed	100.00
		VAT	20.00

Discount allowed

	£		£
Debtors	100.00		

6 Summary

We have covered some fairly tricky ideas in this chapter and it is very important that you really do understand them.

You must ensure you are able to perform VAT calculations from both net and gross amounts.

Also quite tricky is the treatment of settlement discounts.

You have to be able to do two things:

(a) Calculate the VAT on a sale when a settlement discount is offered.

(b) Calculate the amount paid by the customer if he takes a settlement discount. This will be less than the invoice value and you therefore have to account for the discount allowed.

Answers to chapter activities

📝 Activity 1

(i)	£100 × 20/100	=	£20.00
(ii)	£250 × 20/100	=	£50.00
(iii)	£480 × 20/120	=	£80.00
(iv)	£960 × 20/120	=	£160.00

📝 Activity 2

The full invoice value will be:

	£
Sales price (10 × £25)	250.00
Less: Trade discount (250 × 20%)	(50.00)
Net	200.00
VAT	40.00
Gross	240.00

The invoice will also include details of the discounted invoice price payable if the settlement discount is taken by the customer:

	£
Sales value (200 × 90%)	180.00
VAT	36.00
	216.00

7 Test your knowledge

Workbook Activity 3

Calculate the VAT on the following sales:

(a)   A sale for £140.00 plus VAT

(b)   A sale for £560.00 plus VAT

(c)   A sale for £780.00 including VAT

(d)   A sale for £1,020.00 including VAT

Workbook Activity 4

Calculate the VAT on the following sales:

(a)   A sale for £280.00 plus VAT where a settlement discount of 2% is taken.

(b)   A sale for £480.00 plus VAT where a settlement discount of 3% is taken.

(c)   A sale for £800.00 plus VAT where a settlement discount of 5% is offered but not taken.

(d)   A sale of £650.00 plus VAT where a settlement discount of 4% is offered but not taken.

Workbook Activity 5

A sells £600 of goods to B. VAT has to be added and A offers B a settlement discount of 3%. Calculate the amount that B will pay A if:

(a)   B takes the settlement discount; and

(b)   B does not take the settlement discount.

The sales day book – general and subsidiary ledgers

7

Introduction

We have already seen how to calculate the amount of a credit sale, including VAT and any relevant discounts. In this chapter we will deal with the initial recording of credit sales before they are entered into the ledger accounts. We will also consider the treatment of bad debts.

CONTENTS
1   Accounting for credit sales
2   The general and subsidiary ledgers
3   Sales returns
4   The sales returns day book

1 Accounting for credit sales

1.1 Introduction

In a typical business there will be a great number of sales transactions to be recorded. If we were to record each transaction individually, the accounts would be very cluttered.

In order to simplify the process (and exercise greater control) we divide the recording of the transactions into three parts.

(a) The first part is the books of prime entry. We shall study here the sales day book.

(b) The second part is the general ledger itself where the double entry takes place.

(c) The third part is the sales ledger which contains the individual customer/debtor accounts. (**Note:** The sales ledger is also sometimes referred to as the subsidiary (sales) ledger.)

Sales invoices and cheques are the source documents which will form the basis of accounting entries in all these three parts.

1.2 Books of prime entry – the sales day book (SDB)

The sales day book is simply a list of the sales invoices that are to be processed for a given period (e.g. a week).

In its simplest form, the sales day book will comprise just the names of the customers and the amount of the invoices issued in the week.

The SDB is not part of the double entry; it is not part of the general ledger accounts. It is a listing that we shall use to perform the double entry at a later stage. It will look something like this:

Week 1			
Customer	Total £	VAT £	Net £
X	1,200	200	1,000
Y	2,400	400	2,000
Z	3,600	600	3,000
Total	7,200	1,200	6,000

1.3 The analysed sales day book

The sales day book is usually analysed with 'analysis columns' showing how the total value of each customer's invoice is made up.

SALES DAY BOOK								
Date	Customer	Reference	Invoice number	Total £	VAT £	Product 1 £	Product 2 £	Product 3 £
			TOTALS					

(a) The date column details the date of the transaction and the customer column details the name of the customer.

(b) The reference number is the code number of the customer's account in the sales ledger.

(c) The invoice number is the number of the invoice issued for this sale.

(d) The total column is the total value of the goods sold as shown on the invoice:

- after deducting any trade discount that may have been offered

- after deducting any settlement invoice where an invoice is paid on receipt

- including VAT.

💡 Example

An invoice to customer A is made up as follows:

	£
Sale of 50 units at £2 per unit	100.00
Less: 20% trade discount	(20.00)
	80.00
VAT (£80 × 20%)	16.00
Total invoice value	96.00

The £96 would be entered in the 'total' column.

(e) The VAT column – this column is the value of the VAT on the invoice – in this case £16.00.

(f) Product 1, 2, etc columns – these are columns that analyse the net sales value (i.e. the total value after deducting VAT) into groupings that are of interest to the business.

In this introductory section we shall not complicate things by considering more than one type of product so that there will only be one column for sales.

In this case the entry in the sales column would be £80.

(g) The total boxes – at the end of a period (say a week or a month) the sales day book is totalled and the total values of each column are written in the total boxes.

The sales day book would therefore look as follows for the example above:

SALES DAY BOOK								
Date	Customer	Reference	Invoice number	Total £	VAT £	Prod. 1 £	Prod. 2 £	Prod. 3 £
	A			96	16	80		
			TOTALS	96	16	80		

Activity 1

An analysed sales day book has the following totals for a week.

Date	Invoice no	Customer name	Code	Total £	VAT £	Europe £	Asia £	America £
23/04/X0		Total		58.700	4,250	21,250	15,400	17,800

How would the totals be posted to the general ledger accounts?

1.4 Casting and cross casting

Casting is the way accountants refer to adding a vertical column of figures and cross-casting is the way accountants refer to adding a horizontal row of figures.

It is worth very briefly doing a simple example of this just to show how a valuable check of the accuracy of your additions is provided by these two operations.

 Example

The following table of numbers is similar to the contents of accounting records such as the 'sales day book' or the 'analysed cash book' which you will come across in the next few chapters.

This table might represent the sales of products A to E in three geographical areas. We have deliberately chosen some awkward numbers to demonstrate the process.

You should calculate the totals yourself before looking at the solution.

	A	B	C	D	E	Total
UK	221,863	17,327	14,172	189,221	5,863	*448,446*
USA	17,155	14,327	8,962	27,625	73,127	
Africa	18,627	33,563	62,815	1,003	57,100	
Total	*257,645*					

Solution

	A	B	C	D	E	Total
UK	221,863	17,327	14,172	189,221	5,863	**448,446**
USA	17,155	14,327	8,962	27,625	73,127	**141,196**
Africa	18,627	33,563	62,815	1,003	57,100	**173,108**
Total	**257,645**	**65,217**	**85,949**	**217,849**	**136,090**	**762,750**

Your additions should agree to an overall balance of 762,750.

This is a very useful technique and provides an excellent check on the accuracy of your addition.

2 The general and subsidiary ledgers

2.1 Introduction

The general ledger is the place where the double entry takes place in the appropriate ledger accounts. The general ledger contains all the accounts you have become familiar with so far, for example:

- Capital
- Drawings
- Van
- Rent
- Electricity
- Purchases
- Bank

One of these accounts is the debtors account, which henceforth will be referred to as the **sales ledger control account (SLCA)**.

This account contains (for a given period) the **total** value of all the invoices issued to credit customers and the **total** of all the cash received from them. It does not contain any detail.

Note: The general ledger may also be referred to as the 'main ledger' or the 'nominal ledger'. You should be able to use these different terms interchangeably.

2.2 The sales ledger control account

Within the general ledger the total amount outstanding from debtors is shown in the sales ledger control account. The sales ledger control account may also be referred to as the debtors ledger control account.

The totals of credit sales (from the sales day book), returns from customers (from the sales returns day book) and cash received and discounts (from the analysed cash book) are posted to this account. This account therefore shows the total debtors outstanding. It does not give details about individual customers' balances. This is available in the sales ledger for debtors.

However, as both records are compiled from the same sources, the total balances on the customers' individual accounts should equal the outstanding balance on the control account at any time.

2.3 Proforma sales ledger control account

A sales ledger control account normally looks like this.

Sales ledger control account				
	£			£
Balance b/d	X	Returns per sales day book		X
Sales per sales day book	X	* Cash from debtors		X
		* Discounts allowed		X
		Bad debt written off		X
		Contra entry		X
		* VAT adjustments re settlement discounts		X
		Balance c/d		X
	X			X
Balance b/d				

* Per cash receipts book

2.4 Bad debts

 Definition

A bad debt is a debt which is not likely to be received; it is therefore not prudent for the business to consider this debt as an asset.

2.5 Reasons for bad debts

A business may decide that a debt is bad for a number of reasons:

- customer is in liquidation – no cash will be received

- customer is having difficulty paying although not officially in liquidation

- customer disputes the debt and refuses to pay all or part of it.

2.6 Accounting for bad debts

The business must make an adjustment to write off the bad debt from the customer's account in the sales ledger and to write it off in the general ledger. The double entry in the general ledger is:

Dr   Bad debt expense

    Cr   Sales ledger control account

Notice that the bad debt becomes an expense of the business. Writing off bad debts decreases the profits made by a business, but is not deducted from sales. The sale was made in the anticipation of receiving the money but, if the debt is not to be received, this does not negate the sale it is just an added expense of the business.

The bad debt must also be written off in the individual debtor's account in the sales ledger by crediting the customer's account as this amount is not going to be received.

When you invoiced the customer you will have recorded the VAT and paid it to the tax authorities (HMRC). Once the debt is more than 6 months old and it has been determined that the customer is not going to pay you, you can reclaim that VAT back from the tax authorities (HMRC).

Dr	Bad debt expense	Net amount
Dr	VAT control account	VAT amount
	Cr Sales ledger control account	Gross amount

2.7 The sales ledger

As well as information about our debtors in total we have to keep track of each individual debtor. How much have we invoiced? What has he paid? How much does he owe? Is a bad debt write off required?

We do this in the sales ledger. This ledger is not part of the general ledger and it is **not** part of the double entry. (Remember it is also sometimes called the subsidiary (sales) ledger.)

The sales ledger contains a separate ledger account for each individual debtor. Every individual invoice and cash receipt is posted to an individual's account in the sales ledger.

2.8 Fitting it all together

We have now looked at the three elements of a typical accounting system. We must now see how it all fits together.

Consider three credit sales invoices.

Customer	Amount
A	£1,500
B	£2,000
C	£2,500

Step 1

Each invoice is recorded in the sales day book and in the personal account of each debtor in the sales ledger. The entry required for each invoice is a debit in each debtor account to indicate that this is the amount that each one owes us.

Step 2

At the end of the period the sales day book is totalled and the total is entered into the sales ledger control account (SLCA) (total debtors account) in the general ledger.

The full double entry is as we saw in the previous chapter (ignoring VAT at the moment):

Debit   Sales ledger control account

Credit   Sales

Step 3

Now consider the following cheques being received against these debts.

Customer	Amount
A	£1,000
B	£2,000

Each receipt is recorded in the cash book (see later chapter) and in the personal account of each debtor in the sales ledger. The entry for cash received in the individual accounts is a credit entry to indicate that they no longer owe us these amounts.

Step 4

At the end of the period the cash book is totalled and the total is entered into the sales ledger control account (total debtors account) in the general ledger.

The full double entry is:

Debit   Cash account (money in)

Credit   Sales ledger control account

This is illustrated on the next page.

Notes:

1   The invoices are entered into the SDB and the cheques are entered into the cash book.

2   The totals from the cash book and SDB are posted to the SLCA.

3   The individual invoices and cash received are posted to the sales ledger.

Example

Posting the sales day book to the accounts in the ledgers

Consider the following sales transactions made by Roberts Metals.

Customer	Sales value (ex VAT)	Trade discount	Net sales value	VAT	Total
	£	£	£	£	£
A	1,000	10%	900	180.00	1,080.00
B	2,000	20%	1,600	320.00	1,920.00
C	3,000	30%	2,100	420.00	2,520.00

Enter this information in the ledger accounts using the following three steps.

Step 1 Write up the sales day book, and total the columns.

Step 2 Post the totals to the accounts in the general ledger.

Step 3 Post the individual invoices to the sales ledger.

Solution

Step 1

SALES DAY BOOK

Date	Customer	Reference	Invoice number	Total £	VAT £	Sales £
	A			1,080.00	180.00	900.00
	B			1,920.00	320.00	1,600.00
	C			2,520.00	420.00	2,100.00
			TOTALS	5,520.00	920.00	4,600.00

Step 2

General ledger

Sales				**VAT**			
£		£		£		£	
		SDB	4,600.00			SDB	920.00

SLCA			
£		£	
SDB	5,520.00		

Step 3

Sales ledger

A				B		
	£		£		£		£
SDB	1,080.00			SDB	1,920.00		

C		
	£		£
SDB	2,520.00		

Note to solution:

(a) The totals of the SDB are entered in the general ledger.

(b) The individual invoices (total value including VAT) are entered in the individual debtors accounts in the sales ledger. This is the amount that the debtor will pay.

(c) Note that there are no entries for trade discounts either in the SDB or in the ledger accounts. The discounted amount after considering the trade discount becomes the new agreed sales price.

(d) The narrative in the ledger accounts refers to the source of the entries – the sales day book. This is an acceptable alternative to using the name of the ledger to which the corresponding entry has been made.

2.9 Contra entries

A further type of adjustment that may be required to sales ledger and purchases ledger control accounts is a contra entry.

2.10 Why a contra entry is required

In some instances a business will be both a debtor and a creditor of another business as it both buys from the business and sells to it. If this is the case then there will be money owed to the business and money owing from it. This can be simplified by making an adjustment known as a contra entry.

Example

James Associates has a customer, X Brothers. X Brothers also sells goods to James Associates. Therefore X Brothers is both a debtor and a creditor of James Associates. The subsidiary ledger accounts of James Associates show the following position:

Sales ledger – debtors

X Brothers

	£		£
Balance b/d	250		

Purchases ledger – creditors

X Brothers

	£		£
		Balance b/d	100

The problem here is that X Brothers owes James Associates £250 and is owed £100 by James Associates. If both parties are in agreement it makes more sense to net these two amounts off and to say that X Brothers owes James Associates just £150. This is achieved in accounting terms by a contra entry.

Solution

Step 1 Take the smaller of the two amounts and debit the purchases ledger account for the creditor and credit the sales ledger account for the debtor with this amount.

Sales ledger – debtors

X Brothers

	£		£
Balance b/d	250	Contra	100

Purchases ledger – creditors

X Brothers

	£		£
Contra	100	Balance b/d	100

Step 2 Balance off the accounts in the subsidiary ledgers.

Sales ledger – debtors

X Brothers

	£		£
Balance b/d	250	Contra	100
		Balance c/d	150
	———		———
	250		250
	———		———
Balance b/d	150		

Purchases ledger – creditors

X Brothers

	£		£
Contra	100	Balance b/d	100
	———		———

This now shows that X Brothers owes £150 to James Associates and is owed nothing by James Associates.

Step 3 The double entry must also be carried out in the general ledger accounts. This is:

Dr   Purchases ledger control account

Cr   Sales ledger control account

When a contra entry is made you must remember not just to deal with the entries in the subsidiary ledgers but also to put through the double entry in the general ledger accounts, the sales ledger and purchases ledger control accounts.

3   Sales returns

3.1   Introduction

When customers return goods, the accounting system has to record the fact that goods have been returned. If the goods were returned following a cash sale then cash would be repaid to the customer. If goods were returned following a credit sale then the SLCA in the general ledger and the customer's individual account in the sales ledger will need to be credited with the value of the goods returned.

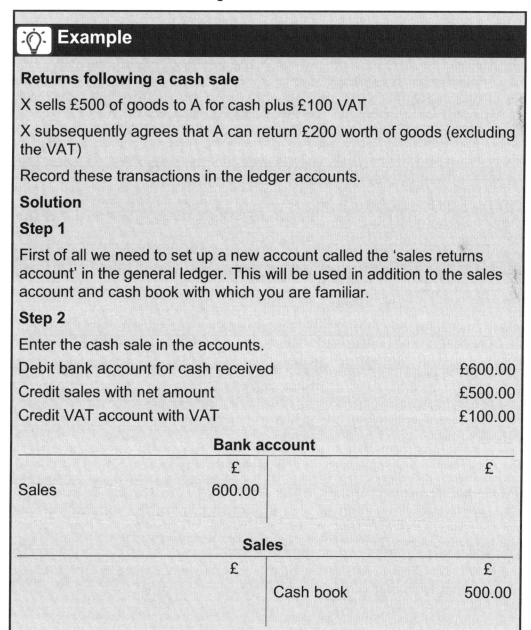

Example

Returns following a cash sale

X sells £500 of goods to A for cash plus £100 VAT

X subsequently agrees that A can return £200 worth of goods (excluding the VAT)

Record these transactions in the ledger accounts.

Solution

Step 1

First of all we need to set up a new account called the 'sales returns account' in the general ledger. This will be used in addition to the sales account and cash book with which you are familiar.

Step 2

Enter the cash sale in the accounts.

Debit bank account for cash received	£600.00
Credit sales with net amount	£500.00
Credit VAT account with VAT	£100.00

Bank account

	£		£
Sales	600.00		

Sales

	£		£
		Cash book	500.00

Sales returns

	£		£

VAT

	£		£
		Cash book	100.00

Step 3

X will repay A £200 plus VAT of (£200 × 20%) = £40. We therefore need to enter the sale return, the cash and the VAT in the accounts.

Debit sales returns account	£200.00
Debit VAT account £200 × 20%	£40.00
Credit bank account with cash paid out	£240.00

Bank account

	£		£
Sales	600.00	Sales returns	240.00

Sales

	£		£
		Cash book	500.00

Sales returns

	£		£
Cash book	200.00		

VAT

	£		£
Cash book	40.00	Cash book	100.00

3.2 Sales returns for credit sales

When a credit customer returns goods, he does not receive cash for the return. Instead the seller will issue a credit note to record the fact that goods have been returned. This credit note is sent to the customer and is entered in the seller's books.

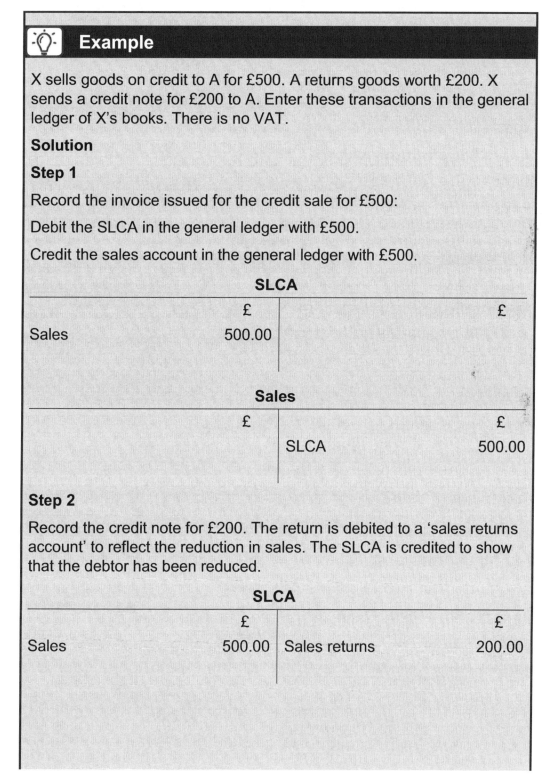

Example

X sells goods on credit to A for £500. A returns goods worth £200. X sends a credit note for £200 to A. Enter these transactions in the general ledger of X's books. There is no VAT.

Solution

Step 1

Record the invoice issued for the credit sale for £500:

Debit the SLCA in the general ledger with £500.

Credit the sales account in the general ledger with £500.

SLCA

	£		£
Sales	500.00		

Sales

	£		£
		SLCA	500.00

Step 2

Record the credit note for £200. The return is debited to a 'sales returns account' to reflect the reduction in sales. The SLCA is credited to show that the debtor has been reduced.

SLCA

	£		£
Sales	500.00	Sales returns	200.00

Sales

	£			£
		SLCA		500.00

Sales returns

	£			£
SLCA	200.00			

3.3 Sales returns with VAT

When a return is made and we include VAT, the VAT has to be accounted for both on the invoice when the sale is made, and on the credit note when the goods are returned. This VAT has to be entered in the books.

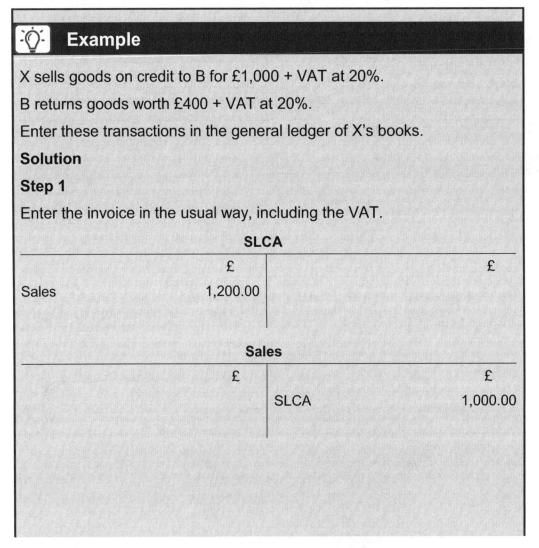

Example

X sells goods on credit to B for £1,000 + VAT at 20%.

B returns goods worth £400 + VAT at 20%.

Enter these transactions in the general ledger of X's books.

Solution

Step 1

Enter the invoice in the usual way, including the VAT.

SLCA

	£			£
Sales	1,200.00			

Sales

	£			£
		SLCA		1,000.00

VAT

	£		£
		SLCA	200.00

Step 2

Enter the credit note. The VAT on the return will be £400 × 20% = £80.

SLCA

	£		£
Sales	1,200.00	Sales returns	480.00

Sales

	£		£
		SLCA	1,000.00

VAT

	£		£
SLCA	80.00	SLCA	200.00

Sales returns

	£		£
SLCA	400.00		

The books will reflect the position after the return. The balance on the SLCA is £720. This is made up as:

	£
Sale	1,000
Sale return	400
	600
VAT 600 × 20%	120
	720

4 The sales returns day book

4.1 The sales returns day book

Sales returns are in practice entered in a 'sales returns day book'. This is similar to the sales day book, and the columns are used in the same way. The only difference is that instead of having a column for the invoice number, there is a column for the 'credit note number'. This is because when the goods are received back the business will issue a credit note.

SALES RETURNS DAY BOOK						
Date	Customer	Reference	Credit note number	Total £	VAT £	Sales returns £

Example

A and B are credit customers of Ellis Electricals. The balances on their accounts in the sales ledger are £1,200 and £2,400 because both A and B have made earlier purchases which have not yet been paid.

A returns goods which cost £600 excluding VAT. B returns goods which cost £400 excluding VAT.

Enter the above returns in the sales returns day book and in the general and sales ledgers of Ellis Electricals. All VAT is at 20%.

Solution

Step 1

Enter the original sales invoices in the general ledger.

SLCA

	£		£
SDB	3,600		

Sales

	£		£
		SDB	3,000.00

VAT

	£		£
		SDB	600.00

Step 2

Write up the sales returns day book.

SALES RETURNS DAY BOOK						
Date	Customer	Reference	Credit note number	Total £	VAT £	Sales returns £
	A			720.00	120.00	600.00
	B			480.00	80.00	400.00
				1,200.00	200.00	1,000.00

Step 3

Enter the SRDB totals in the general ledger accounts.

SLCA

	£		£
SDB	3,600.00	SRDB	1,200.00

Sales

	£		£
		SDB	3,000.00

VAT

	£		£
SRDB	200.00	SDB	600.00

Sales returns

	£		£
SRDB	1,000.00		

Step 4

Enter the individual amounts in the sales ledger.

A

	£		£
SDB	1,200.00	SRDB	720.00

B

	£		£
SDB	2,400.00	SRDB	480.00

4.2 Sales returns in sales day book

In some businesses the level of sales returns are fairly low and therefore it is not justified to keep a separate sales returns day book. In these cases any credit notes that are issued for sales returns are recorded as negative amounts in the sales day book.

 Activity 2

Given below are the totals of an analysed sales returns day book for a week. VAT is at 20%.

Date	Customer name	Credit note no	Code	Total	VAT	Europe	Asia	America
				£	£	£	£	£
23/04/X0				3,091	291	1,458	650	692

Post these totals to the general ledger accounts.

5 Summary

Within this chapter we have studied the sales day book, the analysed sales day book, and the sales returns day book. Remember that these day books are simply lists of invoices/credit notes which simplify posting entries to the general ledger.

We have also considered bad debts and the accounting treatment of them both considering and not considering VAT.

You should make sure that you are comfortable with all the material in this chapter and fully understand how the various parts of the accounting system relate to each other. You will often be required to enter invoices and credit notes into the books of prime entry and then to post the entries to the general ledger and sales ledger.

Answers to chapter activities

Activity 1

The required double entry is as follows:

Debit	Sales ledger control account	£58,700
Credit	VAT	£4,250
	Europe sales	£21,250
	Asia sales	£15,400
	America sales	£17,800

Note carefully that it is the net amount that is credited to each sales account and the gross amount (including VAT) that is debited to the sales ledger control account. The VAT total is credited to the VAT account.

The ledger entries would appear as follows:

Sales ledger control account

	£		£
SDB	58,700		

VAT

	£		£
		SDB	4,250

Europe sales

	£		£
		SDB	21,250

Asia sales

	£		£
		SDB	15,400

America sales

	£		£
		SDB	17,800

Activity 2

Sales returns – Europe account

	£		£
SRDB	1,458		

Sales returns – Asia account

	£		£
SRDB	650		

Sales returns – America account

	£		£
SRDB	692		

VAT account

	£		£
SRDB	291		

Sales ledger control account

	£		£
		SRDB	3,091

Note carefully that it is the net amount that is debited to each returns account and the gross amount to the sales ledger control account. The difference, the VAT, is debited to the VAT account.

6 Test your knowledge

 Workbook Activity 3

You work in the accounts department of D F Engineering and one of your tasks is to write up the day books. In your organisation there is no separate sales returns day book and therefore any credit notes are entered as negative amounts in the sales day book.

Given below are the details of the sales invoices and credit notes that have been issued this week. D F Engineering does not offer trade or settlement discounts but is registered for VAT and all sales are of standard rated goods.

Invoices sent out:

		Code	£	Invoice number
20X1				
1 May	Fraser & Co	SL14	128.68 plus VAT	03466 ✓
	Letterhead Ltd	SL03	257.90 plus VAT	03467 ✓
2 May	Jeliteen Traders	SL15	96.58 plus VAT	03468 ✓
3 May	Harper Bros	SL22	268.15 plus VAT	03469 ✓
	Juniper Ltd	SL17	105.38 plus VAT	03470 ✓
4 May	H G Frank	SL30	294.67 plus VAT	03471 ✓
5 May	Keller Assocs	SL07	110.58 plus VAT	03472

Credit notes sent out:

		Code	£	Credit note number
20X1				
2 May	Garner & Co	SL12	68.70 plus VAT	0746 ✓
4 May	Hill Traders	SL26	117.68 plus VAT	0747 ✓

Required:

Write up the sales day book given for the week ending 5 May 20X1 and total all of the columns.

Date	Invoice no	Customer name	Code	Total £	VAT £	Net £

Workbook Activity 4

You work in the accounts department of Keyboard Supplies, a supplier of a wide range of electronic keyboards to a variety of music shops on credit. Given below are three sales invoices that you have just sent out to customers and these are to be written up into the sales day book given below.

Sales of four different types of keyboard are made and the sales are analysed into each of these four types and coded as follows:

Atol keyboards	01
Bento keyboards	02
Garland keyboards	03
Zanni keyboards	04

Required:

Write up the analysed sales day book and total each of the columns.

INVOICE

Keyboard Supplies

Invoice to:
BZS Music
42 Westhill
Nutford TN11 3PQ

Trench Park Estate
Fieldham
Sussex TN21 4AF
Tel: 01829 654545
Fax: 01829 654646

Deliver to:
As above

Invoice no:	06116
Tax point:	18 April 20X1
VAT reg no:	466 1128 30
Purchase order no:	77121

Code	Description	Quantity	VAT rate %	Unit price £	Amount excl of VAT £
B4012	Bento Keyboard	3	20	180.00	540.00
Z2060	Zanni Keyboard	6	20	164.00	984.00
					1,524.00
Trade discount 20%					304.80
					1,219.20
VAT					243.84
Total amount payable					1463.04

Deduct discount of 3% if paid within 10 days, net 30 days

A discount of 3% of the full price applies if payment is made within 10 days. No credit note will be issued. Following payment you must ensure you have only recovered the VAT actually paid.

If you pay within 10 days, the discounted price is:

Net	1182.62
VAT	236.52
Gross	1419.14

INVOICE

Keyboard Supplies

Invoice to:
M T Retail
Fraser House
Perley TN7 8QT

Trench Park Estate
Fieldham
Sussex TN21 4AF
Tel: 01829 654545
Fax: 01829 654646

Deliver to:
As above

Invoice no:		06117
Tax point:		18 April 20X1
VAT reg no:		466 1128 30
Purchase order no:		PO4648

Code	Description	Quantity	VAT rate %	Unit price £	Amount excl of VAT £
A6060	Atol Keyboard	1	20	210.00	210.00
Z4080	Zanni Keyboard	1	20	325.00	325.00
					535.00
VAT					107.00
Total amount payable					642.00

Net 30 days

INVOICE

Keyboard Supplies

Invoice to:
Harmer & Co
1 Acre Street
Nutford TN11 6HA

Trench Park Estate
Fieldham
Sussex TN21 4AF
Tel: 01829 654545
Fax: 01829 654646

Deliver to:
As above

Invoice no:		06118
Tax point:		18 April 20X1
VAT reg no:		466 1128 30
Purchase order no:		7486

Code	Description	Quantity	VAT rate %	Unit price £	Amount excl of VAT £
G4326	Garland Keyboard	3	20	98.00	294.00
B2040	Bento Keyboard	5	20	115.00	575.00
					869.00
VAT					173.80
Total amount payable					1042.80

Sales day book									
Date	Invoice no	Customer name	Code	Total £	VAT £	01 £	02 £	03 £	04 £

 ## Workbook Activity 5

Graham Haddow runs a buildings maintenance and decorating business and sends out invoices for the work that he has done. He analyses his sales between the maintenance work and decorating work. You are given three sales invoices that he sent out last week.

Required:

Enter the sales invoice details into the analysed sales day book given and total all of the columns.

INVOICE

Graham Haddow

Invoice to:
Portman & Co
Portman House
Tonbridge TN1 4LL

59 East Street
Medford
MF6 7TL
Tel: 0122 280496

Invoice no:	07891
Tax point:	1 May 20X1
VAT reg no:	431 7992 06
Your reference:	P2

	Amount excl of VAT £
Repair of window	66.00
Clearing of guttering	73.00
	139.00
VAT	27.80
Total amount payable	166.80

Deduct discount of 2% if paid within 14 days, net 30 days

A discount of 2% of the full price applies if payment is made within 14 days. No credit note will be issued. Following payment you must ensure you have only recovered the VAT actually paid.

If you pay within 14 days, the discounted price is:

Net	136.22
VAT	27.24
Gross	163.46

INVOICE

Invoice to:
Stanton Associates
323 Main Road
Tonbridge TN1 6EL

Graham Haddow

59 East Street
Medford
MF6 7TL
Tel: 0122 280496

Invoice no:	07892
Tax point:	3 May 20X1
VAT reg no:	431 7992 06
Your reference:	S3

	Amount excl of VAT £
Decoration of meeting room	1,100.00
VAT	220.00
Total amount payable	1,320.00

Deduct discount of 2% if paid within 14 days, net 30 days

A discount of 2% of the full price applies if payment is made within 14 days. No credit note will be issued. Following payment you must ensure you have only recovered the VAT actually paid.

If you pay within 14 days, the discounted price is:

Net	1,078.00
VAT	215.60
Gross	1,293.60

INVOICE

Graham Haddow

59 East Street
Medford
MF6 7TL
Tel: 0122 280496

Invoice to:
Boreham Bros
40/54 Hill Drive
Medford MF2 8AT

Invoice no:	07893
Tax point:	5 May 20X1
VAT reg no:	431 7992 06
Your reference:	B7

	Amount excl of VAT £
Repair of door frames	106.00
Re-decorating of door frames	130.00
	236.00
VAT	47.20
Total amount payable	283.20

Sales day book

Date	Invoice no	Customer name	Code	Total £	VAT £	Maintenance £	Decorating £

Checking receipts

Introduction

Now that we can account for our sales on both cash and credit terms, the next step in the process would be to account for amounts received in payment. Initially we will look at the receipt of monies in various forms and, in particular, the checking, accounting for and paying in of such receipts.

CONTENTS
1   Receiving money in a retail business
2   Receiving money for credit sales
3   Settlement (cash) discounts

1 Receiving money in a retail business

1.1 Introduction

Different types of business will receive money in different forms. For example a retail organisation will receive cash, cheques, credit card and debit card payments through the till.

In contrast a totally credit sales based organisation will rarely receive cash and credit/debit card payments but will receive cheques through the post to pay sales invoices which have been sent to customers or be in receipt of electronic bank payments such as BACS.

In this section we will start with a look at the checks that should be carried out by a retailer receiving various types of payment through the till.

1.2 Receiving cash

If cash payments are made for goods then the till operator should input the correct price for the goods, check the amount of money offered by the customer, enter this amount in the till or cash register, put the money into the till and pay out to the customer the correct change which will have been calculated by the till.

1.3 Accepting cheques

If a cheque is accepted as payment from an individual rather than a business, then it must be accompanied by a cheque guarantee card.

If a cheque is accepted with a valid cheque guarantee card, this means that the bank will pay the cheque; the cheque is guaranteed. We will go into detail later with regard to ensuring the validity of the cheque itself.

1.4 Cheque guarantee card

- For a £100 cheque guarantee card, this card guarantees that a cheque for up to £100 will be paid by the bank, regardless of the amount of money in that account.

- Only one £100 cheque for each transaction is allowed.

- The cheque must not exceed £100, or the bank can refuse to pay anything.

- The cheque guarantee card is usually the same card as the individual's debit card.

1.5   Checks to carry out on a cheque guarantee card

Look at the following cheque which is supported by a cheque guarantee card, and think of the checks that must be carried out before the cheque is accepted.

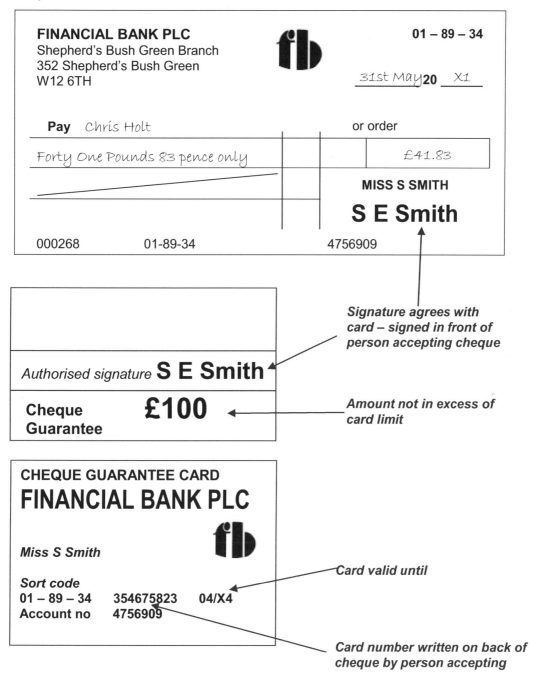

Note: Cheques from companies cannot be guaranteed by a cheque guarantee card.

If the retailer is suspicious in any way he should contact the bank which has issued the card.

1.6 Summary of checks

Card

- Card is valid (start and expiry date).
- Signature agrees with signature on cheque.
- Details agree with the cheque (e.g. account number, sort code).

Cheque

- Correct date.
- Amount does not exceed the amount on the cheque guarantee card.
- Amount is the same in both words and figures.
- Cheque signed in presence of person accepting it.
- Cheque guarantee card number written on back by person accepting it.
- Only one cheque for the purchase.

1.7 Payment by credit card

A customer may choose to pay using a credit card. Most retailers today will be linked to the credit card company by computer rather than needing to manually issue a credit card voucher.

1.8 Computerised credit card payments

Many retail businesses have taken the opportunity offered by the new information technology system EFTPOS (Electronic Funds Transfer at the Point of Sale) to simplify the procedure for accepting payment by credit card.

The retailer installs a terminal which is generally attached to the electronic cash register or is part of the cash register itself.

```
1900 2359
CASA ITALIA PIZZERIA
05/07/X1 21:58
Express: 2554006633579400

TOTAL £15.80

Auth code: 54662
THANK YOU SIGN BELOW
Please debit my account as shown

_____
```

The terminal is linked directly to the credit card company's computer at its operations centre by telephone line.

The exact format of the credit card sales voucher depends upon the equipment used, but it will normally have only two copies. The cardholder signs at least one of the copies which is returned to the retailer for the retailer's records. The other copy is for the cardholder's records.

Most retailers have introduced the PIN system whereby the customer simply enters their PIN into the credit card machine rather than having to sign the credit card voucher.

No banking of the vouchers need be done by the retailer because all transactions are immediately transferred electronically by the terminal via the telephone line.

The terminal automatically performs any authorisation procedures by contacting the computer at the operation centre.

1.9   What is EFTPOS?

Electronic Funds Transfer at Point of Sale (EFTPOS) is a system which uses advanced information technology.

EFTPOS – A national scheme which links terminals in shops and supermarkets with the processing department of banks, building societies and credit card companies.

The system is very flexible because it allows almost any type of credit card or debit card to be accepted by one system.

 Example

- Janet is a 27-year-old nurse from South Wales. She has gone into a petrol filling station on the M3 and filled her car with petrol.

- She wishes to pay by credit card. The filling station is linked up to the EFTPOS system.

- Janet's credit card is a Visa card. The filling station's bank is Lloyds TSB Bank in Gravesend, Kent.

Explain the sequence of transactions.

Solution

- Janet produces her card at the cash desk (point of sale).

- The sales assistant swipes or puts the card into a card reader on a terminal attached to the cash register.

- The sales assistant enters the amount of the purchase into the cash register.

- The information on the magnetic strip on the card is read by the retailer's terminal. A coded message (scrambled for security) is sent by telephone line to the central EFTPOS processing centre. This includes details of the amount. The card details are recorded and the request is sent to Visa for authorisation by telephone line.

- The Visa processing computer checks certain details.

- The customer is asked to enter her PIN followed by enter which is validated by the credit card company.

- In this case, the Visa processing computer authorises the purchase and updates its records. It notifies the central EFTPOS processing centre of the authorisation.

- The central EFTPOS processing centre transmits the authorisation to the retailer's terminal.

- A two-part credit card sales voucher is printed out and one copy given to Janet.

- The cash register also prints a receipt.

- After authorisation, the central EFTPOS processing centre sends details of the purchase to Lloyds Bank where the money is transferred into the filling station's account.

- The sales assistant gives Janet her card, her copy of the credit card sales voucher and her receipt.

This has all taken a matter of minutes.

1.10 Floor limits

Often credit card companies will set a maximum floor limit on amounts that can be accepted on a credit card for payment e.g. no purchases over £200. However if a customer wishes to use a card for a higher value purchase the company can be contacted for authorisation.

1.11 Checks to be made on the credit card

When accepting payment by credit card, the retailer must check that the card has not reached its expiry date and that the signature on the voucher matches that on the card, or that the PIN has been accepted. If authorisation is not given for a transaction by the credit card company then the credit card should not be accepted as this will mean that the credit limit has been exceeded or else that the card has been notified as having been stolen.

 Activity 1

A customer wishes to purchase £320 of clothes from a shop using a credit card for payment. The floor limit set by the credit card company is £100.

(a) Is it possible that the transaction can still go ahead despite the floor limit?

(b) Briefly explain the reason for your answer.

1.12 Debit cards

Debit cards – The debit card is a method of making payments direct from a bank account without having to write a cheque or produce a cheque guarantee card.

The payments are made by the customer using the EFTPOS technology described above. Payments made appear on the customer's bank statement alongside any other payments made by cheque, standing order, direct debit, etc.

If the payment is not authorised by the bank then the debit card should not be accepted for payment as this may mean that the customer does not have enough funds in their account.

Whatever method is used to pay for retail sales it is vital that the person receiving the payment checks all cheques, guarantee cards and credit/debit cards thoroughly to ensure they are valid. Otherwise the business may not receive payment for the goods sold.

2 Receiving money for credit sales

2.1 Introduction

When a business makes credit sales then it normally receives money from debtors in the post. This will normally be in the form of cheques and it is important that there is strict control of these cheques.

2.2 Remittance lists

All cash received should be listed on a **remittance list** (sometimes known as a **cheques received list).** The list should give details of:

- the customer
- the invoice numbers to which the payment relates (if known)
- the amount paid; and
- any discount allowed (see later in this chapter).

The list should be totalled and signed.

2.3 Using remittance advices

When a business issues an invoice to a customer, the invoice will often have a detachable slip. This slip is called a **remittance advice.**

This **remittance advice** is a slip returned by the customer when paying an invoice so as to identify what the payment is for. This makes it much easier for the business receiving the cheque to know which outstanding invoices are actually being paid by this cheque.

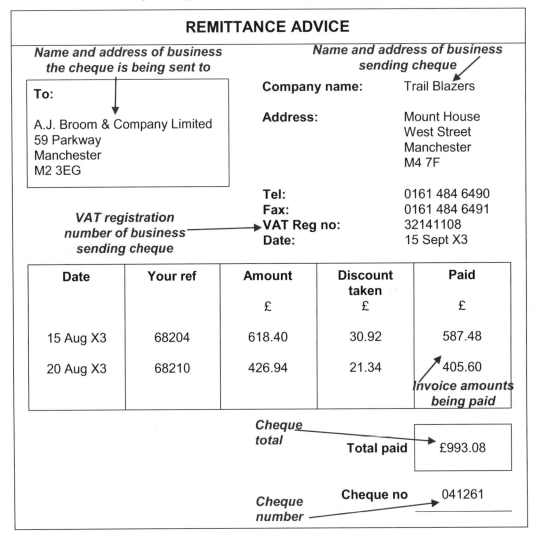

When receiving cheques from a customer it is vital to ensure that the correct amount has been paid. This can be done by agreeing the amount of the cheque to the details on the remittance advice and to the invoices themselves.

Activity 2

A remittance advice is a document sent by a supplier to a customer to advise the customer that goods ordered have been sent off to the customer. True/False

 Example

This morning the following cheques and supporting remittance advices were received in the post by your organisation, A. J. Broom & Company Ltd.

You are required to check the remittance advice and cheque amounts to the invoices given to ensure that the correct amount has been received.

WESTERN BANK		20 – 16 – 80
21 High Street		
Bristol		
BS1 4TZ		14 Sept **20** X3

Pay A.J. Broom & Company — or order

Two Thousand and nine pounds and four pence — Account Payee — £2,009.04

P Smithson

PATRICK CARPENTERS

046178   20–16–80   41643121

CENTRAL BANK
52 Warwick Road
Birmingham
B13 4XT

40 – 18 – 30

15 Sept **20** X3

Pay A.J. Broom & Company   or order

One thousand two hundred and

Twenty eight pounds and 74 pence

Account Payee

£1,228.74

J P Roberts

ROBERTS CONSTRUCTION

020106   40–18–30   31164992

REMITTANCE ADVICE

To:		Company name:	Patrick Carpenters
		Address:	Samba Industrial Est. Leeds
A.J. Broom & Company Limited 59 Parkway Manchester M2 6EG		Tel:	0714 304 2990
		Fax:	0714 304 2963
		VAT Reg no:	318 4861 27
		Date:	14 Sept 20X3

Date	Your ref	Amount	Discount taken	Paid
		£	£	£
23 Aug	68229	1,649.04	–	1,649.04
23 Aug	3217	(360.00)	–	(360.00)
4 Sept	68237	720.00	–	720.00
			Total paid	£ 2,009.04
			Cheque no	046178

REMITTANCE ADVICE

To:	Company name:	Roberts Construction
A.J. Broom & Company Limited 59 Parkway Manchester M2 6EG	Address: Tel: Fax: VAT Reg no: Date:	Chillian Park Oldham 0201 632 497 0201 632 498 331 4986 91 15 Sept 20X3

Date	Your ref	Amount	Discount taken	Paid	
		£	£	£	
23 Aug	68230	1,228.74	–	1,228.74	
			Total paid	£ 1,228.74	
			Cheque no	020106	

Invoice 68229

A.J. Broom & Company Limited

	59 Parkway
	Manchester
	M2 6EG
	Tel: 0161 560 3392
Patrick Carpenters	Fax: 0161 560 5322
Samba Industrial Estate	Tax Point: 23 August 20X3
Leeds	VAT reg no: 452 4585 48

Code	Supply	Description	Quantity	VAT rate %	Unit price £	Amount excl of VAT £
336 BTB	Sale	Roof tiles – black	10	20	123.00	1,230.00
667 LL5	Sale	Softwood plank – 20 cm	14	20	10.30	144.20
						1,374.20
VAT						274.84
Total amount payable						**1,649.04**

Invoice 68237

A.J. Broom & Company Limited

59 Parkway

Manchester

M2 6EG

Tel: 0161 560 3392

Fax: 0161 560 5322

Patrick Carpenters
Samba Industrial Estate
Leeds

| | | | | | Tax Point: | 4 September 20X3 |
| | | | | | VAT reg no: | 452 4585 48 |

Code	Supply	Description	Quantity	VAT rate %	Unit price £	Amount excl of VAT £
630 CC4	Sale	Oak veneer in Panels	3	20	200.00	600.00
VAT						120.00
Total amount payable						**720.00**

Credit note 3217

A.J. Broom & Company Limited

59 Parkway

Manchester

M2 6EG

Tel: 0161 560 3392

Fax: 0161 560 5322

Patrick Carpenters
Samba Industrial Estate
Leeds

| | | | | | Tax Point: | 23 August 20X3 |
| | | | | | VAT reg no: | 452 4585 48 |

Code	Supply	Description	Quantity	VAT rate %	Unit price £	Amount excl of VAT £
950 BB3	Return	Cotswold bricks	1	20	300.00	300.00
VAT						60.00
Total amount credited						**360.00**

						Invoice 68230

A.J. Broom & Company Limited

	59 Parkway	
	Manchester	
	M2 6EG	
	Tel: 0161 560 3392	
Roberts Construction	Fax: 0161 560 5322	
Chillian Park	Tax Point:	23 August 20X3
Oldham	VAT reg no:	452 4585 48

Code	Supply	Description	Quantity	VAT rate %	Unit price £	Amount excl of VAT £
160 TT7	Sale	Insulation	5	20	95.50	477.50
632 BS4	Sale	Brick tiles	20	20	33.25	665.00
						1,142.50
Trade discount 4%						45.70
						1,096.80
VAT						219.36
Total amount payable						**1,316.16**

Solution

From Patrick Carpenters

	£
Invoice number 68229	1,649.04
Invoice number 68237	720.00
Credit note 3217	(360.00)
	2,009.04

This agrees with the cheque.

From Roberts Construction

Invoice number 68230 £1,316.16

This does not agree with the cheque as the cheque is made out for £1,228.74. This discrepancy should be brought to the attention of the manager responsible for credit control at Roberts Construction and a polite letter should be written to the customer explaining the error that has been made. Request can be made for payment but if this is a regular customer then the additional amount may simply be added to the next cheque that Roberts Construction sends.

2.4 Cheque received with no accompanying remittance advice

If a cheque arrives in the post from a customer with no remittance advice or other confirmation of which invoices are being paid then it will be necessary to examine the details of this customer's transactions in the sales ledger.

The name of the customer should be fairly obvious from the name of the payer on the cheque – this will be printed by the bank as well as signed by the customer. The individual account for this debtor must then be extracted from the subsidiary ledger in an attempt to match the payment received to invoices and credit notes.

 Example

A cheque has been received in the post this morning from A J Holland, a credit customer, for £878.00 but it is not supported by any other documentation.

The individual debtor account for A J Holland has been found in the sales ledger.

A J Holland

	£		£
13/05/X2 Invoice 2256	336.67	20/05/X2 Credit 249	54.09
18/05/X2 Invoice 2271	846.23		
20/05/X2 Invoice 2280	447.69		
25/05/X2 Invoice 2288	147.73		

Solution

By a process of trial and error it can be discovered that the invoices that are being paid off are number 2256, 2280 and 2288 less the credit note. It would appear therefore that the cheque is for the correct amount although there might be some concern as to why invoice 2271 has not been paid, maybe there is some dispute over the amount of this invoice which should be investigated.

Always check figures carefully as such errors are often easy to miss.

2.5 Checking cheques

When cheques are received in the post it is important that they are checked for their validity, particularly in respect of:

- the date; a cheque can become out of date as it is only valid for 6 months from the date of issue

- the payee's name: should be the same as the one shown on the account into which the cheque is being paid

- the words and figures agree; if they disagree the cheque should be returned by the bank for amendment or for a new cheque to be issued

- the cheque is signed.

Example

The following three cheques were received in the post today, 3 June 20X6, by your organisation, L L Traders.

Check each one carefully to ensure that they are valid.

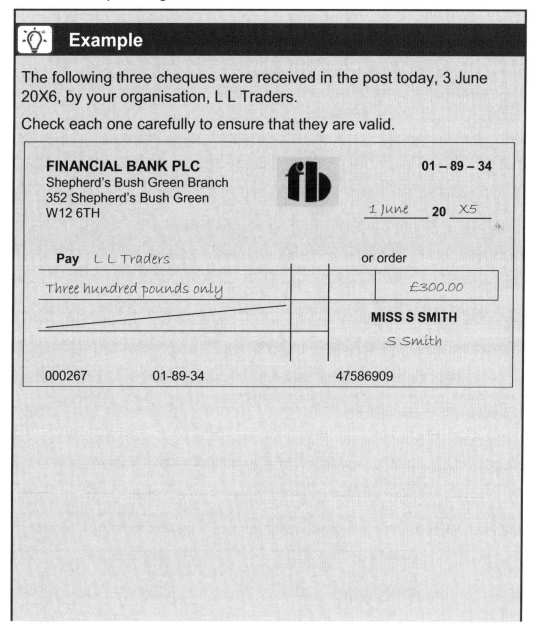

WESTERN BANK PLC
Stevenage Branch
29 High Street
Stevenage SG5 1BJ

WB

23 – 90 – 34

22 May **20** X6

Pay   L J Traders   or order

Two hundred and forty three pounds and   £243.18

18 pence   **J LEONARD**

J Leonard

000341   23-90-34   37586261

NORTHERN BANK PLC
Ealing Branch
15 London Road
W5 4DT

NB

23 – 47 – 34

30 May **20** X6

Pay   L L Traders   or order

One hundred and ninety six pounds   £169.23

23 pence   **P BUTLER**

P Butler

000476   22-47-34   20586484

Solution

The first cheque is dated 1 June 20X5 whereas today's date is 3 June 20X6. Therefore this cheque is out of date and must be returned to the customer requesting a replacement cheque.

The second cheque is made out to L J Traders instead of L L Traders. Again this must be returned to the customer with a request for a replacement cheque.

The third cheque is made out for £196.23 in words but £169.23 in figures. This cheque must also be returned to the customer with a request for a replacement cheque.

You must always be very thorough in assessments: check carefully each aspect of the cheque: date, words and figures, payee, signature etc.

Activity 3

(a) Today is the 15 March 20X3. Would the cheque below be accepted for payment if it were now presented to the National Bank plc?

(b) Give two reasons for your answer.

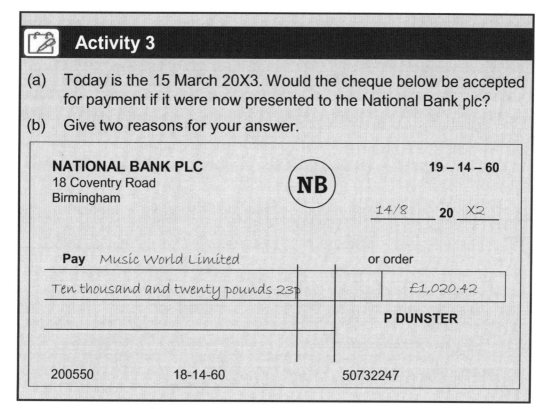

NATIONAL BANK PLC
18 Coventry Road
Birmingham

NB

19 – 14 – 60

14/8　**20** *X2*

Pay *Music World Limited*　or order

Ten thousand and twenty pounds 23p　£1,020.42

P DUNSTER

200550　18-14-60　50732247

3 Settlement (cash) discounts

3.1 Introduction

When a settlement discount is offered to a customer, this will normally be offered as a percentage amount. If a customer takes advantage of the discount, it is important to check that this is correct.

3.2 Checks to make

Where a payment is received after deducting a settlement discount then great care should be taken in checking this receipt.

Step 1　Check back to the original invoice to ensure that the discount is valid, i.e. that the customer has paid within the stated period.

Step 2　Check that the correct percentage discount has been taken and that it has been correctly calculated (this will usually be shown on the sales invoice as seen in earlier chapters).

Example

Cheques have been received from two credit customers. Today's date is 3 October 20X3.

Garden Supplies Ltd	£2,214.96
Porter & Co	£981.36

The invoices that these cheques are paying are given below.

You are required to check that the receipt is for the correct amount.

						Invoice 66293

	A.J. Broom & Company Limited	
	59 Parkway	
	Manchester	
	M2 6EG	
	Tel: 0161 560 3392	
Garden Supplies Ltd	Fax: 0161 560 5322	
Grange Hill	Tax Point:	20 September 20X3
Chester	VAT reg no:	452 4585 48

Code	Supply	Description	Quantity	VAT rate %	Unit price £	Amount excl of VAT £
950 BB3	Sale	Cotswold bricks	2	20	300.00	600.00
159 504	Sale	Roof tiles – red	6	20	195.50	1,173.00
874 KL5	Sale	Brick tiles	3	20	56.65	169.95
						1,942.95
VAT						388.59
Total amount payable						**2,331.54**

A discount of 5% of the full price applies if payment is made within 10 days. No credit note will be issued. Following payment you must ensure you have only recovered the VAT actually paid

If you pay within 10 days, the discounted price is:

Net	1845.80
VAT	369.16
Total amount payable	**2,214.96**

					VAT rate	Unit price	Amount excl of VAT

Invoice 66299

A.J. Broom & Company Limited

	59 Parkway		
	Manchester		
	M2 6EG		
	Tel: 0161 560 3392		
Porter & Co	Fax: 0161 560 5322		
Cunard Place	Tax Point:	26 September 20X3	
Manchester	VAT reg no:	452 4585 48	

Code	Supply	Description	Quantity	VAT rate %	Unit price £	Amount excl of VAT £
262 BPT	Sale	Lined Oak Panels 1m^2	6	20	145.00	870.00
VAT						174.00
						————
Total amount payable						**1,044.00**

A discount of 5% of the full price applies if payment is made within 10 days. No credit note will be issued. Following payment you must ensure you have only recovered the VAT actually paid

If you pay within 10 days, the discounted price is:

Net	826.50
VAT	165.30
	————
Total amount payable	**991.80**

Solution

The invoice to Garden Supplies Ltd is dated 20 September. As today's date is 3 October then the payment has not been received within 10 days of the invoice date which are the stated terms for the settlement discount. Therefore the customer should be politely informed of this fact and a request made for the balance of the invoice to be paid, £2,331.54 – £2,214.96 = £116.58.

The invoice to Porter & Co is dated 26 September and therefore is valid in terms of date. However, the customer has made an error and deducted a discount of 6% instead of 5% and paid £981.36 instead of £991.80. Again the customer must be informed of the error and the balance requested. For a small amount such as this, £10.44 (£991.80 – £981.36), the credit controller may decide that this amount can be added to the next payment from Porter & Co if they are regular customers.

In assessments you must always check all discount calculations and dates very thoroughly.

3.3 Recording any settlement discounts taken

When the settlement discounts have been checked and are valid it is important that the amount of the discount is noted. This should be either on the back of the cheque or on the remittance list. This is necessary because when the primary records are written up for these receipts (see next chapter) the amount of the discount must be recorded. A note should also be made of the adjustment required to the VAT account, in respect of the lower Output VAT paid when a settlement discount is taken.

3.4 Automated payments

It is entirely possible that a customer might pay an amount due with a bank giro credit. A bank giro credit is a method of transferring money into someone else's bank account in any bank in the country. This amount would then appear as a credit in the bank statement. Just as with a cheque receipt this automated receipt must be checked back to the original invoices to ensure that it is for the correct amount and to check for items such as settlement discounts deducted.

4 Summary

This chapter has concentrated on all of the important checks that must be made when receiving money from customers to ensure that the correct amounts have been paid and that the payment method is valid. Cash, cheques and credit card payments must be carefully checked by a retailer. A supplier on credit terms has to make a number of checks when cheques are received from a customer. Is the cheque for the correct amount given the invoices that are paid? Is any settlement discount valid and correctly calculated? Are the cheques that have been received correctly made out so that they can be paid into the organisation's bank account?

Answers to chapter activities

Activity 1

(a) Yes

(b) The credit card company can be contacted by phone to authorise use of the card for the purchase.

Activity 2

False. A remittance advice is a slip that the customer can send back to the supplier with his payment to identify what the payment is for.

Activity 3

(a) No

(b) Any two from the following:

    (i) The cheque has not been signed.

    (ii) The cheque is out of date.

    (iii) The words and figures on the cheque are not the same.

5 Test your knowledge

Workbook Activity 4

Simon Harris is a self-employed accountant who has a number of clients who all pay by cheque. Today's date is 5 May 20X1 and in the last week he has received the following cheques.

Required:

Inspect each one carefully to ensure that it is valid and make a note of any problems that you find.

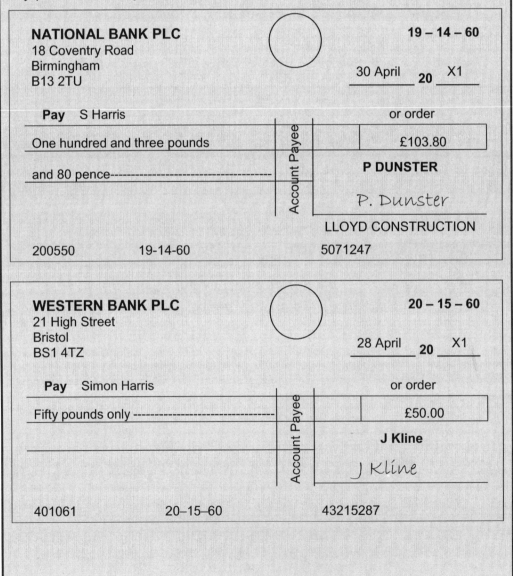

NATIONAL BANK PLC
18 Coventry Road
Birmingham
B13 2TU

19 – 14 – 60

30 April 20 X1

Pay   S Harris   or order

One hundred and three pounds   £103.80

and 80 pence----------------------------------   **P DUNSTER**

P. Dunster

LLOYD CONSTRUCTION

200550   19-14-60   5071247

WESTERN BANK PLC
21 High Street
Bristol
BS1 4TZ

20 – 15 – 60

28 April 20 X1

Pay   Simon Harris   or order

Fifty pounds only -------------------------------   £50.00

J Kline

J Kline

401061   20–15–60   43215287

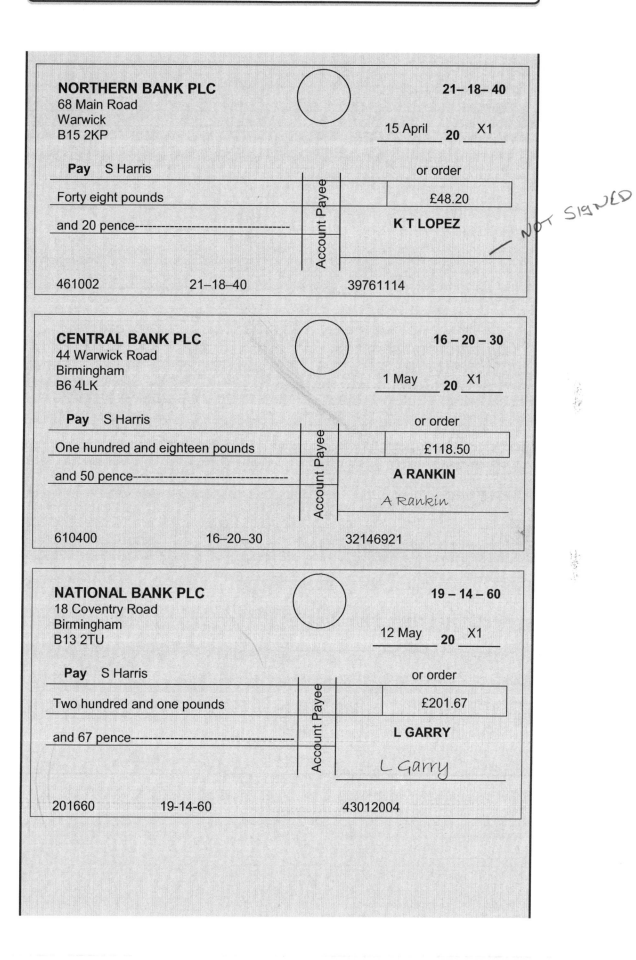

NORTHERN BANK PLC
68 Main Road
Warwick
B15 2KP

21– 18– 40

15 April 20 X1

Pay S Harris   or order

Forty eight pounds   £48.20

and 20 pence----------------------------------   **K T LOPEZ**

Account Payee

461002   21–18–40   39761114

✓ NOT SIGNED

CENTRAL BANK PLC
44 Warwick Road
Birmingham
B6 4LK

16 – 20 – 30

1 May 20 X1

Pay S Harris   or order

One hundred and eighteen pounds   £118.50

and 50 pence----------------------------------   **A RANKIN**

A Rankin

Account Payee

610400   16–20–30   32146921

NATIONAL BANK PLC
18 Coventry Road
Birmingham
B13 2TU

19 – 14 – 60

12 May 20 X1

Pay S Harris   or order

Two hundred and one pounds   £201.67

and 67 pence----------------------------------   **L GARRY**

L Garry

Account Payee

201660   19-14-60   43012004

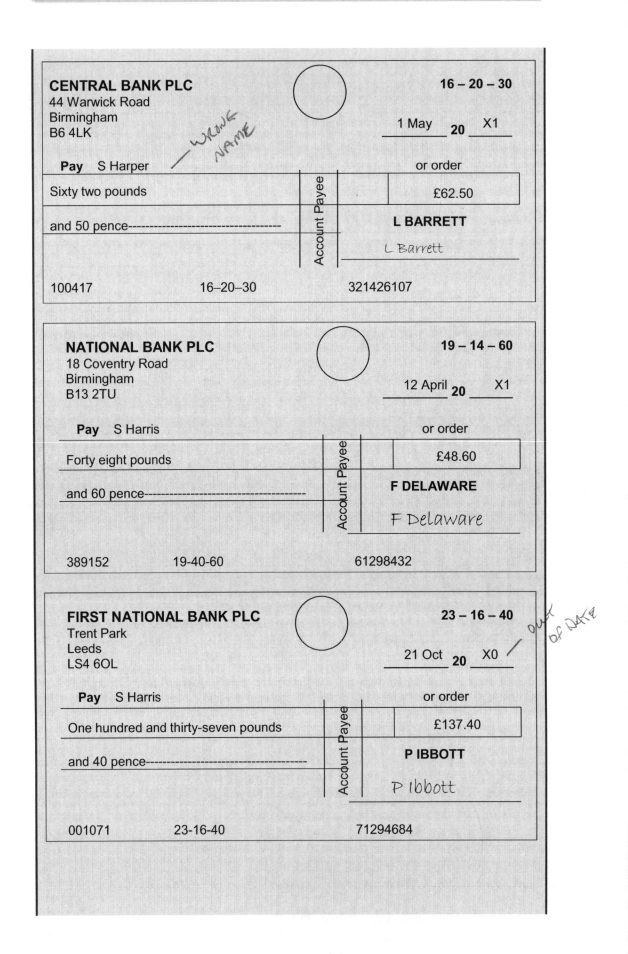

CENTRAL BANK PLC
44 Warwick Road
Birmingham
B6 4LK

16 – 20 – 30

1 May **20** X1

— WRONG NAME

Pay S Harper   or order

Sixty two pounds   £62.50

and 50 pence----------------------------------   **L BARRETT**

                                                   L Barrett

Account Payee

100417   16–20–30   321426107

NATIONAL BANK PLC
18 Coventry Road
Birmingham
B13 2TU

19 – 14 – 60

12 April **20** X1

Pay S Harris   or order

Forty eight pounds   £48.60

and 60 pence----------------------------------   **F DELAWARE**

                                                   F Delaware

Account Payee

389152   19-40-60   61298432

FIRST NATIONAL BANK PLC
Trent Park
Leeds
LS4 6OL

23 – 16 – 40

21 Oct **20** X0

OUT OF DATE

Pay S Harris   or order

One hundred and thirty-seven pounds   £137.40

and 40 pence--------------------------------   **P IBBOTT**

                                                   P Ibbott

Account Payee

001071   23-16-40   71294684

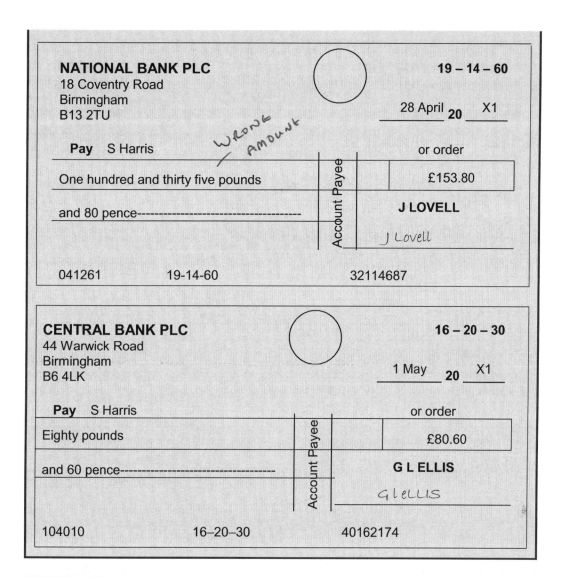

NATIONAL BANK PLC
18 Coventry Road
Birmingham
B13 2TU

19 – 14 – 60

28 April **20** X1

WRONG AMOUNT

Pay S Harris

or order

One hundred and thirty five pounds

£153.80

and 80 pence---------------------------------------

J LOVELL

J Lovell

Account Payee

041261   19-14-60   32114687

CENTRAL BANK PLC
44 Warwick Road
Birmingham
B6 4LK

16 – 20 – 30

1 May **20** X1

Pay S Harris

or order

Eighty pounds

£80.60

and 60 pence---------------------------------------

G L ELLIS

G l eLLiS

Account Payee

104010   16–20–30   40162174

📝 Workbook Activity 5

Today's date is 12 May 20X1 and the following five cheques have arrived in this morning's post. You have found the invoices that these payments relate to – these are also given.

Required:

Check that each receipt is correct and make a note of any problems that you find.

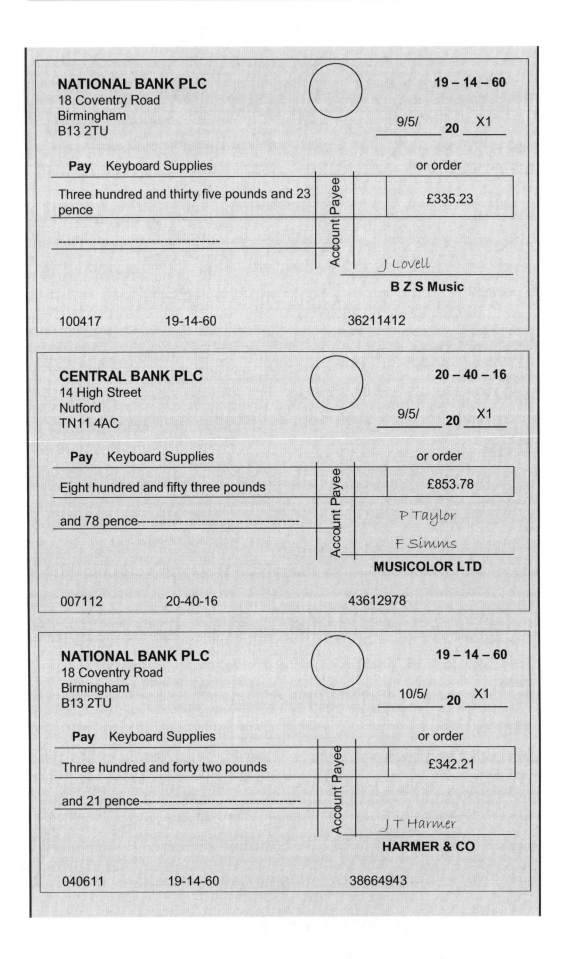

NATIONAL BANK PLC
18 Coventry Road
Birmingham
B13 2TU

19 – 14 – 60

9/5/ 20 X1

Pay Keyboard Supplies

Three hundred and thirty five pounds and 23 pence

----

or order

Account Payee

£335.23

J Lovell

B Z S Music

100417   19-14-60   36211412

CENTRAL BANK PLC
14 High Street
Nutford
TN11 4AC

20 – 40 – 16

9/5/ 20 X1

Pay Keyboard Supplies

Eight hundred and fifty three pounds

and 78 pence-------------------------------------

or order

Account Payee

£853.78

P Taylor

F Simms

MUSICOLOR LTD

007112   20-40-16   43612978

NATIONAL BANK PLC
18 Coventry Road
Birmingham
B13 2TU

19 – 14 – 60

10/5/ 20 X1

Pay Keyboard Supplies

Three hundred and forty two pounds

and 21 pence-------------------------------------

or order

Account Payee

£342.21

J T Harmer

HARMER & CO

040611   19-14-60   38664943

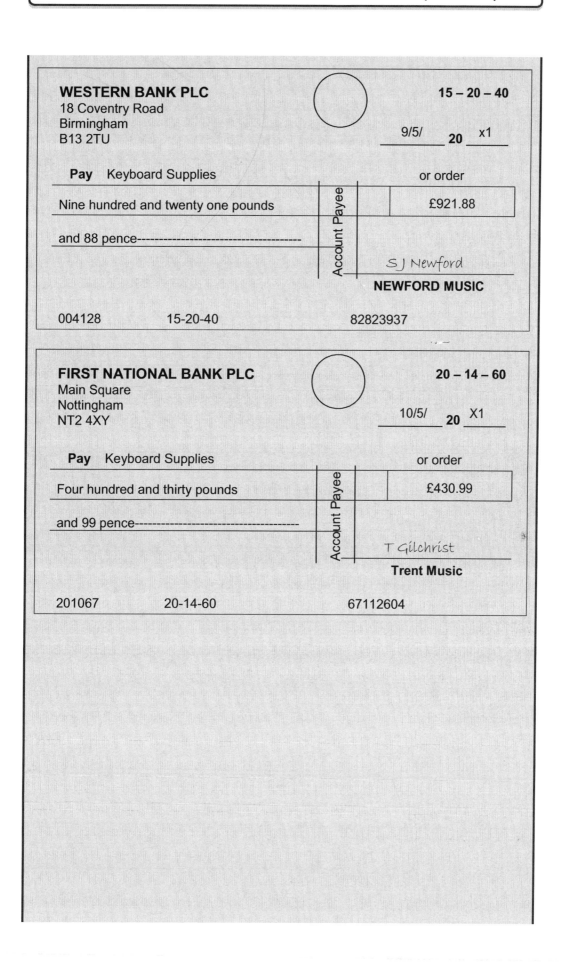

WESTERN BANK PLC
18 Coventry Road
Birmingham
B13 2TU

15 – 20 – 40

9/5/ **20** x1

Pay   Keyboard Supplies

or order

Nine hundred and twenty one pounds

£921.88

and 88 pence-----------------------------------

Account Payee

S J Newford

NEWFORD MUSIC

004128   15-20-40   82823937

FIRST NATIONAL BANK PLC
Main Square
Nottingham
NT2 4XY

20 – 14 – 60

10/5/ **20** X1

Pay   Keyboard Supplies

or order

Four hundred and thirty pounds

£430.99

and 99 pence-----------------------------------

Account Payee

T Gilchrist

Trent Music

201067   20-14-60   67112604

INVOICE

Invoice to:
BZS Music
42 Westhill
Nutford TN11 3PQ

Deliver to:

Keyboard Supplies

Trench Park Estate
Fieldham
Sussex TN21 4AF
Tel: 01829 654545
Fax: 01829 654646

Invoice no:	06180
Tax point:	3 May 20X1
VAT reg no:	466 1128 30
Your reference:	SL01
Purchase order no:	77147

Code	Description	Quantity	VAT rate %	Unit price £	Amount excl of VAT £
B4012	Bento Keyboard	2	20	180.00	360.00
					360.00
Trade discount 20%					72.00
					288.00
VAT					57.60
Total amount payable					345.60

A discount of 3% of the full price applies if payment is made within 10 days. No credit note will be issued. Following payment you must ensure you have only recovered the VAT actually paid.

If you pay within 10 days, the discounted price is:

Net	279.36
VAT	55.87
Total amount payable	335.23

INVOICE

Keyboard Supplies

Invoice to:
Musicolor Ltd
23 High Street
Nutford TN11 4 TZ

Trench Park Estate
Fieldham
Sussex TN21 4AF
Tel: 01829 654545
Fax: 01829 654646

Deliver to:

As above

Invoice no:	06176
Tax point:	1 May 20X1
VAT reg no:	466 1128 30
Your reference:	SL06
Purchase order no:	6362

Code	Description	Quantity	VAT rate %	Unit price £	Amount excl of VAT £
Z4600	Zanni Keyboard	3	20	185.00	555.00
A4802	Atol Keyboard	2	20	130.00	260.00
					815.00
Trade discount 10%					81.50
					733.50
VAT					146.70
Total amount payable					880.20

A discount of 3% of the full price applies if payment is made within 10 days. No credit note will be issued. Following payment you must ensure you have only recovered the VAT actually paid.

If you pay within 10 days, the discounted price is

Net	711.49
VAT	142.29
Total amount payable	853.78

INVOICE

Invoice to:
Harmer & Co
1 Acre Street
Nutford TN11 0HA

Deliver to:

As above

Keyboard Supplies

Trench Park Estate
Fieldham
Sussex TN21 4AF
Tel: 01829 654545
Fax: 01829 654646

Invoice no:	06183
Tax point:	3 May 20X1
VAT reg no:	466 1128 30
Your reference:	SL17
Purchase order no:	047786

Code	Description	Quantity	VAT rate %	Unit price £	Amount excl of VAT £
G4326	Garland Keyboard	3	20	98.00	294.00
					294.00

VAT	58.80
Total amount payable	352.80

A discount of 3% of the full price applies if payment is made within 10 days. No credit note will be issued. Following payment you must ensure you have only recovered the VAT actually paid.

If you pay within 10 days, the discounted price is
Net

Vat	285.18
Total amount payable	57.03
	342.21

INVOICE

Keyboard Supplies

Invoice to:
Newford Music
32/34 Main Street
Welland
Sussex TN4 6BD

Trench Park Estate
Fieldham
Sussex TN21 4AF
Tel: 01829 654545
Fax: 01829 654646

Deliver to:

As above

Invoice no:	06171
Tax point:	30 April 20X1
VAT reg no:	466 1128 30
Your reference:	SL18
Purchase order no:	47202

Code	Description	Quantity	VAT rate %	Unit price £	Amount excl of VAT £
Z4406	Zanni Keyboard	6	20	165.00	990.00
					990.00
Trade discount 20%					198.00
					792.00
VAT					158.40
Total amount payable					950.40

A discount of 3% of the full price applies if payment is made within 10 days. No credit note will be issued. Following payment you must ensure you have only recovered the VAT actually paid.

If you pay within 10 days, the discounted price is
Net
Vat

Total amount payable	768.24
	153.64
	921.88

INVOICE

Invoice to:
Trent Music
Trent House
Main Street
Fieldham TN21 6ZF

Keyboard Supplies
Trench Park Estate
Fieldham
Sussex TN21 4AF
Tel: 01829 654545
Fax: 01829 654646

Deliver to:

Invoice no:	06184
Tax point:	3 May 20X1
VAT reg no:	466 1128 30
Your reference:	SL41
Purchase order no:	93754

Code	Description	Quantity	VAT rate %	Unit price £	Amount excl of VAT £
G4030	Garland Keyboard	4	20	105.00	420.00
					420.00
Trade discount 10%					42.00
					378.00
VAT					75.60
Total amount payable					453.60

A discount of 3% of the full price applies if payment is made within 10 days. No credit note will be issued. Following payment you must ensure you have only recovered the VAT actually paid.

If you pay within 10 days, the discounted price is

Net	
Vat	366.66
Total amount payable	73.33
	439.99

The analysed cash receipts book

Introduction

Once we have carried out all relevant checks on our receipts, we need to record these transactions within our accounting records. As we have seen before, however, if we were to do this individually, the accounting records would become cluttered. In this chapter we will look at the use of a cash book and then review in more detail the recording of cash receipts, particularly from credit customers. The analysed cash payments book is reviewed in later in this book.

CONTENTS
1   The cash book
2   The analysed cash receipts book
3   Settlement discounts allowed to customers
4   Cash and credit sales contrasted

1 The cash book

1.1 The cash book

One of the most important books used within a business is the cash book. There are various forms of cash book, a 'two column' and a 'three column' cash book.

> ### Definition
>
> A cash book is a record of cash receipts and payments that forms part of the double entry system.

1.2 Two column cash book

A proforma two column cash book is shown below.

CASH BOOK							
Date	Narrative	Cash £	Bank £	Date	Narrative	Cash £	Bank £

Notes:

(a) The left hand side of the cash book represents the debit side – money received.

(b) The right hand side of the cash book represents the credit side – money paid out.

(c) The date column contains the date of the transaction.

(d) The narrative column describes the transactions – typically the name of the customer who is paying. It would also contain the sales ledger code of the debtor.

(e) The cash column on the debit side represents cash received, whereas the cash column on the credit side represents cash paid.

(f) The bank column on the debit side represents money received in the bank account (by cheque or other bank payment) whereas the bank column on the credit side represents money paid from the bank account(by cheque or other bank payment).

A business may operate a bank current account as a means to settle business transactions. Receipts may be made in the form of a cheque, cash may be deposited into the current account and payment may be made by drawing a cheque against the current account.

To be able to record these bank specific transactions, a separate column must be introduced to the cash book to account for them. This is what leads to the use of a two column cash book; a column for cash transactions and a column for transactions made through the bank current account. Each column represents a separate account, cash account and bank account, each with its own double entry.

As well as being aware of the use of two columns for bank and cash, you should also be aware that a cash book may have additional columns for the purpose of analysing the receipts and payments in terms of sources and types of income and expenditure.

 Definition

An analysed cash book is a cash book with additional columns for analysing receipts and payments in terms of their source and the type of income and expenditure.

1.3 Three column cash book

The three column cash book incorporates the cash discounts for each relevant entry into a third column. At the end of a certain period of time, when the cash book is balanced off, the totals from these discount columns would then be transferred to the discount accounts in the general ledger. Discounts received are entered in the discounts column on the credit side of the cash book, and discounts allowed in the discounts column on the debit side of the cash book.

A proforma three column cash book is shown below.

CASH BOOK									
Date	Narrative	Cash £	Bank £	Discount £	Date	Narrative	Cash £	Bank £	Discount £

The purpose of each of the columns is consistent to that of a two column cash book with the addition of the discount columns in both the receipts (debit) side and the payments (credit) side. It is important to note that cash books can be in different formats with different numbers of analysis columns.

We will now focus on the cash receipts book. The cash payments book will be reviewed in a later chapter.

2 The analysed cash receipts book

2.1 Layout

A proforma analysed cash receipts book is shown below.

CASH RECEIPTS BOOK								
Date	Narrative	Reference	Total £	VAT £	SLCA £	Cash sales £	Discount allowed £	VAT adjustment £
		TOTALS						

Notes:

(a) The date column records the date of the transaction.

(b) The narrative column describes the transactions – typically the name of the customer who is paying. It would also contain the sales ledger code of the debtor.

(c) The reference column contains any other information that may be helpful e.g. 'cash', 'cheque', 'BACS' etc.

(d) The total column contains the total cash received (including any VAT).

(e) The VAT column contains the VAT on the transaction but not if the VAT has already been entered in the sales day book. This is a tricky point and is dealt with later.

(f) The SLCA column contains any cash received that has been received from a debtor. The total received including VAT is entered in this column.

(g) The cash sales, discount allowed and VAT adjustment columns will be dealt with later.

💡 **Example**

The following is an example of the general and sales ledgers, including entries from the sales and sales returns day books.

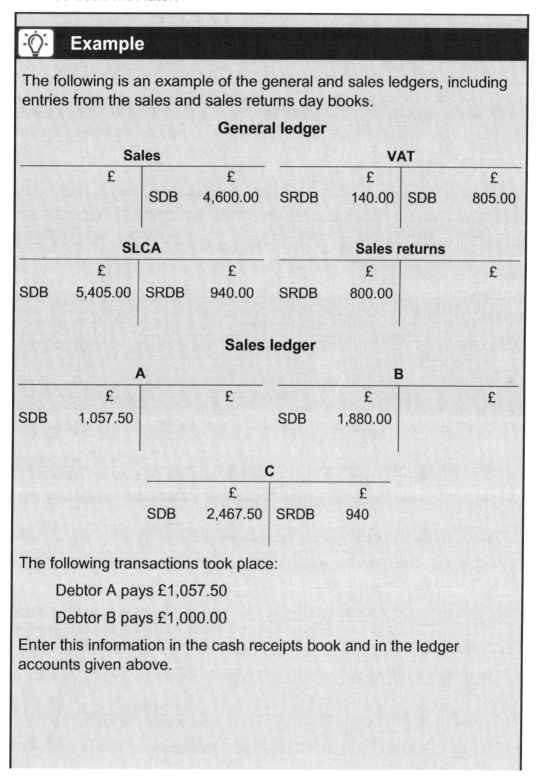

General ledger

Sales				VAT			
£		£		£		£	
		SDB	4,600.00	SRDB	140.00	SDB	805.00

SLCA				Sales returns			
£		£		£		£	
SDB	5,405.00	SRDB	940.00	SRDB	800.00		

Sales ledger

A				B			
£		£		£		£	
SDB	1,057.50			SDB	1,880.00		

C			
£		£	
SDB	2,467.50	SRDB	940

The following transactions took place:

Debtor A pays £1,057.50

Debtor B pays £1,000.00

Enter this information in the cash receipts book and in the ledger accounts given above.

Solution

The following steps are needed.

Step 1 Enter these transactions in the cash book.

Step 2 Total the cash book and post the totals to the general ledger.

Step 3 Post the individual amounts of cash paid by debtors to the individual accounts in the sales ledger.

Step 1

CASH RECEIPTS BOOK

Date	Narrative	Ref	Total	VAT	SLCA	Cash sales	Discount allowed	VAT adjustment
			£	£	£	£	£	£
	A		1,057.50	See Note 2 of Step 2	1,057.50			
	B		1,000.00		1,000.00			
		TOTALS	2,057.50		2,057.50			

Step 2

We have brought forward the balances from the general ledger in the earlier example and now post the cash received book (CRB) totals to the general ledger.

General ledger

Sales			
£		£	
		SDB	4,600.00

VAT			
£		£	
SRDB	140.00	SDB	805.00

SLCA			
£		£	
SDB	5,405.00	SRDB	940.00
		CRB	2,057.50

Sales returns			
£		£	
SRDB	800.00		

Note 1: We have posted the total of the SLCA column of the CRB to the sales ledger control account. This is the same as the total column in this example, but in more complex examples it need not be. The entry to the sales ledger control account is a credit entry as this reduces the amount owed by our debtors.

Note 2: A common confusion is for people to wonder about the VAT – surely some of the money paid by A and B is actually paying the VAT part of the invoice. Yes it is, but we have already accounted for this VAT element when we entered the invoices themselves into the ledger accounts via the sales day book.

The total of the invoices in the SDB were debited to the SLCA and the VAT and sales were the corresponding credits. We therefore now post the total cash including VAT to the sales ledger control account but nothing is posted to the VAT account as this has already been done when dealing with the invoices.

Note 3: This is now the full double entry for the cash received completed.

Debit   Bank account (cash receipts book)

Credit   Sales ledger control account

We have credited the sales ledger control account and the entry in the cash receipts book itself is the related debit entry. So there is no need for any further debit entry.

Step 3

We have brought forward the balance from the sales ledger in the earlier example and now post the cash received to the individual sales ledger accounts. Again, as with the sales ledger control account, this is a credit entry in each case as the cash received is reducing the amount owed by each debtor.

A				B		
	£		£		£		£
b/f	1,057.50	CRB	1,057.50	b/f	1,880.00	CRB	1,000.00

C			
	£		£
b/f	2,467.50	SRDB	940.00

2.2 Balancing the accounts

Below we reproduce some of the accounts as they have been written up above and we then balance the accounts and bring down the balances.

General ledger

SLCA

	£		£
SDB	5,405.00	CRB	2,057.50
		SRDB	940.00
		c/d	2,407.50
	5,405.00		5,405.00
b/d	2,407.50		

Sales ledger

A

	£		£
SDB	1,057.50	CRB	1,057.50
	1,057.50		1,057.50

B

	£		£
SDB	1,880.00	CRB	1,000.00
		c/d	880.00
	1,880.00		1,880.00
b/d	880.00		

C

	£		£
SDB	2,467.50		940.00
		c/d	1,527.50
	2,467.50		2,467.50
b/d	1,527.50		

Note: The balance on the sales ledger control account in the general ledger (£2,407.50) is the same as the total balances of the individual accounts in the subsidiary sales ledger (£880.00 + £1,527.50 = £2,407.50).

3 Settlement discounts allowed to customers

3.1 Introduction

Settlement discounts are a small but tricky complication when dealing with the analysed sales day book and cash book.

We shall consider the same example as before with only one change – customer A is offered an additional 5% settlement discount if he pays his invoice within 30 days.

Example

The sales day book with settlement discounts.

Consider the following sales transactions made by Roberts Metals.

Customer	Sales value (ex VAT)	Trade discount	Net sales value	VAT	Total
	£	£	£	£	£
A	1,000	10%	900	180.00	1,080.00
B	2,000	20%	1,600	320.00	1,920.00
C	3,000	30%	2,100	420.00	2,520.00

In addition to the trade discount, customer A has been offered an additional 5% discount if he pays his invoice within 30 days.

Enter this information in the sales day book and ledger accounts.

Solution

The following steps are needed.

Step 1   Write up the sales day book.

Step 2   Post the totals to the accounts in the general ledger.

Step 3   Post the individual invoices to the sales ledger.

The solution is the same as before as it is not yet known whether or not Customer A will take up the discount.

SALES DAY BOOK

Date	Customer	Reference	Invoice number	Total £	VAT £	Sales £
	A			1,080.00	180.00	900.00
	B			1,920.00	320.00	1,600.00
	C			2,520.00	420.00	2,100.00
			TOTALS	5,520.00	920.00	4,600.00

Step 2

General ledger

Sales				VAT			
£		£		£		£	
		SDB	4,600.00			SDB	920.00

SLCA			
£		£	
SDB	5,520.00		

Sales ledger

A				B			
£		£		£		£	
SDB	1,080.00			SDB	1,920.00		

C			
£		£	
SDB	2,520.00		

As you can see the offering of the settlement discount has had no effect on the entries to the sales day book or the ledgers as it is not yet known whether the discount will be taken.

Example

The analysed cash receipts book with settlement discounts

Now we will look at the cash receipts book.

Debtor A pays his debt within 30 days and therefore takes the 5% discount and debtor B pays £1,000 on account.

Enter these transactions in the cash receipts book and the ledger accounts.

Solution

Notes:

The entries in the cash receipts book are different when a debtor takes a settlement discount because two new columns are added to the CRB – the 'discount allowed' column and the 'VAT adjustment' columns. In addition, a new account is opened in the general ledger – the 'discount allowed ledger account'.

The steps are now:

Step 1   Calculate the cash that A pays after allowing for the discount.

Step 2   Enter the cash received in the CRB (with the additional columns for 'discounts allowed' and 'VAT adjustment'). Total the columns.

Step 3   Enter the totals in the general ledger (including the 'discount allowed account' and 'VAT adjustment').

Step 4   Enter the individual cash received from debtors A and B in the sales ledger account.

Step 1

Calculate the cash paid by A.

	£
Net sale value after trade discount (as entered in SDB)	900.00
Less: 5% settlement discount (900 × 5%)	(45.00)
Amended invoice value	855.00
Amended VAT on invoice	171.00
Cash paid by A	1,026.00

Step 2

Enter cash received in the CRB.

CASH RECEIPTS BOOK

Date	Narrative	Ref	Total	VAT	SLCA	Cash sales	Discount allowed	VAT Adjustment
			£	£	£	£	£	£
	A		1,026.00		1,026.00		45.00	9.00
	B		1,000.00		1,000.00			
	TOTALS		2,026.00		2,026.00		45.00	9.00

Note: The CRB does not 'cross-cast', i.e. if you add the totals across (SLCA + discounts + VAT adjustments) this does not equal the total column.

The discount allowed and VAT adjustment columns are known as 'memorandum columns' – they are not really part of the cash book – they are simply there to remind the bookkeeper to make an entry in the general ledger as we shall see below.

The VAT adjustment required is as follows:

The VAT on the full sales value was £180.00. This is the VAT which has been recorded in the SDB.

The VAT on the sales value after deducting the settlement discount is £171.00.

Therefore, an adjustment of £9.00 is required to correct the output VAT paid by the customer.

Step 3 – Posting the CRB totals

The CRB totals are posted as follows to the general ledger.

	Sales				VAT		
	£		£		£		£
		SDB	4,600.00	CRB	9.00	SDB	920.00

	SLCA				Discount allowed		
	£		£		£		£
SDB	5,520.00	CRB	2,026.00	CRB	45.00		
		CRB	45.00				
		CRB	9.00				

Note that the discount allowed figure in the CRB is entered in the SLCA (to acknowledge the fact that the discount has been taken) and is debited to the discount allowed account.

This debit is an expense of the business – allowing the discount has cost the business £45.

The VAT adjustment figure is also entered in the SLCA to reflect the fact that the customer has paid less VAT as a result of taking up the discount, and is debited to the VAT account to reduce the overall VAT liability of the company.

Step 4 – Posting to the sales ledger

	A	£		£		B	£		£
SDB		1,080.00	CRB	1,026.00	SDB		1,920.00	CRB	1,000.00
			Disc	45.00				c/d	920.00
			VAT adj	9.00					
		1,080.00		1,080.00			1,920.00		1,920.00
					b/d		920.00		

	C	£		£
SDB		2,520.00		

Note again that the discount and the VAT adjustment are both credited to the account of A to show that he has taken the £45 discount, and paid less VAT as a result, which clears his account.

Note also that there is no corresponding debit entry of £45 to a discount account or of £9 to a VAT adjustment account in the sales ledger. The sales ledger is simply there to show the detail in the general ledger SLCA. The double entry for the £45 discount and the £9 VAT adjustment only takes place in the general ledger, as we have seen above, between the SLCA and the discounts allowed account, and the SLCA and the VAT account.

4 Cash and credit sales contrasted

4.1 Introduction

We studied cash sales at the very start of double entry bookkeeping and saw that the entries were very simple – debit cash and credit sales. Nothing has happened to change that but it is worth looking at cash and credit sales 'side by side' to appreciate the difference in their treatment, when we consider the sales day book and cash receipts book.

 Example

Linda's Electricals sells goods to three customers.

Customer A buys an electric fire for £100 cash plus VAT of £20.

Customer B buys rolls of electrical wiring on credit for £1,000 plus VAT of £200.

Customer C buys 100 switches on credit for £200 plus VAT of £40. Customer B pays his debt in full.

There are no trade or settlement discounts. Write up the books in the following steps.

Step 1   Enter the cash sale in the analysed cash receipts book in the general ledger.

Step 2   Enter the credit sales in the SDB and cash received in the analysed cash receipts book in the general ledger.

Step 3   Post the totals of the SDB and cash book to the accounts in the general ledger.

Step 4   Post the individual amounts in the SDB and cash book to the sales ledger.

Solution

Step 1

Enter the cash sale in the cash book.

CASH RECEIPTS BOOK							
Date	Narrative	Total	VAT	SLCA	Cash sales	Discount allowed	VAT adjustment
		£	£	£	£	£	£
	A	120.00	20.00		100.00		

This is a very simple entry. At the moment of course it is only half of the double entry (the debit side of the entry). We have yet to do the credit entries (see Step 3).

Step 2

Enter the credit sales into the SDB and the cash received into the analysed cash receipts book (which already has the cash received from A per Step 1).

SALES DAY BOOK						
Date	Customer	Reference	Invoice number	Total £	VAT £	Net sales value £
	B			1,200.00	200.00	1,000.00
	C			240.00	40.00	200.00
			TOTALS	1,440.00	240.00	1,200.00

CASH RECEIPTS BOOK							
Date	Narrative	Total	VAT	SLCA	Cash sales	Discount allowed	VAT adjustment
		£	£	£	£	£	£
	A	120.00	20.00		100.00		
	B	1,200.00		1,200.00			
		1,320.00	20.00	1,200.00	100.00		

Note the different treatment of VAT for a cash and credit sale. For the cash sale, the VAT paid by A is entered in the VAT column of the cash book. For the credit sales of B and C, the VAT is entered in the VAT column of the SDB, and because it has already been 'captured' in the books it is not entered again in the cash book when the debt is paid by B.

In Step 3, we will see how the double entry is completed to ensure that all amounts are correctly treated.

Step 3

Post the SDB totals and cash book totals to the general ledger.

Sales				VAT			
£		£		£		£	
		SDB	1,200.00			SDB	240.00
		CRB	100.00			CRB	20.00

SLCA			
£		£	
SDB	1,440.00	CRB	1,200.00

Step 4

In step 4, the individual amounts from the Sales Day Book and the Cash Book should be entered into the subsidiary sales ledgers for customers B, & C. The transaction with customer A was a cash sale and therefore no entry is required into the subsidiary ledger.

B				C			
£		£		£		£	
SDB	1,200.00	CRB	1,200.00	SDB	240		

Note 1: The VAT on the three sales are all now correctly credited to the VAT account, either by way of the SDB for credit sales or the CRB for cash sales.

Remember that the CRB is part of the double entry. The total column in the CRB is the debit entry that tells us how much cash has been paid in (£1,320), and the entries from the CRB to the other general ledger accounts are the balancing credit entries.

	£
Sales	100.00
VAT	20.00
SLCA	1,200.00
Total credits	1,320.00

5 Summary

This has been quite a difficult chapter which has addressed some of trickier topics. There are two points which typically cause trouble and which you should get to grips with.

(a)   Accounting for VAT on cash received from debtors and cash received from cash sales.

(b)   Accounting for discounts allowed and the related VAT adjustment in the analysed cash book and general ledger accounts.

If you have any doubt at all about the treatment of these you should go back and study these two points in the chapter.

6 Test your knowledge

 Workbook Activity 1

Ellis Electricals makes the following credit sales to A and B giving a 20% trade discount plus a 5% settlement discount if customers pay their invoices within 30 days.

	Customer A £	Customer B £
Sales value	1,000	4,000
Trade discount (20%)	200	800
Net sales value	800	3,200
VAT	160	640
Total invoice value	960	3,840

The invoices also include the following detail.

A discount of 5% of the full price applies if payment is made within 30 days. No credit note will be issued. Following payment you must ensure you have only recovered the VAT actually paid.

If you pay within 30 days, the discounted price is:

	Customer A £	Customer B £
Net sales value	760	3,040
VAT	152	608
Total invoice value	912	3,648

Ellis Electricals also makes a cash sale to C for £300 plus VAT.

Customer A pays his invoice in full within 30 days and takes the settlement discount. Customer B pays £2,000 on account.

Required:

Write up the SDB and the CRB and post the entries to the general and sales ledgers.

Workbook Activity 2

Your organisation receives a number of cheques from debtors through the post each day and these are listed on the cheque listing. It also makes some sales to non-credit customers each day which include VAT at the standard rate of 20% and are paid for by cheque.

Today's date is 28 April 20X1 and the cash receipts book is given below:

Cash receipts book									
Date	Narrative	SL Code	VAT adj £	Discount £	Bank £	SLCA £	Sales £	VAT £
20X1								
28/4	G Heilbron	SL04			108.45✓	108.45		
	L Tessa	SL15	0.66✓	3.31✓	110.57✓	110.57		
	J Dent	SL17	1.26✓	6.32✓	210.98✓	210.98		
	F Trainer	SL21			97.60✓	97.60		
	A Winter	SL09	0.63✓	3.16✓	105.60✓	105.60		
	Non-credit sales				270.72		225.60	45.12
			2.55✓	12.79✓	903.92	633.20✓	225.60✓	45.12✓

Required:

Show what the entries in the sales ledger will be:

Account name	Amount £	Dr ✓	Cr ✓

Show what the entries in the general ledger will be:

Account name	Amount £	Dr ✓	Cr ✓

✎ Workbook Activity 3

Given below is the debit side of the cash book completed for transactions that took place on 15th May:

Cash Book – Debit side					
Date	Narrative	SL Code	VAT adj £	Discount £	Bank £
20X1					
15/5	McCaul & Partners	M04	0.59 ✓	2.95 ✓	147.56 ✓
	P Martin	M02			264.08 ✓
	F Little	L03			167.45 ✓
	D Raine	R01	1.59	7.97 ✓	265.89 ✓
			2.18	10.92 ✓	844.98

Required:

Show what the entries in the sales ledger will be:

Account name	Amount £	Dr ✓	Cr ✓

Show what the entries in the general ledger will be:

Account name	Amount £	Dr ✓	Cr ✓

Debtors' statements

Introduction

In this chapter we consider communication with debtors. If a business is to collect the money owed to it on a timely basis it is important to ensure that the customers are fully aware of the amounts outstanding that they owe and the credit terms of relevant transactions.

CONTENTS

1 Accounting for credit sales and receipts from customers

2 Debtors' statements

3 Aged debtor analysis

1 Accounting for credit sales and receipts from customers

1.1 Introduction

Before we consider the preparation of debtors' statements, we will firstly bring together all of the accounting that has taken place for credit sales and receipts from credit customers in one example so that you can see how it all fits together. It is important that you understand how the amount owed by customers is calculated and recorded.

 Example

Given below is the sales day book, sales returns day book and cash receipts book for the first month of trading by Nick Brookes.

SALES DAY BOOK

Date	Invoice No	Customer name	Code	Total	VAT	Net
20X2				£	£	£
03/04	001	Mayer Ltd	SL1	189.60	31.60	158.00
04/04	002	Elizabeth & Co	SL2	264.00	44.00	220.00
07/04	003	Hofen Partners	SL3	132.00	22.00	110.00
10/04	004	Penken Bros	SL4	162.00	27.00	135.00
14/04	005	Mayer Ltd	SL1	211.20	35.20	176.00
18/04	006	Hofen Partners	SL3	124.80	20.80	104.00
21/04	007	Mayer Ltd	SL1	259.20	43.20	216.00
24/04	008	Penken Bros	SL4	171.60	28.60	143.00
26/04	009	Mayer Ltd	SL1	196.80	32.80	164.00
28/04	010	Elizabeth & Co	SL2	240.00	40.00	200.00
28/04	011	Penken Bros	SL4	141.60	23.60	118.00
				2,092.80	348.80	1,744.00

SALES RETURNS DAY BOOK

Date	CN No	Customer name	Code	Total	VAT	Net
20X2				£	£	£
10/04	CN001	Mayer Ltd	SL1	50.40	8.40	42.00
17/04	CN002	Penken Bros	SL4	40.80	6.80	34.00
				91.20	15.20	76.00

CASH RECEIPTS BOOK							
Date	Narrative	Total	VAT	SLCA	Cash sales	Discount	VAT adj
		£	£	£	£	£	£
20X2							
07/04	Cash sales	382.20	63.70		318.50		
15/04	Elizabeth & Co	256.08		256.08		6.60	1.32
18/04	Mayer Ltd	139.20		139.20			
21/04	Cash sales	579.00	96.50		482.50		
21/04	Penken Bros	117.56		117.56		3.03	0.61
28/04	Hofen Partners	132.00		132.00			
		1,606.04	160.20	644.84	801.00	9.63	1.93

Solution

First we must post the totals from each of the books of prime entry to the general ledger accounts. As this is the first month of trading there will of course be no opening balances on any of the ledger accounts.

Sales ledger control account

		£			£
30/04	SDB	2,092.80	30/04	SRDB	91.20
			30/04	CRB	644.84
			30/04	CRB – discount	9.63
			30/04	CRB – VAT adj	1.93

VAT account

		£			£
30/04	SRDB	15.20	30/04	SDB	348.80
30/04	CRB	1.93	30/04	CRB	160.20

Sales account

		£			£
			30/04	SDB	1,744.00
			30/04	CRB	801.00

Sales returns account

		£			£
30/04	SRDB	76.00			

Discounts allowed account

		£			£
30/04	CRB	9.63			

Once the entries have been made in total to the general ledger accounts then each individual invoice, credit note, cash receipt and discount must be entered into the individual debtor accounts in the sales ledger.

Mayer Ltd

		£			£
03/04	001	189.60	10/04	CN001	50.40
14/04	005	211.20	18/04	CRB	139.20
21/04	007	259.20			
26/04	009	196.80			

Elizabeth & Co

		£			£
04/04	002	264.00	15/04	CRB	256.08
28/04	010	240.00	15/04	CRB – discount	6.60
			15/04	CRB – VAT adj	1.32

Hofen Partners

		£			£
07/04	003	132.00	28/04	CRB	132.00
18/04	006	124.80			

Penken Bros

		£			£
10/04	004	162.00	17/04	CN002	40.80
24/04	008	171.60	21/04	CRB	117.56
28/04	011	141.60	21/04	CRB – discount	3.03
			21/04	CRB – VAT adj	0.61

From this you can see how the system for credit sales works and the information contained in the individual accounts in the sales ledger.

2 Debtors' statements

2.1 Introduction

The sales ledger clerk prepares monthly statements to send to debtors:

- **to remind them that certain invoices are due for payment**

- **to reconfirm amounts outstanding where credit notes have been issued.**

 Definition

A statement is a document issued (normally monthly) by a supplier to a customer showing unpaid sales invoices and the amount due in total.

2.2 Layout of statement

Statements can be prepared in a number of different ways. Some also have remittance advices attached to them in order to encourage early payment.

A remittance advice is a blank document that the customer fills out when making a payment to the supplier. It shows the total payment being made and which invoices (less credit notes) the payment is paying off.

2.3 Preparing a debtors' statement

A debtors' statement will normally be prepared from the information in the debtors' individual account in the sales ledger. Different businesses will use different formats but the basics that must be shown are all invoices, credit notes, payments received and discounts for the period together with usually a running total of the balance.

2.4 Procedure for preparing a debtors' statement

When preparing a statement for a credit customer, it is important that all details are correct, therefore a logical and accurate approach is required.

Step 1 Find the customer's account in the filing system for the sales ledger.

Step 2 Work through the account by date order listing each transaction in turn on the statement – invoices as a debit and credit notes, payments and discounts as credits.

Step 3 Return to the start of the statement and calculate the balance at each transaction date to appear in the balance column.

Example

Given below are the sales ledger accounts for two of Nick Brookes' customers. We will start by balancing each account to show the total amount due by each customer.

		Mayer Ltd			**SL01**
		£			£
03/04	001	189.60	10/04	CN001	50.40
14/04	005	211.20	18/04	CRB	139.20
21/04	007	259.20			
26/04	009	196.80	Balance c/d		667.20
		───────			───────
		856.80			856.80
		───────			───────
Balance b/d		667.20			

		Penken Bros			**SL04**
		£			£
10/04	004	162.00	17/04	CN002	40.80
24/04	008	171.60	21/04	CRB	117.56
28/04	011	141.60	21/04	CRB – discount	3.03
			21/04	CRB – VAT adj	0.61
			Balance c/d		313.20
		───────			───────
		475.20			475.20
		───────			───────
Balance b/d		313.20			

We can now use this information to prepare statements for these two customers as at the end of April 20X2.

Solution

To: Mayer Ltd			NICK BROOKES	
			225 School Lane	
			Weymouth	
			Dorset WE36 5NR	
			Tel: 0149 29381	
			Fax: 0149 29382	
			Date: 30/04/X2	

STATEMENT

Date	Transaction	Debit £	Credit £	Balance £
03/04	INV001	189.60		189.60
10/04	CN001		50.40	139.20
14/04	INV005	211.20		350.40
18/04	Payment		139.20	211.20
21/04	INV007	259.20		470.40
26/04	INV009	196.80		667.20

May we remind you that our credit terms are 30 days with 3% discount for payment within 14 days

To: Penken Bros			NICK BROOKES	
			225 School Lane	
			Weymouth	
			Dorset WE36 5NR	
			Tel: 0149 29381	
			Date: 30/04/X2	

STATEMENT

Date	Transaction	Debit £	Credit £	Balance £
10/04	INV004	162.00		162.00
17/04	CN002		40.80	121.20
21/04	Payment		117.56	
21/04	Discount		3.03	
21/04	VAT adj		0.61	0.00
24/04	INV008	171.60		171.60
28/04	INV011	141.60		313.20

May we remind you that our credit terms are 30 days with 3% discount for payment within 14 days

These are documents that are being sent to customers; therefore it is extremely important that it is completely accurate. Always check your figures and additions.

Activity 1

You are to prepare a statement to be sent out to one customer, Jack Johnson, for the month of May 20X6. At the start of May this customer did not owe your business, Thames Traders, any money. The sales ledger account for Jack for the month of May is given below.

Jack Johnson

Date		£	Date		£
03 May	Invoice 1848	38.79	08 May	Credit note 446	12.40
07 May	Invoice 1863	50.70	15 May	Cash receipt	77.09
10 May	Invoice 1870	80.52	24 May	Credit note 458	16.50
18 May	Invoice 1881	42.40			
23 May	Invoice 1892	61.20			
30 May	Invoice 1904	27.65			

You are required to prepare a statement for Jack on the blank statement given below.

Thames Traders

To: Date:

STATEMENT

Date	Transaction	Debit £	Credit £	Balance £

May we remind you that our credit terms are 30 days

3 Aged debtor analysis

3.1 Introduction

An aged debt analysis shows the age of invoices making up each customer's balance. This can be used to identify debtors who need chasing and a suitable letter can then be written to the customer.

3.2 What an aged debt analysis looks like

An aged debt analysis takes the total debt due from a customer and splits it into the amount of invoices that are dated within the current month, the amounts that are normally more than 30 days old and amounts that are more than 60 days old.

The layouts will differ from business to business but in general terms a typical aged debt analysis may look like this:

Customer	Total £	Current £	> 30 days £	> 60 days £
H Hardy	689.46	368.46	321.00	–
L Farmer	442.79	379.60	–	63.19
K Knight	317.68	–	169.46	148.22

3.3 How to use an aged debt analysis

The aged debt analysis can be used to indicate any customers who may be a problem in terms of credit control by giving an indication of their payment patterns.

Example

Given below is a typical extract from an aged debt analysis. What might the figures indicate about each of the debtors?

	Total £	Current £	> 30 days £	> 60 days £
H Hardy	689.46	368.46	321.00	–
L Farmer	442.79	379.60	–	63.19
K Knight	317.68	–	169.46	148.22

Solution

H Hardy – It would appear that this customer tends to take more than 30 days of credit – this may be acceptable to your business or it may be felt that a reminder that credit terms are 30 days may be appropriate.

L Farmer – The vast amount of this debt is current but £63.19 is from more than 60 days old – there may be a dispute about this invoice and the customer would normally be contacted in order to determine what the problem is.

K Knight – This is a worrying picture as there have been no sales to the customer in the current period but older amounts are still owing – this may be due to the fact that your organisation has stopped sales to this customer until payment is received for the older debts or it may be that the customer has not wished to make any further purchases – this should be investigated.

3.4   Communication with customers

If there is a problem with a customer's balance then it will be normal practice to write a polite letter to the customer requesting payment and enquiring if there is any problem with the amounts shown in the statement. If there are no problems or disputed invoices but payment is still not received within a reasonable time then this initial letter should be followed by a letter with a firmer tone requesting payment. This may include a statement that the matter will be put into the hands of your business's solicitors if payment is not received. However, this will be a matter of policy within each business.

 Example

You are the credit controller for GoGo Limited, a wholesaler of discount children's clothing. You have been reviewing the aged debtors' listing. The following customer is causing you concern:

	Total £	Current £	30+ days £	60+ days £
Candy Limited	556.78	0	0	556.78

You must write a letter to this customer to ask for payment.

Solution

GoGo Limited
225 Western Road
Anytown
Anyshire AN1 2RN

Creditors' Ledger Clerk
Candy Limited
53 High Street Anytown
Anyshire AN1 6BN

23 August 20X4

Dear Sir

Outstanding balance

According to our records your company has an outstanding balance of £556.78.

Our normal credit terms are 30 days. As this debt is now over 60 days old we would be very grateful if you could send us your payment immediately.

If you have any queries please do not hesitate to contact me.

Yours faithfully

AN Smith
Credit Controller

Do not be tempted to write a letter that sounds angry or threatening. Polite efficiency is what is required.

Activity 2

The following is an extract from an aged debt analysis report prepared on 1 June.

Name	Balance	Up to 1 month	Up to 3 months	Over 3 months
	£	£	£	£
West & Co	4,860	3,400	1,460	0
Star Limited	2,719	0	0	2,719
Norwood Limited	3,116	1,200	1,900	16
Just Electric	1,391	1,320	0	71

(a) With which one of the four accounts might you be most concerned?

(b) Explain briefly the reason for your answer.

4 Summary

In this chapter all of the accounting entries for sales invoices, credit notes and receipts from debtors were brought together. We also saw how to produce a statement to be sent to a customer from the customer's account in the sales ledger.

We have also introduced an aged debt analysis. You do not need to be able to produce one but you do need to be able to use it to determine any customers who appear to be causing problems with debt collection. It is important when communicating with customers that you deal effectively but politely at all times.

Answers to chapter activities

 Activity 1

Thames Traders

To: Jack Johnson

Date: 31 May 20X6:

STATEMENT

Date	Transaction	Debit £	Credit £	Balance £
03 May	Inv 1848	38.79		38.79
07 May	Inv 1863	50.70		89.49
08 May	CN 446		12.40	77.09
10 May	Inv 1870	80.52		157.61
15 May	Payment		77.09	80.52
18 May	Inv 1881	42.40		122.92
23 May	Inv 1892	61.20		184.12
24 May	CN 458		16.50	167.62
30 May	Inv 1904	27.65		195.27

May we remind you that our credit terms are 30 days

 Activity 2

(a) Star Limited.

(b) The balance has been outstanding for over three months with no sales since.

5 Test your knowledge

Workbook Activity 3

You work in the accounts department of Farmhouse Pickles Ltd and given below are two debtors' accounts from the sales ledger.

		Grant & Co			SL07
		£			£
1 April	Balance b/d	337.69	12 April	SRDB – 0335	38.70
4 April	SDB 32656	150.58	20 April	CRB	330.94
18 April	SDB 32671	179.52	20 April	CRB – discount	6.75
			20 April	CRB – VAT adj	1.35
25 April	SDB 32689	94.36	24 April	SRDB – 0346	17.65

		Mitchell Partners			SL10
		£			£
1 April	Balance b/d	180.46	12 April	SRDB – 0344	66.89
7 April	SDB 32662	441.57	21 April	CRB	613.58
20 April	SDB 32669	274.57	21 April	CRB – discount	8.45
			21 April	CRB – VAT adj	1.69

Required:

Prepare statements to be sent to each of these customers at the end of April 20X1 on the blank statements provided.

To:

FARMHOUSE PICKLES LTD

225 School Lane
Weymouth
Dorset
WE36 5NR
Tel: 0261 480444
Fax: 0261 480555
Date:

STATEMENT

Date	Transaction	Debit £	Credit £	Balance £

May we remind you that our credit terms are 30 days

To:

225 School Lane
Weymouth
Dorset
WE36 5NR
Tel: 0261 480444
Fax: 0261 480555
Date:

STATEMENT

Date	Transaction	Debit £	Credit £	Balance £

May we remind you that our credit terms are 30 days

Workbook Activity 4

Shown below is a customer's account from the sales ledger of Ryan's Toy Shop Ltd, along with a statement of account to be sent to that customer.

Arnold's Toys Ltd							
Dr				**Cr**			
Date	Transaction	£		Date	Transaction	£	
19/11	Invoice 2195	118	08 ✓	20/11	Credit note 2198	323	60 ✓
20/11	Invoice 2198	2,201	95 ✓	22/11	Cheque	118	08 ✓
				22/11	Balance c/d	1,878	35
		2,320	03			2,320	03
23/11	Balance b/d	1,878	35				

Required:

Complete the statement of account below.

Ryan's Toy Shop LTD					
125 Finchley Way Bristol BS1 4PL Tel: 01272 200299					
STATEMENT OF ACCOUNT					
Customer name: Arnold's Toys Ltd					
Customer address: 14 High Street, Bristol, BS2 5FL					
Statement date 1st December		**Amount**		**Balance**	
Date	**Transaction**	£	p	£	P

Credit purchases – discounts and VAT

Introduction

In this chapter we move on from considering the accounting entries for sales and look here at the equivalent accounting entries for purchases.

1 Discounts and VAT

1.1 Introduction

We studied discounts and VAT when studying sales. The calculation of VAT and discounts are **exactly** the same when considering purchases. Remember that it is the seller who offers the discounts and it is the seller who charges the VAT, so the fact that we are now studying purchases does not change how these things are calculated.

The purchaser will receive a 'sales invoice' from the seller. This will have details of discounts and VAT exactly as we saw before when studying sales. The purchaser will call this a 'purchase invoice' and enter it in the books accordingly as we shall see.

When a purchaser receives an invoice offering a settlement discount (prompt payment discount), they will need to account for it as follows:

- If the purchaser pays the full price for the goods, and does not take up the settlement discount, they will record the invoice at full price in their records and no VAT adjustment will be needed.

- If the customer pays the discounted price in accordance with the terms of the settlement discount **on receipt of the invoice**, they will record the discounted price and VAT on this in their accounts, and no further VAT adjustment will be needed.

- If the customer does not pay on receipt of the invoice, they must record the invoice at full price. If they subsequently decide to take up the settlement discount, they must adjust the VAT they claim as input VAT as follows:

  (a) If the customer has received an invoice setting out the terms of the settlement discount which states that no credit note will be issued, they will adjust the VAT in their records when payment is made. They should retain evidence which shows the date and amount of the payment, such as a bank statement, as well as the invoice as evidence of the discount taken.

  (b) If the supplier's invoice does **not** state that a credit note will not be issued, the customer must adjust the VAT they claim as input VAT when the credit note is received. They should retain the credit note as evidence of the discount taken.

Example

Carl buys £1,000.00 of goods from Susan on credit. Susan sends a sales invoice with the goods offering a 5% discount if Carl pays within 30 days. VAT is at 20%.

Calculate:

(a) the VAT claimed if the settlement discount is not taken

(b) the VAT claimed if the settlement discount is taken and the invoice is paid on receipt

(c) the VAT claimed if the settlement discount is taken and the invoice is paid 20 days after receipt.

Solution

(a) VAT = £1,000.00 × 20% = £200.00.

(b) VAT = (£1,000.00 – (5% × £1,000.00)) × 20% = £190.00. The discounted price and VAT will be recorded in the accounts as the invoice is paid on receipt.

(c) When the invoice is initially recorded, VAT of £1,000.00 × 20% = £200.00 will be recorded. This will be reduced to £190.00 (as above) when the invoice is paid and the settlement discount claimed in accordance with the terms of the invoice. A VAT adjustment of £200.00 - £190.00 = £10.00 will be required to correct the Input VAT claimed in respect of the invoice.

2 Credit purchases – double entry

2.1 Basic double entry

The basic double entry for credit purchases with VAT is as follows:

Debit   Purchases account with the net amount

Debit   VAT account with the VAT

Credit   Creditors account with the gross amount

Purchases have been debited with the net amount as the VAT is not a cost to the business. Instead the VAT is an amount that can be set off against the amount of VAT due to HM Revenue and Customs and therefore the VAT is a debit entry in the VAT account. The creditors account is credited with the gross amount as this is the amount that must be paid to the supplier.

As with debtors and the sales ledger control account we will now be calling the creditors account the purchases ledger control account (PLCA).

Work through the following examples to practise the double entry for credit purchases.

Example 1

B sells goods on credit to Y for £500 plus VAT at 20%. Y pays B the full amount due. Record these transactions in the accounts of Y.

Solution

Step 1   Calculate the VAT on the purchase and enter the transaction in the PLCA, purchases and VAT accounts.

Calculation of VAT

	£
Net value of sale	500.00
VAT at 20%	100.00
Gross value of purchase	600.00

PLCA

	£		£
		Purchases and VAT	600.00

Purchases

	£		£
PLCA	500.00		

VAT

	£		£
PLCA	100.00		

Step 2   Enter £600.00 paid by Y in the PLCA and the bank account.

PLCA

	£		£
Bank	600.00	Purchases and VAT	600.00

Purchases

	£		£
PLCA	500.00		

VAT

	£		£
PLCA	100.00		

Bank

	£		£
		PLCA	600.00

Example 2

B sells £1,000 of goods to Y net of VAT on credit. He gives Y a deduction of 20% trade discount from the £1,000 net value. Y pays his account in full. Enter these amounts in the accounts of Y. VAT is at 20%.

Solution

Step 1 Calculate the value of the sale net of discount and the VAT at 20% thereon.

	£
Sales value	1,000
Less: 20% discount	200
Net value	800
VAT at 20%	160
Total invoice value	960

Step 2 Enter the invoice in the PLCA, purchases and VAT accounts.

PLCA

	£			£
			Purchases and VAT	960

Purchases

	£		£
PLCA	800		

VAT

	£		£
PLCA	160		

Note: The trade discount does not feature at all in the accounts. The invoice value is expressed after deduction of the trade discount and it is this invoiced amount that is entered in the accounts.

Step 3   Enter the cash paid by Y.

PLCA

	£		£
Bank	960	Purchases and VAT	960

Purchases

	£		£
PLCA	800		

VAT

	£		£
PLCA	160		

Bank

	£		£
		PLCA	960

Example 3

C sells £2,000.00 of goods net of VAT to Z on credit. He offers Z a 5% settlement discount if Z pays within 30 days. C's invoices state that a credit note will not be issued in respect of the settlement discount. Z pays his account within 30 days and takes the settlement discount. Enter these transactions in the accounts of Z.

Solution

Step 1   Calculate the VAT on the purchase.

	£
Invoice value net of VAT	2,000.00
VAT = 20% × 2,000.00	400.00
	————
Invoice value	2,400.00
	————

Step 2   Enter the invoice in the accounts of Z.

PLCA

	£		£
		Purchases and VAT	2,400.00

Purchases

	£		£
PLCA	2,000.00		

VAT

	£		£
PLCA	400.00		

Step 3   Calculate the amount paid by Z.

	£
Invoice value net of VAT	2,000.00
Less: settlement discount = 5% × 2,000.00	(100.00)
VAT ((2,000.00 – 100.00) × 20%)	380.00
Amount paid by Z	2,280.00

Step 4   Calculate the VAT adjustment as a result of the settlement discount being taken which must be recorded by Z.

VAT on original invoice	400.00
Less: VAT on discounted invoice	(380.00)
VAT adjustment	20.00

Step 5   Enter these amounts in the accounts.

PLCA

	£		£
Bank	2,280.00	Purchases and VAT	2,400.00
Discount received	100.00		
VAT	20.00		

Purchases

	£		£
PLCA	2,000.00		

VAT

	£		£
PLCA	400.00	PLCA	20.00

Bank

	£		£
		PLCA	2,280.00

Discount received

	£		£
		PLCA	100.00

Note: Because Z takes the settlement discount, he pays C £120.00 less than the invoice value.

In order to clear the PLCA we have to debit that account with the £120.00, and credit a discount received account with £100.00 as well as crediting the VAT account with the £20.00 reduction in Input VAT.

The £100.00 recorded in discounts received is income (reduction of an expense) of the business as the business is paying less than the face value of the invoice.

3 Summary

The topics covered in this chapter will have been familiar to you as you have already studied the similar topics for sales.

Make sure you understand the point about the VAT adjustment when there is a settlement discount offered. You must also understand the double entry for settlement discounts.

4 Test your knowledge

Workbook Activity 1

Calculate the VAT for the following:

(a) X purchases £400.00 goods from Y net of VAT.

(b) X purchases £650.00 goods from Y net of VAT.

(c) X purchases £528.00 goods from Y including VAT.

(d) X purchases £120.00 goods from Y including VAT.

Workbook Activity 2

Calculate the VAT on the following:

(a) X purchases £850.00 goods from Y and subsequently takes the 3% settlement discount offered.

(b) X purchases £600.00 goods from Y and subsequently takes the 5% settlement discount offered.

(c) X purchases £325.00 goods from Y and does not take the 2% settlement discount offered.

(d) X purchases £57.00 goods from Y and does not take the 4% settlement discount offered.

Workbook Activity 3

Z buys £600.00 of goods net of VAT from A on 1.10.X5 and takes the 3% settlement discount offered when payment is made on 10.10.X5.

Post these transactions in the ledger accounts of Z.

The purchases day book – general and subsidiary ledgers

Introduction

Just as we did for sales on credit we will now consider how purchases on credit are recorded in the books of prime entry and the ledger accounts.

CONTENTS
1 Accounting for credit purchases
2 The analysed purchases day book
3 Purchases returns – cash suppliers
4 Purchases returns – credit suppliers
5 Purchases returns day book

1 Accounting for credit purchases

1.1 Introduction

When we studied accounting for sales in the earlier chapters of this book, we dealt with the three parts of the accounting records as they affected sales.

In the case of purchases, the parts are exactly the same except that instead of a 'sales day book' we have the 'purchases day book', and instead of the sales ledger we have the purchases ledger. The third part, namely the general ledger, is exactly the same and contains all the general ledger accounts with which you are familiar. Remember that, as for sales, the double entry goes through the general ledger, and the purchases ledger is just a memorandum ledger that holds the details of the individual creditor's accounts (it is sometimes called the subsidiary (purchases) ledger).

1.2 Proforma purchases ledger control account

A purchases ledger control account normally appears like this.

Purchases ledger control account			
	£		£
Payments to suppliers per analysed cash book:		Balance b/d	X
Cash	X	Purchases per purchases day book	X
Discount received	X		
VAT adjustment	X		
Returns per purchases returns day book	X		
Contra entry	X		
Balance c/d	X		
	──		──
	X		X
	──		──
		Balance b/d	X

If all of the accounting entries have been correctly made then the balance on this purchases ledger control account should equal the total of the balances on the individual supplier accounts in the purchases ledger.

1.3 Fitting it all together

Consider these three credit purchases invoices.

Supplier	Amount
X	£4,000
Y	£5,000
Z	£6,000

Step 1

Each invoice is recorded in the purchases day book by the purchaser.

Step 2

At the end of the period the purchases day book is totalled and the total is entered into the purchases ledger control account in the general ledger. The individual entries are recorded in the individual creditor accounts in the purchases ledger.

Now consider these cheques being paid to the creditors.

Supplier	Amount
X	£2,000
Y	£3,000

Step 1

Each payment is recorded in the cash book.

Step 2

At the end of the period the cash book is totalled and the total is entered into the purchases ledger control account in the general ledger. The individual entries are recorded in the individual creditor accounts in the purchases ledger.

This is illustrated below.

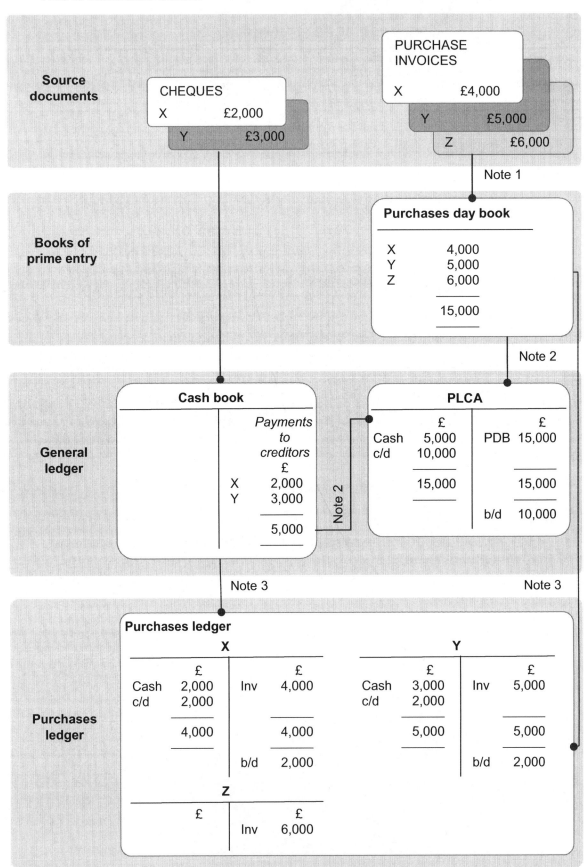

Notes:

1 The invoices are entered into the PDB and the cheques are entered into the cash book.

2 The totals from the cash book and PDB are posted to the PLCA.

3 The individual invoices and cash paid are posted to the purchases ledger.

2 The analysed purchases day book

2.1 Layout

The purchases day book is usually analysed with 'analysis columns' showing how the total value of each supplier's invoice is made up.

PURCHASES DAY BOOK								
Date	Supplier	Reference	Invoice number	Total £	VAT £	Product 1 £	Product 2 £	Product 3 £
			TOTALS					

(a) The date and supplier columns are self explanatory.

(b) The reference number is the number of the supplier's account in the purchases ledger.

(c) The invoice number is the number of the invoice from the supplier.

(d) The total column is the value of the goods purchased:

- after deducting any trade discount that may have been offered

- including VAT

- and including (i.e. not deducting) any settlement discount that may be offered to the purchaser (we shall not complicate things at this stage by considering this further).

> ### 💡 Example
>
> Customer B receives an invoice as follows from supplier X:
>
> | | £ |
> |---|---|
> | 50 units at £6 per unit | 300 |
> | Less: 20% trade discount | 60 |
> | | 240 |
> | VAT @ 20% (£240 × 20%) | 48 |
> | Total invoice value | 288 |
>
> The £288 would be entered in the 'total' column.

(e) The VAT column – this column is the value of the VAT on the invoice – in this case £48.

(f) Product 1, 2, etc columns – these are columns that analyse the net purchases value (i.e. the total value after deducting VAT) into groupings that are of interest to the business.

In this introductory section we shall not complicate things by considering more than one type of product so that there will only be one column for purchases.

In this case the entry in the purchases column would be £240.

(g) The total boxes – at the end of a period (say a week or a month) the purchases day book is totalled and the total values of each column are written in the total boxes.

The purchases day book would therefore look as follows for the example above:

PURCHASES DAY BOOK

Date	Supplier	Reference	Invoice number	Total £	VAT £	Product 1 £	Product 2 £	Product 3 £
	X			288	48	240		
			TOTALS	288	48	240		

Note: In the pages that follow we shall concentrate on the basic entries in the purchases day book using only the supplier, total, VAT and one purchases column. This will enable us to concentrate on the simple double entry.

Example

Posting the purchases day book to the accounts in the ledgers.

Consider the following purchase invoices received from suppliers by Roberts Metals.

Customer	Purchases value (ex VAT)	Trade discount	Net purchases value	VAT	Total
	£	£	£	£	£
X	500	10%	450.00	90.00	540.00
Y	1,750	20%	1,400.00	280.00	1,680.00
Z	5,000	30%	3,500.00	700.00	4,200.00

The following three steps are needed to enter this information in the ledger accounts.

Step 1 Write up the purchases day book, and total the columns.

Step 2 Post the totals to the accounts in the general ledger.

Step 3 Post the individual invoices to the purchases ledger.

Solution

Step 1

PURCHASES DAY BOOK

Date	Supplier	Reference	Invoice number	Total £	VAT £	Purchases £
	X			540.00	90.00	450.00
	Y			1,680.00	280.00	1,400.00
	Z			4,200.00	700.00	3,500.00
			TOTALS	6,420.00	1,070.00	5,350.00

Step 2

General ledger

Purchases

£		£
PDB 5,350.00		

VAT

£		£
PDB 1,070.00		

PLCA

£		£
	PDB	6,420.00

Step 3

Purchases ledger

X

£		£	
		PDB	540.00

Y

£		£	
		PDB	1,680.00

Z

£		£	
		PDB	4,200.00

Note to solution:

(a)   The totals of the PDB are entered in the general ledger.

(b)   The individual invoices (total value including VAT) are entered in the individual creditor accounts in the purchases ledger. This is the amount that will be paid to the creditor.

(c)   Note that there are no entries for trade discounts either in the PDB or in the ledger accounts.

Activity 1

Date	Invoice no	Supplier	Code	Total	VAT	Dept 1	Dept 2	Dept 3
				£	£	£	£	£
		Total		90,000	15,000	20,000	15,000	40,000

How would the totals be posted to the general ledger accounts?

3 Purchases returns – cash suppliers

3.1 Introduction

When a business buys and then returns goods to a supplier, the accounting system has to record the fact that goods have been returned. If the goods were returned following a cash purchase then cash would be repaid by the supplier to the customer who had bought the goods. If goods were returned following a credit purchase then the PLCA in the general ledger will need to be debited and the individual supplier's account in the purchases ledger will need to be debited with the value of the goods returned (we shall see the other entries required below).

 Example

Returns following a cash purchase

Y buys £1,000 of goods from B for cash plus £200 VAT (at 20% standard rated).

B subsequently agrees that Y can return £500 worth of goods (excluding VAT).

Record these transactions in the ledger accounts of Y.

Solution

Step 1

First of all we need to set up a new account called the 'purchases returns account' in the general ledger.

Step 2

Enter the cash purchases in the accounts of Y.

Credit cash book for cash paid	£1,200.00
Debit purchases with expense	£1,000.00
Debit VAT account with VAT	£200.00

Cash book

£		£
	Purchases and VAT	1,200.00

Purchases

	£		£
Cash book	1,000.00		

Purchases returns

	£		£

VAT

	£		£
Cash book	200		

Step 3

B will repay Y £500 plus VAT of £100 (VAT rate 20%). We therefore need to enter the purchases returns, the cash and the VAT in the accounts.

Cash book

	£		£
Purchases return + VAT	600.00	Purchases and VAT	1,200.00

Purchases

	£		£
Cash book	1,000.00		

Purchases returns

	£		£
		Cash book	500.00

VAT

	£		£
Cash book	200.00	Cash book	100.00

4 Purchases returns – credit suppliers

4.1 Introduction

When a credit customer returns goods, he does not receive cash for the return; the seller will issue a credit note to record the fact that goods have been returned. This credit note is sent to the customer and is entered in the customer's books.

4.2 Purchases returns with VAT

When a return is made we include VAT; the VAT was accounted for on the invoice when the purchase was made, and now has to be accounted for on the credit note when the goods are returned. This VAT has to be entered in the books.

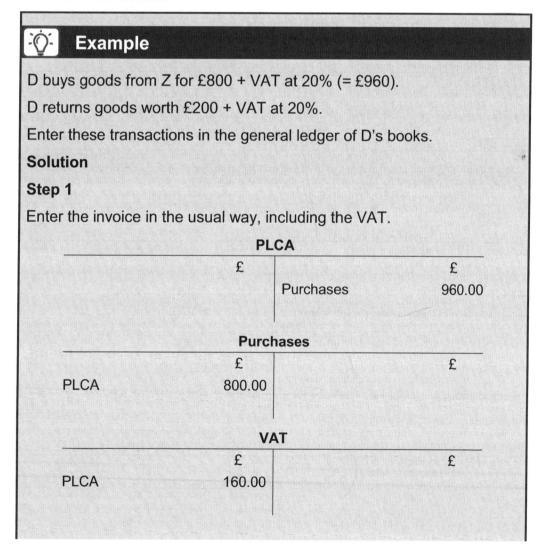

Example

D buys goods from Z for £800 + VAT at 20% (= £960).

D returns goods worth £200 + VAT at 20%.

Enter these transactions in the general ledger of D's books.

Solution

Step 1

Enter the invoice in the usual way, including the VAT.

PLCA			
	£		£
		Purchases	960.00

Purchases			
	£		£
PLCA	800.00		

VAT			
	£		£
PLCA	160.00		

Step 2

Enter the credit note. The VAT on the return will be £200 × 20% = £40. This gives a total credit note of £240.

PLCA

	£		£
Purchases returns + VAT	240.00	Purchases	960.00

Purchases

	£		£
PLCA	800.00		

VAT

	£		£
PLCA	160.00	PLCA	40.00

Purchases returns

	£		£
		PLCA	200.00

The books will reflect the position after the return. The balance on the PLCA is £720. This is made up as:

	£
Purchase	800
Purchase return	200
	———
	600
VAT 600 × 20%	120
	———
	720
	———

5 Purchases returns day book

5.1 Introduction

Purchases returns are in practice entered in a 'purchases returns day book'. This is similar to the purchases day book, and the columns are used in the same way. The only difference is that instead of having a column for the invoice number, there is a column for the 'credit note number'. This is because when the goods are sent back the business will receive a credit note from the supplier.

PURCHASES RETURNS DAY BOOK						
Date	Supplier	Reference	Credit note number	Total £	VAT £	Purchases returns £

💡 Example

John bought goods for £750 + VAT from X and £1,000 + VAT from Y.

John returns goods which cost £200 excluding VAT to X, and goods which cost £400 excluding VAT to Y.

Enter the above purchases and returns in the general and purchases ledger of John, using a purchases returns day book.

Solution

Step 1

Enter the original purchases invoices in the general ledger.

PLCA

	£		£
		PDB	2,100.00

Purchases

	£		£
PDB	1,750.00		

VAT

	£		£
PDB	350.00		

Step 2

Write up the purchases returns day book.

PURCHASES RETURNS DAY BOOK						
Date	Supplier	Reference	Credit note number	Total £	VAT £	Purchases returns £
	X			240.00	40.00	200.00
	Y			480.00	80.00	400.00
				720.00	120.00	600.00

Step 3

Enter the PRDB totals in the general ledger accounts.

PLCA

	£		£
PRDB	720.00	PDB	2,100.00

Purchases

	£		£
PDB	1,750.00		

VAT

	£		£
PDB	350.00	PRDB	120.00

Purchases returns

	£		£
		PRDB	600.00

Step 4

Enter the individual amounts in the purchases ledger. The amounts will be debited to the individual creditor accounts as the return is reducing the amount that is owed to the creditor.

X

	£		£
PRDB	240.00	PDB (£750 + VAT)	900.00

Y

	£		£
PRDB	480.00	PDB (£1,000 + VAT)	1,200.00

5.2 Purchases returns in purchases day book

In some businesses the level of purchases returns are fairly low and therefore it is not justified to keep a separate purchases returns day book. In these cases any credit notes that are received for purchases returns are recorded as negative amounts in the purchases day book. If this is the case then you will be told that this is the policy of the business. Care should be taken, however, when adding up the columns in the purchases day book as any credit notes must be deducted rather than added in.

Activity 2

Given below are the totals of an analysed purchases returns day book for a week.

Date	Supplier	Credit note no	Code	Total	VAT	Dept 1	Dept 2	Dept 3
				£	£	£	£	£
23/04/X0				9,600	1,600	1,000	2,000	5,000

Post these totals to the general ledger accounts.

6 Summary

The purchases day book and the purchases returns day book are simple devices for grouping together purchases invoices for goods purchased and credit notes for goods returned. The topics you need to practise are:

(a)   posting the total of these day books to the general ledger accounts; and

(b)   posting the individual invoices and credit notes to the creditors accounts in the purchases ledger.

It is also useful if you understand how the accounts fit together as shown in the diagram in Section 1.3 of this chapter.

Answers to chapter activities

📝 Activity 1

The required double entry is as follows:

Debit	VAT	£15,000
	Department 1 purchases	£20,000
	Department 2 purchases	£15,000
	Department 2 purchases	£40,000
Credit	Purchases ledger control account	£90,000

Note carefully that it is the net amount that is debited to each purchases account and the gross amount (including VAT) that is credited to the purchases ledger control account. The VAT total is debited to the VAT account.

The ledger entries would appear as follows:

Purchases ledger control account

	£		£
		PDB	90,000

VAT

	£		£
PDB	15,000		

Department 1 purchases

	£		£
PDB	20,000		

Department 2 purchases

	£		£
PDB	15,000		

Department 3 purchases

	£		£
PDB	40,000		

Activity 2

Purchases returns – Department 1 account

	£			£
			PRDB	1,000

Purchases returns – Department 2 account

	£			£
			PRDB	2,000

Purchases returns – Department 3 account

	£			£
			PRDB	5,000

VAT account

	£			£
			PRDB	1,600

Purchases ledger control account

	£		£
PRDB	9,600		

Note carefully that it is the net amount that is credited to each returns account and the gross amount that is debited to the purchases ledger control account. The difference, the VAT, is credited to the VAT account.

7 Test your knowledge

Workbook Activity 3

Curtain Decor is a business that makes curtains and blinds to order. Its purchases are analysed between fabric purchases, header tape purchases and others. A separate purchases returns day book is not kept so any credit notes received are recorded as negative amounts in the purchases day book. The business only has five credit suppliers and they are as follows:

Mainstream Fabrics	PL01
C R Thorne	PL02
Fabric Supplies Ltd	PL03
Lillian Fisher	PL04
Headstream & Co	PL05

Today's date is 12 April 20X1 and given below are three invoices and a credit note. These are to be entered into the analysed purchases day book and each column is to be totalled.

INVOICE

Invoice to:
Curtain Décor
Field House
Warren Lane
Hawkhurst TN23 1AT

Fabric Supplies Ltd
12/14 Tike Road
Wadfield
TN11 4ZP
Tel: 01882 467111
Fax: 01882 467112

Deliver to:

As above

Invoice no:	06783
Tax point:	7 April 20X1
VAT reg:	532 6741 09

Code	Description	Quantity	VAT rate %	Unit price £	Amount excl of VAT £
B116-14	Header Tape 14cm	30 m	20	4.62	138.60
P480-G	Fabric – Green	56 m	20	14.25	798.00
					936.60

VAT	187.32
Total amount payable	1,123.92

A discount of 2% of the full price applies if payment is made within 10 days. No credit note will be issued. Following payment you must ensure you have only recovered the VAT actually paid

If you pay within 10 days, the discounted price is:

Net	917.87
VAT	183.57
Total amount payable	1101.44

INVOICE

Lillian Fisher

Invoice to:
Curtain Décor
Field House
Warren Lane
Hawkhurst TN23 1AT

61 Park Crescent
Hawkhurst
TN23 8GF
Tel: 01868 463501
Fax: 01868 463502

Deliver to:

As above

Invoice no:	0328
Tax point:	7 April 20X1
VAT reg:	469 7153 20

Code	Description	Quantity	VAT rate %	Unit price £	Amount excl of VAT £
TB06	Tie Back Cord – Yellow	10 m	20	6.55	65.50
TB09	Tie Back Cord – Green	4 m	20	6.55	26.20
					91.70
VAT					18.34
Total amount payable					110.04

CREDIT NOTE

Headstream & Co

Credit note to:
Curtain Décor
Field House
Warren Lane
Hawkhurst TN23 1AT

140 Myrtle Place
Fenham
TN16 4SJ
Tel: 01842 303136
Fax: 01842 303137

Credit note no:	CN0477
Tax point:	7 April 20X1
VAT reg:	663 4892 77

Code	Description	Quantity	VAT rate %	Unit price £	Amount excl of VAT £
HT479	Header Tape 22 cm	2 m	20	8.30	16.60
CCF614Y	CC Fabric – Yellow	4 m	20	12.85	51.40
					68.00
VAT					13.60
Total credit					81.60

INVOICE

Invoice to:
Curtain Décor
Field House
Warren Lane
Hawkhurst TN23 1AT

Mainstream Fabrics
Tree Tops House
Farm Road
Tonbridge
TN2 4XT
Tel: 01883 214121
Fax: 01883 214122

Deliver to:

As above

Invoice no:	07359
Tax point:	8 April 20X1
VAT reg:	379 4612 04

Code	Description	Quantity	VAT rate %	Unit price £	Amount excl of VAT £
DG4167F	Design Guild Fabric – Fuchsia	23 m	20	13.60	312.80
					312.80
Trade discount 10%					31.28
					281.52
VAT					56.30
Total amount payable					337.82

Purchases day book

Date	Invoice no	Code	Supplier	Total	VAT	Fabric	Header tape	Other

KAPLAN PUBLISHING

Workbook Activity 4

Kingdon Builders analyse their purchases into wood, bricks and cement, and small consumables such as nails and screws. You are given three purchase invoices, recently received, to enter into the purchases day book given.

An extract from the purchase ledger coding manual is given:

Supplier	Purchase ledger code
JR Ryan & Co	PL08
HT Todd Plc	PL13
Magnum Supplies	PL16

Today's date is 3 May 20X1.

Enter the invoices into the analysed purchases day book and total each of the columns.

INVOICE

Invoice to:
Kingdon Builders
Brecon House
Stamford Road
Manchester
M16 4PL

Magnum Supplies
140/150 Park Estate
Manchester
M20 6EG
Tel: 0161 561 3202
Fax: 0161 561 3200

Deliver to:

As above

Invoice no:	077401
Tax point:	1 May 20X1
VAT reg no:	611 4337 90

Code	Description	Quantity	VAT rate %	Unit price £	Amount excl of VAT £
BH47732	House Bricks – Red	400	20	1.24	496.00
					496.00
Trade discount 15%					74.40
					421.60
VAT					84.32
Total amount payable					505.92

INVOICE

J.R. Ryan & Co

Invoice to:
Kingdon Builders
Brecon House
Stamford Road
Manchester
M16 4PL

59 Parkway
Manchester
M2 6EG
Tel: 0161 560 3392
Fax: 0161 560 5322

Deliver to:

As above

Invoice no:				046193	
Tax point:				1 May 20X1	
VAT reg no:				661 2359 07	

Code	Description	Quantity	VAT rate %	Unit price £	Amount excl of VAT £
DGT 472	SDGS Softwood × 225 mm	47 11.2 m	20	8.44	94.53
NBD021	Oval Wire Nails	7 boxes	20	2.50	17.50
					112.03
Trade discount 10%					11.20
					100.83
VAT					20.16
Total amount payable					120.99

INVOICE

Invoice to:
Kingdon Builders
Brecon House
Stamford Road
Manchester
M16 4PL

HT Todd Plc
30 Longfield Park
Kingsway
M45 2TP
Tel: 0161 511 4666
Fax: 0161 511 4777

Deliver to:

As above

Invoice no:	47823
Tax point:	1 May 20X1
VAT reg no:	641 3229 45
Purchase order no:	7211

Code	Description	Quantity	VAT rate %	Unit price £	Amount excl of VAT £
PLY8FU	Plywood Hardboard	16 sheets	20	17.80	284.80
BU611	Ventilator Block	10	20	8.60	86.00
					370.80

VAT	74.16
Total amount payable	444.96

A discount of 3% of the full price applies if payment is made within 14 days. No credit note will be issued. Following payment you must ensure you have only recovered the VAT actually paid

If you pay within 14 days, the discounted price is:

Net	359.68
VAT	71.94
Total amount payable	431.62

Purchases day book								
Date	Invoice no	Code	Supplier	Total	VAT	Wood	Bricks/ Cement	Consum- ables

Workbook Activity 5

Kingdon Builders have recently received the three credit notes given. They are to be recorded in the analysed purchases returns day book given.

An extract from the purchase ledger coding manual shows:

Supplier	Purchase ledger code	Settlement discount on original purchase
HT Todd Plc	PL13	3%
BL Lukey Ltd	PL03	2%
Magnum Supplies	PL16	2%

Today's date is 3 May 20X1.

You are required to enter the credit notes into the analysed purchases returns day book and to total each of the columns.

CREDIT NOTE

HT Todd Plc

Credit note to:
Kingdon Builders
Brecon House
Stamford Road
Manchester
M16 4PL

30 Longfield Park
Kingsway
M45 2TP
Tel: 0161 511 4666
Fax: 0161 511 4777

Deliver to:

As above

Credit note no:	CN06113
Tax point:	28 April 20X1
VAT reg no:	641 3229 45
Purchase order no:	47792

Code	Description	Quantity	VAT rate %	Unit price £	Amount excl of VAT £
PL432115	Door Lining Set – wood 32 × 115 mm	1	20	30.25	30.25
					30.25
Trade discount 15%					4.54
					25.71
VAT					4.98
Total amount of credit					30.69

CREDIT NOTE

BL Lukey Ltd
The White House
Standing Way
Manchester
M13 6FH
Tel: 0161 560 3140
Fax: 0161 560 6140

Credit note to:
Kingdon Builders
Brecon House
Stamford Road
Manchester
M16 4PL

Deliver to:

As above

Credit note no:	06132
Tax point:	28 April 20X1
VAT reg no:	460 3559 71

Code	Description	Quantity	VAT rate %	Unit price £	Amount excl of VAT £
PLY8FE1	Plywood Hardwood 2440 × 1220 mm	2	20	17.80	35.60
					35.60
VAT					6.97
Total amount of credit					42.57

CREDIT NOTE

Magnum Supplies

Credit note to:
Kingdon Builders
Brecon House
Stamford Road
Manchester
M16 4PL

140/150 Park Estate
Manchester
M20 6EG
Tel: 0161 561 3202
Fax: 0161 561 3200

Deliver to:

Credit note no: C4163
Tax point: 30 April 20X1
VAT reg no: 611 4337 90

As above

Code	Description	Quantity	VAT rate %	Unit price £	Amount excl of VAT £
BU1628	Ventilator Brick	5	20	9.20	46.00
					46.00
Trade discount 15%					6.90
					39.10
VAT					7.66
Total amount of credit					46.76

Purchases returns day book								
Date	Credit note no	Code	Supplier	Total	VAT	Wood	Bricks/ Cement	Consum- ables

Making payments

13

Introduction

Once the invoice for purchases has been received then payment must be made for the goods or services. In this chapter we will consider the different methods of payment, the most appropriate methods of payment, the timing of payments and how the payment procedure works.

1 Payments by cheque

1.1 Introduction

Most payments that a business makes are either electronic (e.g. BACS), online payments (e.g. made through PayPal, Worldpay or NetBank) or a business may use a more traditional method of paying by cheque.

1.2 Writing a cheque

The detailed legal requirements relating to cheques were covered in an earlier chapter and therefore we will only cover these requirements briefly.

When a cheque is written out by a business it is important that it is correctly drawn up. The main factors to consider are:

- The cheque must be **dated** with the date on which it is written – a cheque is only valid for six months after the date on the cheque and most suppliers would not accept a post-dated cheque so care should be taken when writing the date onto the cheque.

- The **payee's name** must be correct – the supplier's name will be on the purchase invoice and this should be correctly reproduced on the cheque otherwise the supplier will not be able to pay the cheque into his bank account.

- The **amount** of the cheque in words and figures must agree with each other – if there is a difference then the cheque cannot be paid into the supplier's account and will be returned by the bank to your business.

- The cheque must be **signed** by the appropriate cheque signatory within the business – in many businesses it will be the organisation's policy that cheques, particularly if they exceed a certain limit, must be signed by more than one cheque signatory.

- If any alterations are made to the cheque then these must be **initialled** by the cheque signatory.

1.3 Stopped cheques

If a cheque is written by your business and sent out to a supplier it can be stopped at any point in time right up until the bank pays it. In order to stop a cheque your business must write to the bank and give clear details of the payee's name, the cheque's number and the amount payable.

Activity 1

You are writing out a cheque for £374 as payment for goods. As you write out the cheque you do not notice that you have dated it 1 June 20X1. Today's date is 1 June 20X2.

Will payment of the cheque by the drawer's bank be affected by the incorrect date? Yes/No

Having noticed the error, is it acceptable for you to alter the cheque to the correct date? Yes/No

2 Transferring money by different methods

2.1 Introduction

A bank customer can transfer money from his account to another person's account by a number of other methods which do not involve writing cheques.

2.2 The appropriate method of payment

There are a number of methods available to businesses of making payments – by cheque, standing order, direct debit, bank giro credit, BACS, CHAPS. The organisation will normally have policies regarding which method of payment is to be used for different types of payment.

Most credit suppliers are likely to require payment by cheque or by direct bank giro credit.

Many organisations such as gas, telephone and electricity providers will encourage customers to pay by direct debit. This means that once the direct debit has been set up then this will automatically be taken from your bank account on the agreed day with no action necessary for your business.

Any fixed periodic payments however might be more appropriately made by standing order, which is for a fixed amount on a fixed periodic date.

Often the wages and salaries payments of a business will be one of the largest and most regular of payments that must be made. The most common method of making the regular wages and salaries payments to employees is using the BACS system.

In the age of e-commerce, more and more businesses may opt to make and receive payments using such facilities as Worldpay or Paypal. They offer domestic and multi currency payment processing for online vendors, auction sites and other commercial users. They charge fees for receiving money proportionate to the amount received, currency used, the payment option used, the country of the sender, the country of the recipient and the recipient's account type.

3 Payments to credit suppliers

3.1 Authorised documentation

A business must make a payment only if there is authorised documentation to show that the payment is genuine. Authorised documentation might include:

- an invoice which has been signed or stamped by a responsible official

- a cheque requisition form

- a memo from a responsible official.

Cheques are normally prepared by the cashier. The cashier should ensure that the amount of the cheque agrees to the authorised documentation.

3.2 Methods of scheduling payments

Different businesses will have different policies for determining the timing of payments to credit suppliers. Some of the most common methods are:

- to pay each invoice that arrives at the latest possible date according to the credit terms

- to pay a number of invoices at the same time when the supplier's statement is received

- to make payments on a set day, such as every Friday, and to pay all of those invoices that will have exceeded their credit terms by the following Friday.

4 Payment by invoice

4.1 Introduction

When each invoice is received it is looked at and the latest date on which it can be paid according to the credit terms of the supplier will be determined. The invoice will then be scheduled for payment on this date.

4.2 Invoices and cash discounts

When the cashier is dealing with writing a cheque for payment of an invoice, then the invoice should already be marked as authorised by the appropriate person in the organisation, having checked it against appropriate documentation such as the purchase order and delivery note. The only remaining task is to deal with any cash or settlement discounts.

Firstly it must be checked that it is company policy to take cash discounts. If this is the case then it must be determined whether there is time to make the payment on time and claim the discount. Finally the amount of the cash discount and the net amount that is to be paid should be calculated. This will usually be shown on the invoice, as shown in the previous chapters.

Example

An invoice shows the following details:

Date: 3 June 20X6

	£
List price of goods	4,000.00
Trade discount 5%	200.00
	3,800.00
VAT (20%)	760.00
Invoice total	4,560.00

A discount of 4% of the full price applies if payment is made within 10 days. No credit note will be issued. Following payment you must ensure you have only recovered the VAT actually paid.

If you pay within 30 days, the discounted price is:

	£
Net	3,648.00
VAT (20%)	729.60
Invoice total	4,377.60

Suppose that today's date is 7 June.

Solution

Today is 7 June and in order to claim the settlement discount the payment must arrive with the supplier by 13 June. Provided that the payment is made in the next few days and posted to the supplier immediately then the settlement discount can be claimed and £4,377.60 paid to the supplier.

An adjusted will also be required to the VAT account, in respect of the lower Input VAT reclaimed when a settlement discount is received.

 Activity 2

A company has recently purchased supplies from International Toiletries Ltd for £250.00, less 20% trade discount, plus VAT. International allow 2.5% settlement discount for payment within seven days of the receipt of their invoice.

(a) State which of the following total amounts is due for payment by the company if they take advantage of the settlement discount.

    A   £240.00

    B   £234.00

    C   £195.00

(b) What would be the VAT inclusive total shown on the original invoice before deducting the settlement discount?

Activity 3

You have received the following invoices from suppliers who offer settlement discounts. You must calculate the discount offered and decide whether or not you can take the discount if you send a cheque today. Today is 21 June 20X9.

	Supplier	Invoice date	Net invoice amount	Discount terms	
(a)	ABC Fencing	20 May 20X9	£239.50	2.5%	30 days ◡
(b)	Brown & Black	15 June 20X9	£458.63	1.5%	28 days Y
(c)	Peter's Wood Products	10 June 20X9	£168.00	2.0%	14 days Y
(d)	S J Lever	15 May 20X9	£391.48	2.0%	30 days √
(e)	A J Bennett	1 June 20X9	£56.91	2.5%	14 days ◡

5 Payment of suppliers' statements

5.1 Introduction

A supplier's statement can also be used to request a cheque to be drawn. It will have the same form as the customer's statement that we considered in an earlier chapter. The supplier's statement could be used when the intention is to pay a number of invoices to this supplier with just one cheque.

5.2 Checking suppliers' statements

Before any payments are made it is important to check that the supplier's statement is correct. Each invoice and credit note should be checked either to the original documentation or to the supplier's account in the purchases ledger.

When the accuracy of the statement has been ascertained then it must be determined exactly which invoices from the statement are to be paid.

Example

Given below is a statement from a supplier together with that supplier's account from the purchases ledger.

To:	Scott Brothers		Nemo Limited		
	34 Festival Way		Date: 31 August 20X3		
	Oldham				
	OL2 3BD				

STATEMENT

Date	Transaction	Total £	Current £	30+ £	60+ £
12 May 20X3	Invoice 2569	92.35			92.35
13 June 20X3	CN 2659	(23.60)			(23.60)
09 July 20X3	Invoice 2701	102.69		102.69	
18 July 20X3	Invoice 2753	133.81		133.81	
02 Aug 20X3	Invoice 2889	56.50	56.50		
10 Aug 20X3	Invoice 2901	230.20	230.20		
28 Aug 20X3	Invoice 3114	243.24	243.24		
	TOTALS	835.19	529.94	236.50	68.75

May we remind you our credit terms are 30 days

Nemo Ltd

		£			£
13 June	CN 2659	23.60	12 May	Invoice 2569	92.35
			09 July	Invoice 2701	102.69
			18 July	Invoice 2753	133.81
			02 Aug	Invoice 2889	56.50
			10 Aug	Invoice 2901	203.20
			28 Aug	Invoice 3114	243.24

To check that the supplier's statement is correct prior to paying any amounts, the statement should be carefully checked to the supplier's account in the purchases ledger.

Solution

The invoice dated 10 August is in the purchases ledger at a total of £203.20 whereas it appears on the supplier's statement as £230.20.

The purchase invoice itself should be accessed from the filing system to determine whether the amount is £203.20 or £230.20. If the supplier's statement is incorrect then a polite telephone call should be made or letter sent to the supplier, Nemo Ltd, explaining the problem.

5.3   Which invoices to pay

Once the supplier's statement has been checked for accuracy then it has to be decided which invoices shall be paid. Most organisations will have a policy regarding the payment of supplier's invoices or, alternatively, a fairly senior figure in the business will decide each month which invoices are to be paid.

 Example

Using the supplier's statement shown above suppose that payment has been authorised for all amounts that have been outstanding for 30 days or more. What amount should the cheque be made out for?

Solution

	£
60+ days total	68.75
30+ days total	236.50
Cheque amount	305.25

5.4   Remittance advices

Some suppliers will attach a remittance advice to the bottom of their statement so that the customer can indicate which invoices less credit notes are being paid with this cheque.

 Example

Given on the next page is a supplier's statement from Bart & Partners. Attached to it is the remittance advice. The policy of the business is to pay all of the January and February invoices less credit notes.

Complete the remittance advice on the basis that the payment was made by cheque number 047732 on 4 April 20X2.

Bart & Partners
Spring House
Park Estate
Oldham OL2 3CF

To: Fells Brothers
Simpfield House
Oldham
OL1 3XJ

Date: 31 March 20X2

STATEMENT

Date	Transaction	Total £	Current £	30+ £	60+ £
15 Jan 20X2	INV 12611	308.50			308.50
01 Feb 20X2	CN 04779	(112.60)		(112.60)	
20 Feb 20X2	INV 12683	419.80		419.80	
02 Mar 20X2	INV 12710	384.20	384.20		
14 Mar 20X2	INV 12748	116.88	116.88		
		1,116.78	501.08	307.20	308.50

May we remind you our credit terms are 30 days

REMITTANCE ADVICE

To:

Company name:

Address:

Date:

Date	Our ref	Amount £	Discount taken £	Paid £
15 Jan 20X2	INV 12611	308.50		
01 Feb 20X2	CN 04779	(112.60)		
20 Feb 20X2	INV 12683	419.80		
02 Mar 20X2	INV 12710	384.20		
14 Mar 20X2	INV 12748	116.88		

Total paid
Cheque no

Solution

REMITTANCE ADVICE

| **To:** | Bart & Partners
Spring House
Park Estate
Oldham
OL2 3CF | **Company name:** Fells Brothers

Address: Simpfield House
Oldham OL1 3XJ
Date: 4 April 20X2 |

Date	Our ref	Amount £	Discount taken £	Paid £
15 Jan 20X2	INV 12611	308.50		308.50
01 Feb 20X2	CN 04779	(112.60)		(112.60)
20 Feb 20X2	INV 12683	419.80		419.80
02 Mar 20X2	INV 12710	384.20		
14 Mar 20X2	INV 12748	116.88		

			Total paid	£615.70

Cheque no 047732

6 Payment on a set date

6.1 Introduction

The problem with paying each invoice on the last possible date that it can be paid is that this means that someone in the organisation is tied up with invoice payments every day. However, the other alternative of paying when the supplier's statement is received means that in many cases the opportunity to take advantage of any settlement discount offered is lost.

6.2 Alternative method

Therefore an alternative method is to set a day each week/fortnight for payment of invoices. On that day all invoices that would have exceeded their credit limit or lost the chance of the settlement discount by the next payment date would be paid.

Example

Your business has the policy of paying invoices each Friday and on that day to pay all invoices that would either exceed their settlement discount period or that would be exceeding their credit period by the following Friday.

Today is Friday 7 May. The following invoices are in the pile of unpaid invoices. Indicate which invoices would be paid today and why.

Supplier	Date	Amount £	Settlement terms
K Fielden	30 Apr	376.90	2% discount for payment within 14 days
Giles Associates	12 Apr	269.46	Net 30 days
Penfold Ltd	05 May	316.58	3% discount for payment within 14 days
Yalders Partners	06 May	146.37	4% discount for payment within 10 days

Solution

K Fielden	30 Apr	376.90	2% discount for payment within 14 days

– in order to take the discount the payment must be received by the supplier by 14 May. As next Friday will be 14 May it is too late to make the payment then so, if the discount is to be taken, payment must be made today.

Giles Associates	12 Apr	269.46	Net 30 days

– as April has 30 days the payment must be received by 12 May. Therefore payment must be made today in order to remain within the stated credit terms.

Penfold Ltd	5 May	316.58	3% discount for payment within 14 days

– in order to take the discount the payment must be received by the supplier by 19 May. Next Friday will be 14 May which should give enough time for the cheque to be drawn and sent to the supplier to arrive by 19 May.

Yalders Partners	6 May	146.37	4% discount for payment within 10 days

– in order to take the discount the payment must be received by the supplier by 16 May. As next Friday is the 14 May, making 16 May the Sunday, it would seem unlikely that if payment were put off until next week, it would reach the supplier in time. Therefore if the discount is to be taken it should be paid today.

7 Authorisation of invoices

7.1 Introduction

In an earlier chapter we saw how all purchase invoices should be thoroughly checked to ensure that they are for goods or services that have been received by the business, that the goods and services have been charged at the correct rate and that all discounts and calculations are correct.

7.2 Authorisation stamp

At this point in the checking process the invoice was stamped with an authorisation stamp or grid stamp which showed that the invoice had been checked and also coded the invoice for the information required for entering it into the accounting records. A typical authorisation stamp at this stage in the process is shown following.

Purchase order no	436129
Invoice no	388649
Cheque no	
Account code	PL70
Checked	J Wilmber
Date	03/05/X4
ML account	006

7.3 Authorisation for payment

As we have seen, different organisations will have different methods of determining precisely when invoices will be paid. The only invoices that will be paid are ones that have already been checked and the authorisation stamp completed. The next stage, however, is for today's list of invoices to be paid to be authorised by the appropriate person within the organisation.

In a small organisation the appropriate person may be the cashier who will write out the cheques. Provided the cashier knows that the invoice has been checked and coded then he/she will determine which invoices need paying and will write out the cheque. At this stage the cheque number is the final entry on the authorisation stamp to show that the cheque has been paid and to ensure that it is not paid a second time in error.

In a larger organisation it may be that a more senior member of the management team must review the invoices due for payment before they are paid. In this case there may be an additional entry on the authorisation stamp for the signature of the manager or he may just initial the stamp itself to indicate to the cashier that payment is to be made.

8 Cheque requisitions

8.1 Introduction

In some instances a payment will need to be made but there is no invoice or bill as yet. Such payments can be made but must be requested by a completed and authorised cheque requisition form.

8.2 Cheque requisition

 Definition

A cheque requisition is a request for a cheque for payment to a third party where there is no invoice or bill to support this payment.

The cheque requisition is a request for a cheque for a certain amount for a payment that does not work its way naturally through the purchase invoice system.

Once a cheque requisition has been completed it must be authorised by an appropriate senior person within the organisation and then the cheque can be issued.

Example

The managing director's company car is in the garage for a service. At 4 o'clock the garage telephones to say that the car is ready to be collected and the cost of the service has been £342.60. It is necessary to give the garage a cheque for this amount upon collection of the car.

A cheque requisition form must be completed.

Solution

CHEQUE REQUISITION FORM

CHEQUE DETAILS

Date .... 3 June 20X6 ....

Payee .... Ricky's Garage ....

Amount £ .... 342.60 ....

Reason .... Service of MD's car .... Account code.... ML03 ....

Invoice no. (attached/to follow) ....

Receipt (attached/to follow) ....

Required by (Print) .... M. PLUMMER ....

                Signature.... M. Plummer ....

Authorised by: .... J.Swain ....

9 Capital and revenue expenditure

9.1 Introduction

Most payments that are made by a business are for day-to-day expenses. These may be for:

- goods for resale

- materials to be used in production

- general expenses.

9.2 Revenue expenditure

These types of everyday expenses for the general running of the business are known as revenue expenditure. The other type of expenditure that a business might incur is capital expenditure.

9.3 Capital expenditure

Capital expenditure is payments for fixed assets. Fixed assets are long term assets for use in the business rather than for items that are either to be sold or to be used in the short term within the business. Typical items of capital expenditure are land and buildings, plant and machinery, office equipment, salesmen's cars, delivery vehicles or fixtures and fittings.

9.4 Payments for capital expenditure

In most cases the appropriate method of payment for a fixed asset will be by payment of a cheque. The procedure is exactly the same as for payments to credit suppliers for goods. The payment must be authorised and the cheque must be correctly prepared.

10 Summary

In this chapter we considered the authorisation of the actual payments to be made to suppliers for goods, services and expenses. Remember that the invoices have already been checked for their accuracy and therefore the key to authorisation of payments is which invoices are to be paid. This will often depend upon the method of payment of invoices that it is the policy of the organisation to use. In some businesses all invoices are checked upon arrival to determine the latest date on which they can be paid in order to either validly claim a settlement discount or stay within the supplier's stated credit terms.

An alternative is to wait until the statement is received from the supplier at the end of the month. Once the statement has been checked to ensure that it is correct, it will be determined which invoices minus credit notes are to be paid. The statement may be accompanied by a remittance advice which should be completed in order to show which invoices less credit notes are being paid.

The problem with waiting until the supplier's statement is received is that many settlement discounts that are offered are lost due to the payment only being made every month. Therefore an alternative is for the business to set a day each week or possibly every two weeks on which invoices are paid in order either to take advantage of the settlement discount or to ensure that the payment does not exceed the stated credit terms.

Prior to the payment of the invoice it must be authorised. In many small organisations the process of checking the invoice to ensure that the goods or services have been received and the checking of all of the details of the invoice for accuracy is all that is required for authorisation. In other organisations more senior managers might be required to authorise the invoices due to be paid.

In some instances a cheque will be required although there is no invoice or bill to support it. In this case a cheque requisition form must be completed and authorised by an appropriate senior person within the organisation before the cheque is issued.

Payments may not only be made for revenue expenditure items but also for capital expenditure on fixed assets.

Answers to chapter activities

 Activity 1

(a)   Yes (since the cheque is more than six months old).

(b)   Yes, provided that you initial the date change.

 Activity 2

(a)   Option B

(£250 × 80% × 97.5% × 1.2) = £234.00

(b)

	£
Supplies (£250 less 20% discount)	200.00
VAT	40.00
Total	240.00

Activity 3

	Discount	*Can take discount?*
(a)	£5.99	No
(b)	£6.88	Yes
(c)	£3.36	Yes
(d)	£7.83	No
(e)	£1.42	No

11 Test your knowledge

 Workbook Activity 4

Given below are four invoices received by Nethan Builders that are to be paid today, 18 May 20X1. It is the business policy to take advantage of any settlement discounts possible.

You are required to complete a remittance advice for each payment.

INVOICE

Invoice to:
Nethan Builders
Brecon House
Stamford Road
Manchester
M16 4PL

Building Contract Supplies
Unit 15
Royal Estate
Manchester
M13 2EF
Tel: 0161 562 3041
Fax: 0161 562 3042

Deliver to:
As above

Invoice no:	07742
Tax point:	8 May 20X1
VAT reg no:	776 4983 06

Code	Description	Quantity	VAT rate %	Unit price £	Amount excl of VAT £
SDGSL6	SDGS Softwood 47 × 225 mm	20.5 m	20	8.30	170.15

	170.15
VAT	34.03
Total amount payable	204.18

A discount of 1.5% of the full price applies if payment is made within 14 days. No credit note will be issued. Following payment you must ensure you have only recovered the VAT actually paid.

If you pay within 14 days, the discounted price is:

Net	167.60
VAT	33.52
Gross	201.12

INVOICE

Jenson Ltd

Invoice to:
Nethan Builders
Brecon House
Stamford Road
Manchester
M16 4PL

Deliver to:
As above

30 Longfield Park, Kingsway
M45 2TP
Tel: 0161 511 4666
Fax: 0161 511 4777

Invoice no: 47811
Tax point: 5 May 20X1
VAT reg no: 641 3229 45
Purchase order no: 7174

Code	Description	Quantity	VAT rate %	Unit price £	Amount excl of VAT £
PL432115	Door Lining set 32 × 115 mm	6	20	30.25	181.50
					181.50
Trade discount 15%					27.22
					154.28
VAT					30.85
Total amount payable					185.13

A discount of 3% of the full price applies if payment is made within 10 days. No credit note will be issued. Following payment you must ensure you have only recovered the VAT actually paid.

If you pay within 10 days, the discounted price is:

Net	149.65
VAT	29.93
Gross	179.58

INVOICE

Magnum Supplies
140/150 Park Estate
Manchester
M20 6EG
Tel: 0161 561 3202
Fax: 0161 561 3200

Invoice to:
Nethan Builders
Brecon House
Stamford Road
Manchester
M16 4PL

Deliver to:
As above

Invoice no:	077422
Tax point:	11 May 20X1
VAT reg no:	611 4337 90

Code	Description	Quantity	VAT rate %	Unit price £	Amount excl of VAT £
BH47732	House Bricks – Red	600	20	1.24	744.00
					744.00
Trade discount 15%					111.60
					632.40
VAT					126.48
Total amount payable					758.88

A discount of 2% of the full price applies if payment is made within 10 days. No credit note will be issued. Following payment you must ensure you have only recovered the VAT actually paid.

If you pay within 10 days, the discounted price is:

Net	619.75
VAT	123.95
Gross	743.70

INVOICE

Haddow Bros

Invoice to:
Nethan Builders
Brecon House
Stamford Road
Manchester
M16 4PL

The White House
Standing Way
Manchester
M13 6FH
Tel: 0161 560 3140
Fax: 0161 560 6140

Deliver to:
As above

Invoice no: G33940
Tax point: 9 May 20X1
VAT reg no: 460 3559 71

Code	Description	Quantity	VAT rate %	Unit price £	Amount excl of VAT £
PLY8FE1	Plywood Hardwood 2440 × 1220 mm	24	20	17.80	427.20
					427.20
VAT					85.44
Total amount payable					512.64

A discount of 2% of the full price applies if payment is made within 10 days. No credit note will be issued. Following payment you must ensure you have only recovered the VAT actually paid.

If you pay within 10 days, the discounted price is:

Net	418.66
VAT	83.73
Gross	502.39

REMITTANCE ADVICE

To: Building Contract Supplies

Nethan Builders
Brecon House
Stamford House
Manchester
M16 4PL

Tel: 0161 521 6411
Fax: 0161 530 6412
VAT reg: 471 3860 42
Date:

Date	Invoice no	Amount £	Discount taken (inc VAT adjustment) £	Paid £
18/5	07742	204.18	3.06	201.12

Total paid £ 201.12

Cheque no

REMITTANCE ADVICE

To: Jenson Ltd

Nethan Builders
Brecon House
Stamford House
Manchester
M16 4PL

Tel: 0161 521 6411
Fax: 0161 530 6412
VAT reg: 471 3860 42
Date:

Date	Invoice no	Amount £	Discount taken (inc VAT adjustment) £	Paid £
18/5	47811	185.13	/	185.13

Total paid £ 185.13

Cheque no

REMITTANCE ADVICE

To: Haddow Bros

Nethan Builders
Brecon House
Stamford House
Manchester
M16 4PL

Tel: 0161 521 6411
Fax: 0161 530 6412
VAT reg: 471 3860 42
Date:

Date	Invoice no	Amount £	Discount taken (inc VAT adjustment) £	Paid £
18/5	G33940	512.64	/	512.64

Total paid £ 512.64

Cheque no

REMITTANCE ADVICE

To: Magum Supplies

Nethan Builders
Brecon House
Stamford House
Manchester
M16 4PL

Tel: 0161 521 6411
Fax: 0161 530 6412
VAT reg: 471 3860 42
Date:

Date	Invoice no	Amount £	Discount taken (inc VAT adjustment) £	Paid £
18/5	07422	758.88	15.18	743.70

Total paid £ 743.70

Cheque no

The analysed cash payments book

Introduction

In this chapter we will consider how cash payments for cash purchases and to credit suppliers are recorded in the cash payments book and in the ledger accounts.

CONTENTS

1   The analysed cash payments book

2   Settlement discounts received from suppliers

---

1 The analysed cash payments book

1.1 Layout

A proforma analysed cash payments book is shown below

CASH PAYMENTS BOOK										
Date	Narrative	Reference	Total £	VAT £	PLCA £	Cash purchases £	Admin £	Rent and rates £	Discount received £	VAT adjust- ment £
		TOTALS								

Notes:

(a) The date column contains the date of the transaction.

(b) The narrative column describes the transactions. The reference column may include a reference to the source of the information or the code of a supplier being paid.

(c) The total column contains the total cash paid (including any VAT).

(d) The VAT column contains the VAT on the transaction but not if the VAT has already been entered in the purchases day book. This is a tricky point but is in principle exactly the same as the treatment of VAT that we studied for the cash receipts book.

(e) The PLCA column contains any cash paid that has been paid to a supplier. The total paid including VAT is entered in this column.

(f) The cash purchases column contains cash paid for purchases that are not bought on credit. This would be the VAT exclusive amount (net). The VAT element would be accounted for in the VAT column.

(g) We saw with the analysed cash receipts book that nearly all receipts come from debtors or cash sales. In the case of payments, there is a great variety of suppliers who are paid through the cash book; rent and rates, telephone, electricity, marketing, etc. The business will have a separate column for the categories of expense that it wishes to analyse.

(h) The discount received column is a memorandum column that contains details of any cash/settlement discounts received. These discounts will need to be entered into the ledger accounts as we shall see.

(i) The VAT adjustment column is also a memorandum column which sets out any VAT adjustments required where a settlement discount has been taken up on a purchase invoice.

1.2 General ledger payments not entered in the PDB

The PDB is often used only for invoices from suppliers of purchases, i.e. goods for resale. Invoices for rent, electricity, telephone, etc will typically not be entered in the PDB. They will be paid by cheque, and the double entry will be made directly between the cash payments book and the relevant expense account in the general ledger.

One reason for this is that the purchases day book (like the sales day book) is used because the business will typically have a large number of similar transactions (e.g. purchases of goods for resale). To simplify the accounting these are all listed in the PDB and posted in total to the general ledger. Payment of rent or telephone only happens once every three months so there is no need to group these together; they are easily dealt with on an individual basis.

 Example

Parma Products buys goods for resale from two suppliers on credit. The business buys £1,000 + VAT at 20% of goods from X and £3,000 + VAT at 20% of goods from Y. Parma receives an invoice and pays £500 + VAT at 20% rent to their landlord. Parma also pays X's invoice in full. Enter these transactions in the accounts of Parma Products. The rent invoice is not entered in the PDB.

Solution

Step 1 Enter the invoices for goods in the PDB.

PURCHASES DAY BOOK

Date	Supplier	Reference	Invoice number	Total £	VAT £	Purchases £
	X			1,200	200	1,000
	Y			3,600	600	3,000
			TOTALS	4,800	800	4,000

Step 2   Enter the totals of the PDB in the general ledger.

Purchases

	£		£
PDB	4,000.00		

VAT

	£		£
PDB	800.00		

PLCA

	£		£
		PDB	4,800.00

Step 3   Enter the cash paid in the analysed cash payments book.

CASH PAYMENTS BOOK								
Date	Narrative	Reference	Total	VAT	PLCA	Rent	Discount received	VAT adj
			£	£	£	£	£	£
	X		1,200.00		1,200.00			
	Rent		600.00	100.00		500.00		
	TOTALS		1,800.00	100.00	1,200.00	500.00		

Note that the VAT on the payment to the supplier has already been accounted for in the general ledger via the entries in the PDB. However, the rent invoice was not entered in the PDB and so the VAT has to be entered in the VAT column of the cash book from where it will be posted to the VAT account (see Step 4).

Step 4   Post the cash paid totals from the cash book to the general ledger.

Purchases

	£		£
PDB	4,000.00		

VAT

	£		£
PDB	800.00		
CPB	100.00		

PLCA

	£		£
CPB	1,200.00	PDB	4,800.00

Rent

	£		£
CPB	500.00		

Note 1: All the VAT paid is now debited to the VAT account. You must make sure that you understand how some is posted via the PDB and some via the cash book.

Note 2: All of the entries made from the cash payments book are debit entries. The credit entry is the total of the cash payments (£1,800) since the cash payments book is part of the double entry.

Step 5:   Enter the amounts in the purchases ledger.

X

	£		£
CPB	1,200.00	PDB	1,200.00

Y

	£		£
		PDB	3,600.00

The entries to the purchases ledger from the cash payments book are debit entries in the individual creditor accounts as the payment means that less is owed to the creditor.

2 Settlement discounts received from suppliers

2.1 Introduction

Settlement discounts are a tricky complication when dealing with the analysed purchases day book and cash book.

 Example

Consider a business run by Francis which buys goods costing £2,000 + VAT from Z. Z offers a 5% settlement discount if Francis pays within 30 days. Francis pays within 30 days.

Enter these new transactions in the books of Francis.

Solution

Step 1 Calculate the value of the invoice.

> **Note:** The invoice is initially recorded at its full price until it is known whether the discount will be taken.

	£
Cost of goods	2,000.00
VAT (2,000 × 20%)	400.00
Total invoice value	2,400.00

Step 2 Enter the invoice from Z in the purchases day book.

PURCHASES DAY BOOK						
Date	Supplier	Reference	Invoice number	Total £	VAT £	Purchases £
	Z			2,400.00	400.00	2,000.00
			TOTALS	2,400.00	400.00	2,000.00

Step 3 Enter the totals of the purchases day book in the general ledger.

Purchases

	£		£
PDB	2,000.00		

VAT

	£		£
PDB	400.00		

PLCA

	£		£
		PDB	2,400.00

Step 4 Calculate the cash paid by Francis.

	£
Cost of goods	2,000.00
5% settlement discount	(100.00)
	1,900.00
VAT (1,900.00 × 20%)	380.00
Total cash paid	2,280.00

Step 5 Enter the cash paid in the analysed cash payments book.

CASH PAYMENTS BOOK

Date	Narrative	Reference	Total	VAT	PLCA	Rent	Discount received	VAT adj
			£	£	£	£	£	£
	Z		2,280.00		2,280.00		100.00	20.00
		TOTALS	2,280.00		2,280.00		100.00	20.00

Note: Remember that the discount received and VAT adjustment columns are 'memorandum' columns. The cash book only cross-casts if you ignore these two columns.

Step 6 Post the cash payments book totals to the general ledger.

Because Francis takes the settlement discount, he pays Z £120 less than the invoice value. In order to clear the creditors account we have to debit that account with the £120, credit the discount received account with £100 and credit the VAT account with £20 to reflect the reduction in Input VAT. This £100 is a reduction in an expense for the business: they have paid the money earlier in order to take advantage of a lower invoice value.

Purchases

	£		£
PDB	2,000.00		

VAT

	£		£
PDB	400.00	PLCA	20.00

PLCA

	£		£
CPB	2,280.00	PDB	2,400.00
Discount received	100.00		
VAT	20.00		

Discount received

	£		£
		PLCA	100.00

Activity 1

FFP makes the following payments in respect of various credit invoices and other items:

- Payment of £4,230 on 23/7/X4 to N Hudson for credit purchases. A settlement discount of £130 was taken and a VAT adjustment of £26 arose in respect of this discount. This was paid by cheque (cheque number 1003). The purchases ledger reference code is P4153.

- On 24/7/X4, £2,350 to G Farr in respect of credit purchases by cheque (cheque number 1004). The purchases ledger reference code is P4778.

- On 28/7/X4, purchase of stock, not on credit, of £960 including VAT of £160 (cheque number 1005).

- On 30/7/X4, payment of a salary by cheque of £2,500, using cheque number 1006. (There is no VAT on wages and salaries.)

Task 1   Enter these transactions in the cash payments book and total the columns.

Task 2   Post the totals to the general ledger.

Task 3   Post the payments to N Hudson and G Farr to the purchases ledger. The opening balances are N Hudson £10,327.00 and G Farr £8,263.00.

Task 1

ANALYSED CASH PAYMENTS BOOK									
Date	Cheque number	Payee/ account number	Total	PLCA	VAT	Wages and salaries	Purchases	Discount received	VAT adj
			£	£	£	£	£	£	£

Task 2

Purchases ledger control account

Date	Details	Folio	£	Date	Details	Folio	

VAT account

Date	Details	Folio	£	Date	Details	Folio	

Wages and salaries account

Date	Details	Folio	£	Date	Details	Folio	

Purchases account

Date	Details	Folio	£	Date	Details	Folio	£

Discount received account

Date	Details	Folio	£	Date	Details	Folio	£

Purchases ledger
N Hudson account

Date	Details	Folio	£	Date	Details	Folio	£

G Farr account

Date	Details	Folio	£	Date	Details	Folio	£

3 Summary

The two main areas covered in this chapter which cause problems are: (a) the treatment of VAT in the cash payments book; and (b) the treatment of discounts received.

Regarding VAT, remember that if an invoice has been entered in the purchases day book, the VAT will have been captured in the PDB and posted to the VAT account from there.

If, however, an invoice is not entered in the purchases day book, the VAT has to be entered in the VAT column of the cash book and posted to the VAT account from there.

Regarding settlement discounts, remember that the discount column in the cash book is simply a memorandum column. The double entry for discount received is entered in the general ledger as: debit PLCA; credit discount received.

Remember also that in the subsidiary purchases ledger, the discount received is entered in the suppliers account but there is no corresponding double entry in the discount received account (it has already been posted from the PLCA).

Any VAT adjustment required in respect of a settlement discount must be recorded in the VAT adjustment column in the cash payments book. The double entry for the VAT adjustment is entered in the general ledger as: debit PLCA; credit VAT.

Remember also that in the subsidiary purchases ledger, the VAT adjustment is entered in the suppliers account but there is no corresponding double entry in the VAT account (it has already been posted from the PLCA).

Answers to chapter activities

Activity 1

Task 1

ANALYSED CASH PAYMENTS BOOK

Date	Cheque number	Payee/ account number	Total £	PLCA £	VAT £	Wages and salaries £	Purchases £	Discount received £	VAT adj £
23/7/X4	1003	N Hudson, P4153	4,230	4,230				130	26
24/7/X4	1004	G Farr, P4778	2,350	2,350					
28/7/X4	1005	Purchases	960		160		800		
30/7/X4	1006	Salary	2,500			2,500			
			10,040	6,580	160	2,500	800	130	26

Task 2

Purchases ledger control account

Date	Details	Folio	£	Date	Details	Folio	£
31/7/X4	Bank	CPB	6,580				
31/7/X4	Discounts received	CPB	130				
31/7/X4	VAT	CPB	26				

VAT account

Date	Details	Folio	£	Date	Details	Folio	£
31/7/X4	Bank	CPB	160	31/7/X4	Bank	CPB	26

Wages and salaries account

Date	Details	Folio	£	Date	Details	Folio	£
31/7/X4	Bank	CPB	2,500				

Purchases account

Date	Details	Folio	£	Date	Details	Folio	£
31/7/X4	Bank	CPB	800				

Discount received account

Date	Details	Folio	£	Date	Details	Folio	£
				31/7/X4	PLC	CPB	130

Purchases ledger
N Hudson account

Date	Details	Folio	£	Date	Details	Folio	£
23/7/X4	Bank	CPB	4,230		b/f		10,327
23/7/X4	Discounts received	CPB	130				
23/7/X4	VAT	CPB	26				

G Farr account

Date	Details	Folio	£	Date	Details	Folio	£
24/7/X4	Bank	CPB	2,350		b/f		8,263

4 Test your knowledge

 Workbook Activity 2

Given below is the cash payments book for a business.

				CASH PAYMENTS BOOK					
Date	Details	Cheque no	Code	VAT adjustment £	Discount £	Bank £	PLCA £	Cash purchases £	VAT £
12/3	Homer Ltd	03648	PL12	1.01 ✓	5.06 ✓	168.70	168.70 ✓		
	Forker & Co	03649	PL07	1.07 ✓	5.38 ✓	179.45	179.45 ✓		
	Purchases	03650				342.00		285.00	57.00
	Print Ass.	03651	PL08			190.45	190.45 ✓		
	ABG Ltd	03652	PL02	1.32 ✓	6.62 ✓	220.67	220.67 ✓		
	Purchases	03653				198.00		165.00	33.00
	G Greg	03654	PL19			67.89	67.89 ✓		
				3.40 ✓	17.06 ✓	1,367.16	827.16 ✓	450.00 ✓	90.00 ✓

Required:

Show what the entries in the purchases ledger will be:

Account name	Amount £	Dr ✓	Cr ✓

Show what the entries in the general ledger will be:

Account name	Amount £	Dr ✓	Cr ✓

Workbook Activity 3

Given below is the credit side of Nethan Builders cashbook.

CASH BOOK – CREDIT SIDE

Date	Details	Cheque no	Code	VAT Adj £	Discount £	Bank £	PLCA £	Cash purchases £	VAT £
20X1									
30/5	J M Bond	200572	PL01			247.56	247.56 ✓		
	Magnum Supplies	200573	PL16	2.65 ✓	13.25 ✓	662.36	662.36 ✓		
	A J Broom	200574	PL08			153.57	153.57 ✓		
	Jenson Ltd	200575	PL13	1.34 ✓	6.73 ✓	336.57	336.57 ✓		
	KKL Traders	200576	PL20	1.77 ✓	8.85 ✓	442.78	442.78 ✓		
	Purchases	200577				110.97		92.48	18.49
				5.76 ✓	28.83 ✓	1,953.81	1,842.84 ✓	92.48 ✓	18.49 ✓
				CL			DR	DR	DR

Required:

Show what the entries in the purchases ledger will be:

Account name	Amount £	Dr ✓	Cr ✓

Show what the entries in the general ledger will be:

Account name	Amount £	Dr ✓	Cr ✓

Petty cash

Introduction

As well as making payments from the business bank account by cheque or other methods, most businesses will also carry a certain amount of cash on the premises known as petty cash. Petty cash is used to make small business payments, for which writing a cheque would not be appropriate, such as payment in the local shop for tea, coffee and milk for the staff kitchen. In this chapter we will consider how a petty cash system will work, the documentation required and how petty cash payments are accounted for.

CONTENTS

1. Petty cash
2. Petty cash systems
3. Maintaining petty cash records
4. Posting the petty cash book
5. Petty cash control account
6. Reconciling the petty cash

1 Petty cash

 Definition

Petty cash is the small amount of cash that most businesses hold in order to make small cash payments.

1.1 Petty cash box

Holding cash on business premises is a security risk and therefore it is important that the petty cash is secure. It should be kept in a locked petty cash box and usually this itself will be held in the safe. Only the person responsible for the petty cash should have access to the petty cash box.

1.2 Payment of petty cash

Petty cash is usually reimbursed to employees who have already incurred a small cash expense on behalf of the business, such as buying coffee and milk in the local shop or paying for a train fare. These payments should only be made for the incurrence of valid business expenses. For this reason, the petty cashier should only pay out to the employee on receipt of an authorised petty cash voucher and, where appropriate, VAT receipt.

 Definition

A petty cash voucher is an internal document that details the business expenditure that an employee has incurred out of his own money.

This voucher must be authorised by an appropriate person before any amounts can be paid to that employee out of the petty cash box.

A typical petty cash voucher is shown below:

Signature of person authorising voucher

Details of expenditure including the date and the nature of the expense

Signature of claimant

Sequential voucher number

Total paid to employee

PETTY CASH VOUCHER				
Authorised by F R Clarke	Received by L Kent		No	4173
Date	Description		Amount	
4 April 20X1	Train Fare		12	50
	Total		12	50

2 Petty cash systems

2.1 Introduction

There are two main types of petty cash systems that a business may use- an imprest system and a non-imprest system.

2.2 The imprest system

Many businesses use the imprest system for petty cash. Using an imprest system makes petty cash easier to control and therefore reduces the possibility of error and fraud.

The business decides on a fixed amount of petty cash (the imprest) which is just large enough to cover normal petty cash requirements for a period (usually a week). This amount of petty cash is withdrawn from the bank.

Claims are paid out of petty cash by a voucher being completed for each amount of petty cash paid out. The vouchers are kept in the petty cash box so that the amount of cash held decreases and is replaced by vouchers.

At any given time, the total contents of the box (i.e. petty cash plus amounts withdrawn represented by vouchers) should equal the amount of the imprest. At the end of the period, a cheque is drawn for the total of the vouchers which restores the petty cash float to the amount of the imprest. The vouchers are removed from the petty cash box and filed.

Example

The imprest amount for a petty cash system is £150, which is the amount paid into the petty cash box on 1 November. At the end of the week the total of the vouchers in the petty cash box is £125.05. How much cash is required in order to replenish the petty cash box to the imprest amount?

Solution

£125.05, the amount paid out on the basis of the petty cash vouchers is the amount that is required to be restored.

 Activity 1

Allsports Limited maintains an imprest amount for the petty cash of £250. During the current period, the sum of £180 is paid out, supported by petty cash vouchers. At the end of the period, what amount should be drawn out of the bank to restore the imprest level?

2.3 Non-imprest petty cash system

An imprest petty cash system as in the previous example is the most common method of dealing with and controlling petty cash. However some businesses may use a non-imprest system. This might be where a set amount of cash is withdrawn each week and paid into the petty cash box no matter what the level of expenditure in that week.

For example it may be an organisation's policy to cash a cheque for £50 each Monday morning for use as petty cash for the week. The danger here is either that petty cash requirements are more than £50 in the week in which case the petty cash box will run out of money. Alternatively week after week expenditure is significantly less than £50 each week, leading to a large amount of cash building up in the petty cash box.

 Activity 2

Give two ways in which the company might attempt to maintain security over petty cash.

3 Maintaining petty cash records

3.1 Introduction

Upon the petty cash vouchers being received and the employees being reimbursed, the details are recorded in their own book of prime entry which is known as the petty cash book. The petty cash book, similar to the cash receipts book and the cash payments book, is not only a primary record but can be kept as part of the main ledger double entry system.

3.2 Layout of the petty cash book

The petty cash book is normally set out as a large ledger account with a small receipts side and a larger analysed payments side. A typical petty cash book is set out below.

Receipts			Payments								
Date	Narrative	Total	Date	Narrative	Voucher no	Total	Postage	Cleaning	Tea & coffee	Sundry	VAT
						£	£	£	£	£	£
1 Nov	Bal b/f	35.50									
1 Nov	Cheque 394	114.50	1 Nov	ASDA	58	23.50			23.50		
			2 Nov	Post Office Ltd	59	29.50	29.50				
			2 Nov	Cleaning materials	60	15.07		12.56			2.51
			3 Nov	Postage	61	16.19	16.19				
			3 Nov	ASDA	62	10.57		8.81			1.76
			4 Nov	Newspapers	63	18.90				18.90	
			5 Nov	ASDA	64	12.10				10.09	2.01

3.3 Receipts side of the petty cash book

The receipts side of the petty cash book only requires one column, as the only receipt into the petty cash box is the regular payment into the petty cash box of cash drawn out of the bank account.

From the example of a typical petty cash book (above), we can see that the balance brought forward was £35.50. The petty cash has then been restored up to £150 by paying in an additional £114.50.

3.4 Payments side of the petty cash book

Payments out of petty cash will be for a variety of different types of expense and an analysis column is required for each type, in the same way as the cash payments book is analysed (as illustrated in the example above).

Note that a column is required for VAT; if an expense includes VAT this must be analysed out. In addition it is important to remember that any VAT included in an expense must be shown separately on the voucher.

Any VAT shown on the petty cash voucher must be analysed out into the VAT column and the net amount shown in the expense analysis column.

3.5 Writing up the petty cash book

When cash is originally paid into the petty cash book then this will be recorded on the receipts side (debit side) of the petty cash book.

Each petty cash voucher will then in turn be written up in the petty cash book on the payments side.

To ensure that no vouchers have been mislaid, petty cash vouchers are pre-numbered sequentially. Each voucher is then entered into the petty cash book in the correct order, with each item of expenditure being recorded in the correct expense analysis column.

Example

A business has just started to run a petty cash system with an amount of £100. £100 is withdrawn from the bank account and paid into the petty cash box on 3 April 20X1. During the first week the following authorised petty cash vouchers were paid. These transactions will now be recorded in the petty cash book.

PETTY CASH VOUCHER				
Authorised by T Smedley	*Received by* P Lannall		*No*	0001
Date	*Description*		*Amount*	
3 April 20X1	Tea/coffee/milk		4	73
		Total	4	73

PETTY CASH VOUCHER

Authorised by	Received by	No	0002
T Smedley	R Sellers		
Date	Description	Amount	
3 April 20X1	Train fare	14	90
	Total	14	90

PETTY CASH VOUCHER

Authorised by	Received by	No	0003
T Smedley	F Dorne		
Date	Description	Amount	
4 April 20X1	Stationery	4	00
	VAT	0	80
	Total	4	80

PETTY CASH VOUCHER

Authorised by	Received by	No	0004
T Smedley	P Dent		
Date	Description	Amount	
5 April 20X1	Postage costs	16	35
	Total	16	35

PETTY CASH VOUCHER

Authorised by	Received by	No	0005
T Smedley	H Polly		
Date	Description	Amount	
7 April 20X1	Train fare	15	30
	Total	15	30

PETTY CASH VOUCHER

Authorised by	Received by	No	0006
T Smedley	P Lannall		
Date	Description	Amount	
8 April 20X1	Milk/biscuits	3	85
	Total	3	85

Solution

Petty cash book											
Receipts			Payments								
Date	Narrative	Total	Date	Narrative	Voucher no	Total	Postage	Travel	Tea & coffee	Sundry	VAT
20X1		£	20X1			£	£	£	£	£	£
03/04	Cash	100.00	03/04	Tea/coffee	0001	4.73			4.73		
			03/04	Train fare	0002	14.90		14.90			
			04/04	Stationery	0003	4.80				4.00	0.80
			05/04	Postage	0004	16.35	16.35				
			07/04	Train fare	0005	15.30		15.30			
			08/04	Milk/biscuits	0006	3.85			3.85		

4 Posting the petty cash book

4.1 Introduction

Once the petty cash book has been written up, we must now post the totals of the petty cash book to the general ledger accounts.

When the petty cash book is not part of the double entry system, the accounting entries must show the impact on the expense accounts, the VAT account and the petty cash control account.

In the event of there being a top up to the petty cash, a separate entry will be required. We would need to show the money being withdrawn from the bank and deposited into petty cash.

When the petty cash book is part of the double entry accounting system as well as being a book of prime entry, there is no need for an entry to the petty cash control account as the petty cash book acts as the general ledger account and the closing balance on the account is taken from it when the trial balance is prepared.

4.2 Posting the petty cash receipt

The receipt into the petty cash box has come from cash being withdrawn from the bank account. This will have been done by writing out a cheque for cash and withdrawing this from the bank. Therefore the cheque should be recorded in the cash payments book as a payment when the cash payments book is written up.

The receipt of the cash into the petty cash box is recorded in the receipts side of the petty cash book, debit side.

As both the petty cash book and the cash payments book are normally part of the general ledger double entry system, the double entry has been completed. The debit is the entry into the petty cash book and the credit entry is the entry in the cash payments book.

4.3 Posting the petty cash payments

When the petty cash book is part of the general ledger double entry system the total column in the petty cash payments side is the credit entry to the petty cash account.

The only additional entries to make are the debits. These entries are taken from the totals of each of the analysis columns. The total from each analysis column is debited to the relevant general ledger account.

Example

The petty cash book written up in an earlier example is given again below. This is to be posted to the general ledger accounts.

Petty cash book											
Receipts			**Payments**								
Date	Narrative	Total	Date	Narrative	Voucher no	Total	Postage	Travel	Tea & coffee	Sundry	VAT
20X1		£	20X1			£	£	£	£	£	£
03/04	Cash	100.00	03/04	Tea/coffee	0001	4.73			4.73		
			03/04	Train fare	0002	14.90		14.90			
			04/04	Stationery	0003	4.80				4.00	0.80
			05/04	Postage	0004	16.35	16.35				
			07/04	Train fare	0005	15.30		15.30			
			08/04	Milk/biscuits	0006	3.85			3.85		

Solution

Step 1 Each of the columns in the petty cash payments side must be totalled.

The accuracy of your totalling should be checked by ensuring that all of the analysis column totals add back to the total of the 'total' column in the petty cash book payments side.

Petty cash book											
Receipts			**Payments**								
Date	Narrative	Total	Date	Narrative	Voucher no	Total	Postage	Travel	Tea & coffee	Sundry	VAT
20X1		£	20X1			£	£	£	£	£	£
03/04	Cash	100.00	03/04	Tea/coffee	0001	4.73			4.73		
			03/04	Train fare	0002	14.90		14.90			
			04/04	Stationery	0003	4.80				4.00	0.80
			05/04	Postage	0004	16.35	16.35				
			07/04	Train fare	0005	15.30		15.30			
			08/04	Milk/biscuits	0006	3.85			3.85		
						59.93	16.35	30.20	8.58	4.00	0.80

Check the totals:

	£
Postage	16.35
Travel	30.20
Tea and coffee	8.58
Sundry	4.00
VAT	0.80
	———
	59.93
	———

Step 2 Each of the analysis column totals must now be entered into the general ledger accounts as debit entries.

VAT account

	£		£
Petty cash book (PCB)	0.80		

The entry has come from the petty cash book and this is the reference – this is now shortened to PCB.

Postage account

	£		£
PCB	16.35		

Travel account

	£		£
PCB	30.20		

Tea and coffee account

	£		£
PCB	8.58		

Sundry expenses account

	£		£
PCB	4.00		

Activity 3

Summary of petty cash vouchers in hand at 31 October 20X7

Date	Description	Total £	VAT included at 20% £
1/10	Envelopes (Administration)	20.10	3.35
4/10	Cleaner (Administration)	8.75	
6/10	Food for staff lunch (Marketing)	17.13	
6/10	Taxi fares (Marketing)	16.23	
6/10	Rail fares (Marketing)	43.75	
10/10	Postage (Administration)	4.60	
15/10	Tea and coffee (Production)	4.39	
17/10	Light bulbs and refuse sacks (Distribution)	8.65	1.44
20/10	Flowers for reception (Administration)	21.23	
26/10	Cleaner (Administration)	8.75	

(a) Write up the payments side of the petty cash book for October 20X7 from the information given.

You should allocate a sequential voucher number to each entry in the petty cash book. The last voucher number to be allocated in September was 6578.

Use the blank petty cash book provided.

(b) Total each of the columns in the petty cash book and cross-cast them.

(c) Post the totals to the general ledger accounts given.

PETTY CASH BOOK – PAYMENTS							
Date	Voucher no	Total	Production	Distribution	Marketing	Administration	VAT
		£	£	£	£	£	£

Production expenses account

£		£

Distribution expenses account

£		£

Marketing expenses account

£		£

Administration expenses account

£		£

VAT account

£		£

5 Petty cash control account

5.1 Introduction

In most cases the petty cash book is not only a book of prime entry but also part of the general ledger. However in other businesses the petty cash book will be simply a book of prime entry and a petty cash control account will be maintained in the general ledger.

5.2 Petty cash control account

The petty cash control account summarises the information in the petty cash book and is posted from the petty cash book. When cash is put into the petty cash box the petty cash control account will be debited and the total of the petty cash payments for the period will be credited to the petty cash control account.

Example

A business runs a petty cash imprest system with an imprest amount of £100. At 1 May there was £32.56 remaining in the petty cash box and £67.44 of cash was withdrawn from the bank and put into the petty cash box to restore the imprest amount. During the month of May the total payments from the petty cash book were £82.16.

Write up the petty cash control account.

Solution

Petty cash control account

	£		£
Balance b/f	32.56	Payments	82.16
Receipt from bank	67.44	Balance c/d	17.84
	———		———
	100.00		100.00
	———		———
Balance b/d	17.84		

6 Reconciling the petty cash

6.1 Introduction

We saw earlier in the chapter that when an imprest system is being used for petty cash then at any point in time the amount of cash in the petty cash box plus the total of the vouchers in the petty cash box should equal the imprest amount.

At regular intervals, usually at the end of each week, this check will be carried out. If there is a difference then this must be investigated.

6.2 Possible causes of difference

If there is more cash in the petty cash box than the balance on the petty cash control account this could be due to an error in writing up the petty cash book (i.e. more has been recorded in payments than has actually been paid out). In this case the entries in the petty cash book should be checked to the underlying petty cash vouchers to discover the error.

If there is less cash in the petty cash box than the balance on the petty cash control account this could also be due to an error in writing up the petty cash book (i.e. less payments have been recorded in the petty cash control account than were actually made). This may be due to a petty cash voucher having been omitted from the petty cash book and therefore again the underlying petty cash vouchers should all be checked to their entries in the petty cash book.

If no accounting errors or posting errors can be found then the cause is likely to be one of the following:

- an error has been made in paying a petty cash voucher and more money was handed out than was recorded on the voucher

- cash has been paid out of the petty cash box without a supporting voucher

- cash could have been stolen from the petty cash box.

In such cases the matter should be investigated and security of the petty cash and petty cash procedures improved.

Example

The petty cash control account from the previous example is reproduced.

Petty cash control account

	£		£
Balance b/f	32.56	Payments	82.16
Receipt	67.44	Balance c/d	17.84
	————		————
	100.00		100.00
	————		————
Balance b/d	17.84		

What action should be taken if when the petty cash was counted at 31 May the amount held in the box was:

(a) £27.84

(b) £7.84

Solution

(a) If the amount of cash in the box was £27.84 then this is £10 more than expected. The following checks should be made:

Has the balance on the petty cash control account been correctly calculated?

Have the receipt and payments totals been correctly posted to the petty cash control account?

Have the payments in the petty cash book been correctly totalled?

Has each individual petty cash voucher been correctly recorded in the petty cash book?

(b) If the amount of cash in the box is only £7.84 then this is £10 less than expected. All of the above checks should be carried out and if no accounting errors can be found then it will have to be assumed that either £10 too much has been paid out on a petty cash voucher, £10 has been paid out of the petty cash box without a supporting voucher or that £10 has been stolen from the petty cash box.

6.3 Procedure for reconciling the petty cash box

The total amount of cash in the petty cash box will be counted. The vouchers that have been paid during the week are also in the petty cash box and they must also be totalled.

When the amount of cash is added to the total of the vouchers in the box they should equal the imprest amount.

The petty cash vouchers for the week will then be removed from the box and filed.

 Example

The amount of cash remaining in a petty cash box at the end of a week is as follows:

Notes/coins	Quantity
£10	1
£5	2
£2	3
£1	7
50p	9
20p	11
10p	15
5p	7
2p	16
1p	23

The imprest amount is £100 and the vouchers in the petty cash box at the end of the week are as follows:

PETTY CASH VOUCHER				
Authorised by	Received by		No	0467
C Alexi	P Trant			
Date	Description		Amount	
4 May 20X3	Window cleaner		15	00
		Total	15	00

PETTY CASH VOUCHER

Authorised by C Alexi	Received by F Saint	No	0468	
Date	Description		Amount	
5 May 20X3	Train fare		9	80
	Total		9	80

PETTY CASH VOUCHER

Authorised by C Alexi	Received by A Paul	No	0469	
Date	Description		Amount	
5 May 20X3	Stationery		8	00
	VAT		1	60
	Total		9	60

PETTY CASH VOUCHER

Authorised by C Alexi	Received by P Peters	No	0470	
Date	Description		Amount	
7 May 20X3	Postage		6	80
	Total		6	80

PETTY CASH VOUCHER				
Authorised by C Alexi	Received by C Ralph		No	0471
Date	Description		Amount	
5 May 20X3	Train fare		16	70
	Total		16	70

The cash and vouchers in the petty cash box at the end of the week are to be reconciled.

Solution

The petty cash must be totalled:

Notes/coins	Quantity	Amount £
£10	1	10.00
£5	2	10.00
£2	3	6.00
£1	7	7.00
50p	9	4.50
20p	11	2.20
10p	15	1.50
5p	7	0.35
2p	16	0.32
1p	23	0.23
		———
		42.10
		———

Now the vouchers must be totalled.

	£
0467	15.00
0468	9.80
0469	9.60
0470	6.80
0471	16.70
	———
	57.90
	———

Finally, total the cash and the vouchers to ensure that they add back to the imprest amount.

	£
Cash	42.10
Vouchers	57.90
	100.00

 Activity 4

Your business runs a petty cash box based upon an imprest amount of £60. This morning you have emptied the petty cash box and found the following notes, coins and vouchers.

Notes
£5 × 2

Coins
£1 × 3
50p × 5
20p × 4
10p × 6
5p × 7
2p × 10
1p × 8

Vouchers	£
2143	10.56
2144	3.30
2145	9.80
2146	8.44
2147	2.62
2148	6.31
2149	1.44

You are required to reconcile the cash and the vouchers in the petty cash box.

7 Summary

In this chapter we have considered the entire petty cash system. Cash is paid into the petty cash box in order to meet the requirements for actual cash in a business's life. This will normally be in the form of reimbursing employees for business expenses that they have incurred on their own behalf. In order to be reimbursed for the expense, the employee must fill out a petty cash voucher which will normally be accompanied by a receipt for the expense and must then be authorised. At this point the employee can be paid the cash out of the petty cash box.

All petty cash is recorded in the petty cash book which is normally both a book of prime entry and part of the general ledger. The cash paid into the petty cash box is recorded as a receipt in the petty cash book and as a payment in the cash payments book, an amount of cash being taken out of the bank account. The payments of petty cash vouchers are recorded as payments in the petty cash book and are analysed as to the type of payment. These payments are then recorded as debit entries in the appropriate expense account.

At the end of a period, a week or a month possibly, the cash in the petty cash box will be counted and reconciled to the vouchers in the box. In an imprest system the total of the vouchers in the box plus the total of the cash in the box should equal the imprest amount.

Answers to chapter activities

Activity 1

£180

Activity 2

Any two from the following:

(i)   Should be kept securely in a locked box or safe, etc.

(ii)   All payments should be properly authorised.

(iii)   Should be the responsibility of one person.

(iv)   The amount of any one payment should be restricted.

Activity 3

(a), (b)

		PETTY CASH BOOK – PAYMENTS											
Date	Voucher no	Total		Production		Distribution		Marketing		Administration		VAT	
		£		£		£		£		£		£	
01/10/X7	6579	20	10							16	75	3	35
04/10/X7	6580	8	75							8	75		
06/10/X7	6581	17	13					17	13				
06/10/X7	6582	16	23					16	23				
06/10/X7	6583	43	75					43	75				
10/10/X7	6584	4	60							4	60		
15/10/X7	6585	4	39	4	39								
17/10/X7	6586	8	65			7	21					1	44
20/10/X7	6587	21	23							21	23		
26/10/X7	6588	8	75							8	75		
		153	58	4	39	7	21	77	11	60	08	4	79

(c)

Production expenses account

	£		£
PCB	4.39		

Distribution expenses account

	£		£
PCB	7.21		

Marketing expenses account

	£		£
PCB	77.11		

Administration expenses account

	£		£
PCB	60.08		

VAT account

	£		£
PCB	4.79		

Activity 4

Notes and coins

	£	£
£5 × 2	10.00	
£1 × 3	3.00	
50p × 5	2.50	
20p × 4	0.80	
10p × 6	0.60	
5p × 7	0.35	
2p × 10	0.20	
1p × 8	0.08	
	———	
		17.53

Vouchers

2143	10.56
2144	3.30
2145	9.80
2146	8.44
2147	2.62
2148	6.31
2149	1.44
	42.47
Imprest amount	60.00

8 Test your knowledge

 Workbook Activity 5

Given below is a business' petty cash book for the week.

Petty cash book											
Receipts			Payments								
Date	Narrative	Total	Date	Details	Voucher no	Amount	Postage	Staff welfare	Station-ery	Travel expenses	VAT
						£	£	£	£	£	£
5/1/X1	Bal b/d	150.00	12/1/X1	Postage	03526	13.68	13.68✓				
				Staff welfare	03527	25.00		25.00✓			
				Stationery	03528	15.12			12.60		2.52
				Taxi fare	03529	12.25				10.21	2.04
				Staff welfare	03530	6.40		6.40			
				Postage	03531	12.57	12.57				
				Rail fare	03532	6.80				6.80	
				Stationery	03533	8.16			6.80		1.36
				Taxi fare	03534	19.20				16.00	3.20
						119.18	26.25	31.40	19.40	33.01	9.12

Required:

Show what the entries in the general ledger will be:

Account name	Amount £	Dr ✓	Cr ✓

Workbook Activity 6

Given below is a completed petty cash book for transactions that took place on 12th April 20X1:

Petty cash book										
Receipts			Payments							
Date	Narrative	Total	Date	Narrative	Voucher no	Total	Postage	Staff welfare	Tea and coffee	Travel expenses	VAT
						£	£	£	£	£	£
12/04	Bal b/d	100.00	12/04	Coffee/milk	2534	4.68		4.68			
				Postage	2535	13.26	13.26				
				Stationery	2536	10.48			8.74		1.74
				Taxi fare	2537	15.32				12.77	2.55
				Postage	2538	6.75	6.75				
				Train fare	2539	7.40				7.40	
				Stationery	2540	3.94			3.29		0.65
						61.83	20.01	4.68	12.03	20.17	4.94

Required:

Post the required entries to the general ledger accounts:

Postage

	£			£
Balance b/f	231.67			

Staff welfare

	£			£
Balance b/f	334.78			

Tea and coffee

	£			£
Balance b/f	53.36			

Travel expenses

	£			£
Balance b/f	579.03			

VAT account

	£			£
			Balance b/f	967.44

VAT and EU issues

Introduction

In this chapter we are firstly going to look at how to prepare the VAT control account. We will then consider the VAT implications of trading with businesses within, and outside of, the EU.

CONTENTS
1   VAT control account
2   Imports and exports
3   Acquisitions and dispatches

1 VAT control account

1.1 Introduction

You have learnt how to calculate and account for output VAT on sales invoices and input VAT on purchase invoices earlier in this study text.

Output VAT is charged on sales or taxable supplies. This is always credited to the VAT control account as this is money that the business must pay over to HM Revenue and Customs.

Input VAT is VAT paid by a business on purchases or expenses. This is always debited to the VAT control account as businesses can reclaim from HMRC the input VAT they have paid by deducting it from the output tax they owe. They will then pay over to HMRC the net amount only.

Note that where input tax exceeds the output tax, then the balance is recoverable from HMRC.

1.2 VAT payable to HMRC

Where the output VAT credited to the VAT control account in a period is greater than the input VAT debited to the VAT control account, there will be a credit balance on the VAT account. This is a liability which the business must pay over to HMRC.

 Example

A business makes sales on credit of £600 and purchases on credit of £120 (both amounts inclusive of VAT). How would these be accounted for in the ledger accounts. Assume a VAT rate of 20%.

Solution

The sales and purchases must be shown net and the VAT entered in the VAT account. As the sales and purchases were on credit the full double entry would be as follows:

Dr	Debtors account	£600
Cr	Sales account	£500
Cr	VAT control account	£100
Dr	Purchases account	£100
Dr	VAT control account	£20
Cr	Creditors account	£120

Sales account

	£		£
		Debtors	500

Debtors account

	£		£
Sales and VAT	600		

Purchases account

	£		£
Creditors	100		

Creditors account

	£		£
		Purchases	120

VAT control account

	£		£
Creditors	20	Debtors	100
Balance c/d	80		
	───		───
	100		100
	───		───
		Balance b/d	80

There is a credit balance on the VAT account. The amount due to be paid to HM Revenue and Customs is £80.

1.3 VAT recoverable from HMRC

Example

A business makes purchases on credit of £600 and sales on credit of £120 (both amounts inclusive of VAT). How would these be accounted for in the ledger accounts. Assume a VAT rate of 20%.

Solution

The sales and purchases must be shown net and the VAT entered in the VAT account. As the sales and purchases were on credit the full double entry would be as follows:

Dr	Debtors account	£120
Cr	Sales account	£100
Cr	VAT control account	£20
Dr	Purchases account	£500
Dr	VAT control account	£100
Cr	Creditors account	£600

Sales account

	£		£
		Debtors	100

Debtors account

	£		£
Sales and VAT	120		

Purchases account

	£		£
Creditors	500		

Creditors account

	£		£
		Purchases	600

VAT control account

	£		£
Creditors	100	Debtors	20
		Balance c/d	80
	___		___
	100		100
	___		___
Balance b/d	80		

There is a debit balance on the VAT account. The amount recoverable from HM Revenue and Customs is £80. This will be refunded by HMRC to the business bank account.

2 Imports and exports

2.1 Introduction

VAT is a tax levied within the European Union (EU). It applies to sales within the EU but not to sales outside the EU (exports).

All purchases made by EU businesses are subject to VAT even if purchased from outside the EU.

The rules for dealing with purchases from outside the EU can be complex, but you only require a broad understanding of how they are dealt with.

Note that the European Union (EU) was previously known as the European Community (EC), and the VAT returns for completion in your assessment still use the old term 'EC'.

2.2 Exports and imports to or from non-EU members

(a) Generally, goods exported from the United Kingdom to a non-EU country are zero-rated (i.e. there is no tax charged on them, even if there normally would be) provided there is documentary evidence of the export.

As no VAT needs to be charged, there will be no output tax to account for. This is the same for all zero-rated sales.

(b) Goods that are imported from outside the EU have to have customs duty paid on them when they enter the country. Customs duty is outside the scope of this syllabus and is not considered further.

However, goods that would be taxed at the standard rate of VAT if supplied in the United Kingdom are also subject to VAT. The amount payable is based on their value including customs duty. This applies to **all goods** whether or not they are for business use. The aim of the charge is to treat foreign goods in the same way as home-produced goods.

The VAT is paid at the port of entry and the goods will typically not be released until it is paid. If the imported goods are for business use and the business uses them to make taxable supplies, it can reclaim the VAT paid in the usual way as input tax. The business will need to obtain an import VAT certificate to show they have paid this VAT.

 Example

Meurig runs a UK VAT registered business. He imports a large amount of goods from outside the EU which would be standard rated if bought in the UK.

All the goods he sells are standard rated items. The VAT rate is 20%.

In the quarter ended 31 December 20X1 he makes sales and purchases as follows:

	£
Sales to UK businesses	70,000 – VAT
Export sales outside the EU	12,400 – NO VAT
Purchases from UK businesses	38,500 – VAT
Imports from outside the EU	17,450 – VAT

All these figures exclude VAT.

(a) How much output VAT will he account for?

(b) How much input VAT will he account for?

Solution

		£
(a)	Output VAT:	
	VAT on standard rated sales	
	20% × £70,000	14,000.00
(b)	Input VAT:	
	VAT on purchases	
	20% × (£38,500 + £17,450)	11,190.00

The sales outside the EU are zero rated so there is no VAT to account for on these.

Imports from outside the EU are treated like normal UK purchases for VAT purposes.

---

3 Acquisitions and dispatches

3.1 Exports and imports to and from countries within the EU

When both the exporting and importing country are EU members, the rules differ according to whether the purchaser is a VAT registered business or not.

Note that movements of goods between EU Member States are not known as imports and exports but as **acquisitions** and **dispatches**.

In what follows we refer to HM Revenue and Customs ('HMRC') as the collecting authority, even though in different countries it will have a different name.

3.2 Sale to a VAT registered business

- When an EU member sells goods to a VAT registered business in another EU country, it is the **buyer** who pays over the VAT to HMRC (or the equivalent in the buyer's country).

- Provided the seller has the buyer's VAT number, the seller sells the goods zero rated to the buyer. The buyer will then pay VAT to HMRC at the appropriate rate. The buyer can also reclaim the VAT from HMRC.

We can summarise this as follows:

The seller

- The seller will supply the goods zero rated.

- The seller will not make account for output tax on the sale in the VAT control account (in common with other zero rated sales).

The buyer

- The VAT registered buyer will pay the seller the sale price of the goods (excluding any VAT).

- The buyer will not account for output tax or input tax in the VAT control account.

- The buyer will however enter the VAT output tax and the VAT input tax on their VAT return. Thus, the net amount of VAT the buyer pays to HMRC is £Nil.

3.3 Sale to a non-VAT registered buyer

- When a sale is made to a non-VAT registered buyer, the seller has to charge VAT at the standard rate.
- The buyer will pay the VAT inclusive price to the seller.

We can summarise this as follows:

The seller

- The seller supplies the goods and charges VAT. The seller will account for this output VAT in their VAT control account.

The buyer

- The non-VAT registered buyer pays the VAT inclusive price to the seller and of course makes no entries in respect of VAT because he is not registered.

- Note that if a UK business has a high level of such sales to another EU country, they may have to register for VAT in that other country.

  However, this is outside the scope of this assessment.

 Example

Trystan runs a UK business selling Welsh handicraft items. He has recently started to sell goods overseas. All the goods he sells are standard rated items. The VAT rate is 20%.

In the quarter ended 31 December 20X1 he makes sales as follows:

	£
Sales to UK businesses	40,000
Sales to EU registered businesses	10,500
Sales to EU non registered customers	21,000
Export sales outside the EU	12,400

All these figures exclude VAT.

Requirement

How much Output VAT will Trystan account for on these sales?

Solution

VAT on standard rated sales

$$20\% \times (\pounds40,000 + \pounds21,000) \quad 12,200.00$$

345

 Activity 1

Bettrys runs a UK business selling standard rated pet accessories. She imports some items from overseas, both from other EU countries and from outside the EU. The VAT rate is 20%.

In the quarter ended 31 December 20X1 her purchases are as follows:

	£
Purchases from UK businesses	27,400
Purchases from EU registered businesses	13,700
Purchases from outside the EU	18,800

All these figures exclude VAT.

How much input VAT can Bettrys reclaim in the quarter ended 31 December 20X1?

4 Summary

In this chapter, the rules on dealing with sales and purchases overseas have been covered.

They can be summarised as follows for a business that only makes standard rated sales and purchases:

Type of transaction	Treatment for VAT purposes
Sales outside EU	Zero rated
Sales within EU – to VAT registered customers	Zero rated
Sales within EU – to non VAT registered customers	Standard rated
Purchases from outside EU	Standard rated
Purchases from within EU	Standard rated

Answers to chapter activities

 Activity 1

Input VAT reclaimed:

20% × (£27,400 + £13,700 + £18,800)	£11,980.00

5 Test your knowledge

Workbook Activity 2

The following accounts have been extracted from a company's ledgers

Date		Dr £	Cr £
Sales: UK			
30.6.X1	Sales day book		60,500
31.7.X1	Sales day book		89,510
31.8 X1	Sales day book		70,400
Sales: Export EU			
30.6.X1	Sales day book		15,150
31.7.X1	Sales day book		20,580
31.8 X1	Sales day book		17,890
Sales: Exports non EU			
30.6.X1	Sales day book		8,500
31.7.X1	Sales day book		7,450
31.8 X1	Sales day book		10,100
Purchases: UK			
30.6.X1	Purchases day book	34,600	
31.7.X1	Purchases day book	31,590	
31.8 X1	Purchases day book	33,670	

Bad debt relief on a sales invoice for £6,000 including VAT is to be claimed this quarter.

Exports within the EU were to VAT registered customers.

(a) How much output VAT will the company account for in respect of the above?

(b) How much input VAT will the company account for in respect of the above?

Workbook Activity 3

Warhorse Ltd runs a UK business selling standard rated horse-riding accessories.

The company imports some items from overseas, both from other EU countries and from outside the EU. The VAT rate is 20%.

In the quarter ended 30 June 20X2 the details of purchases are as follows:

	£
Purchases from UK businesses	31,250
Purchases from EU registered businesses	7,650
Purchases from outside the EU	15,850

All these figures exclude VAT.

How will these purchases be accounted for from a VAT point of view?

 Workbook Activity 4

You are given the following information for Coleman Limited in respect of the quarter ended 31 December 20X8.

1   Of the external sales of £916,000 made during the quarter ended 31 December 20X8, a total of £65,000 relates to exports to EU countries, to VAT registered customers.

     The remainder of this quarter's sales was of standard rated sales to UK customers. All sales figures given exclude VAT.

2   Total purchases by the company in the quarter amounted to £310,000 of standard-rated inputs, and £23,000 of zero-rated inputs (both figures stated are exclusive of VAT).

     All of these purchases were from within the UK.

(a)   How much output VAT must the company pay over to HMRC?

(b)   How much input VAT can the company reclaim from HMRC?

Suspense accounts and errors

Introduction

Accounting errors arise for a number of reasons. Some lead to unbalanced double entries being recorded in the general ledger. In these circumstances a suspense account is opened to temporarily balance the debits and credits in the trial balance. The suspense account cannot be allowed to remain permanently in the trial balance, and must be cleared by correcting all of the errors that have caused the imbalance.

CONTENTS
1   Types of errors
2   Opening a suspense account
3   Clearing the suspense account
4   Redrafting the trial balance

1 Types of errors

1.1 Introduction

We saw in Chapter 4 that one of the purposes of the trial balance is to provide a check on the accuracy of the double entry bookkeeping. If the trial balance does not balance then an error or a number of errors have occurred and this must be investigated and the errors corrected.

1.2 Errors detected by the trial balance

The following types of error will cause a difference in the trial balance and therefore will be detected by the trial balance and can be investigated and corrected:

A single entry – if only one side of a double entry has been made then this means that the trial balance will not balance e.g. if only the debit entry for receipts from debtors has been made then the debit total on the trial balance will exceed the credit balance.

A casting error – if a ledger account has not been balanced correctly due to a casting error then this will mean that the trial balance will not balance.

A transposition error – if an amount in a ledger account or a balance on a ledger account has been transposed and incorrectly recorded then the trial balance will not balance e.g. a debit entry was recorded correctly as £5,276 but the related credit entry was entered as £5,726.

An extraction error – if a ledger account balance is incorrectly recorded on the trial balance either by recording the wrong figure or putting the balance on the wrong side of the trial balance then the trial balance will not balance.

An omission error – if a ledger account balance is inadvertently omitted from the trial balance then the trial balance will not balance.

Two entries on one side – instead of a debit and credit entry, if a transaction is entered as a debit in two accounts or as a credit in two accounts then the trial balance will not balance.

1.3   Errors not detected by the trial balance

Some errors do not lead to an imbalance in the trial balance and are, therefore, not detected by them. These include:

A reversal of entries – this is where debit and credit entries have been made in the correct accounts in the general ledger but have been made to the wrong sides of the accounts. For example, a cash payment for electricity was debited to the cash account and credited to the electricity account. Both debit and credit entries have been posted so the trial balance will still balance but the entry is the incorrect way around.

An error of original entry – this is where the wrong figure is entered as both the debit and credit entry e.g. a payment of the electricity expense was correctly recorded as a debit in the electricity account and a credit to the bank account but it was recorded as £300 instead of £330.

A compensating error – this is where two separate errors are made, one on the debit side of the accounts and the other on the credit side, and by coincidence the two errors are of the same amount and therefore cancel each other out.

An error of omission – this is where an entire double entry is omitted from the ledger accounts. As both the debit and credit have been omitted the trial balance will still balance.

An error of commission – with this type of error a debit entry and an equal credit entry have been made but one of the entries has been to the wrong account e.g. if the electricity expense was debited to the rent account but the credit entry was correctly made in the bank account – here both the electricity account and rent account will be incorrect but the trial balance will still balance.

An error of principle – this is similar to an error of commission but the entry has been made in the wrong type of account e.g. if the electricity expense was debited to a non-current asset account – again both the electricity account and the non-current asset account would be incorrect but the trial balance would still balance.

It is important that a trial balance is prepared on a regular basis in order to check on the accuracy of the double entry. However not all errors in the accounting system can be found by preparing a trial balance.

1.4 Correction of errors

Errors will normally be corrected by putting through a journal entry for the correction.

The procedure for correcting errors is as follows:

Step 1

Determine the precise nature of the incorrect double entry that has been made.

Step 2

Determine the correct entries that should have been made.

Step 3

Produce a journal entry that cancels the incorrect part and puts through the correct entries.

 Example

The electricity expense of £450 has been correctly credited to the bank account but has been debited to the rent account.

Step 1

The incorrect entry has been to debit the rent account with £450.

Step 2

The correct entry is to debit the electricity account with £450.

Step 3

The journal entry required is:

Dr   Electricity account   £450
Cr   Rent account   £450

Note that this removes the incorrect debit from the rent account and puts the correct debit into the electricity account.

 Activity 1

Colin returned some goods to a supplier because they were faulty. The original purchase price of these goods was £8,260.

The ledger clerk has correctly treated the double entry but used the figure £8,620.

What is the correcting entry which needs to be made?

    KAPLAN PUBLISHING

2 Opening a suspense account

2.1 Introduction

A suspense account is used as a temporary account to deal with errors and omissions. It means that it is possible to continue with the production of financial accounts whilst the reasons for any errors are investigated and then corrected.

2.2 Reasons for opening a suspense account

A suspense account will be opened in two main circumstances:

(a) the bookkeeper does not know how to deal with one side of a transaction

or

(b) the trial balance does not balance.

2.3 Unknown entry

In some circumstances the bookkeeper may come across a transaction for which he is not certain of the correct double entry and therefore rather than making an error, one side of the entry will be put into a suspense account until the correct entry can be determined.

Example

A new bookkeeper is dealing with a cheque received from a garage for £800 for the sale of an old car. He correctly debits the bank account with the amount of the cheque but does not know what to do with the credit entry.

Solution

He will enter it in the suspense account:

Suspense account		
£		£
	Bank account – receipt from sale of car	800

2.4 Trial balance does not balance

If the total of the debits on the trial balance does not equal the total of the credits then an error or a number of errors have been made. These must be investigated, identified and eventually corrected. In the meantime the difference between the debit total and the credit total is inserted as a suspense account balance in order to make the two totals agree.

Example

The totals of the trial balance are as follows:

	Debits £	Credits £
Totals as initially extracted	108,367	109,444
Suspense account, to make the TB balance	1,077	
	109,444	109,444

Suspense

	£		£
Opening balance	1,077		

Activity 2

The debit balances on a trial balance exceed the credit balances by £2,600. Open up a suspense account to record this difference.

3 Clearing the suspense account

3.1 Introduction

Whatever the reason for the suspense account being opened it is only ever a temporary account. The reasons for the difference must be identified and then correcting entries should be put through the ledger accounts, via the journal, in order to correct the accounts and clear the suspense account balance to zero.

3.2 Procedure for clearing the suspense account

Step 1

Determine the incorrect entry that has been made or the omission from the ledger accounts.

Step 2

Determine the journal entry required to correct the error or omission – this will not always mean that an entry is required in the suspense account e.g. when the electricity expense was debited to the rent account the journal entry did not require any entry to be made in the suspense account.

Step 3

If there is an entry to be made in the suspense account put this into the suspense account – when all the corrections have been made the suspense account should normally have no remaining balance on it.

 Example

A trial balance has been extracted and did not balance. The debit column totalled £200,139 and the credit column totalled £200,239.

You discover the cash purchases £100 have been correctly entered into the cash account but no entry has been made in the purchases account.

Draft a journal entry to correct this error, and complete the suspense ledger account.

Solution

As the debit entries and credit entries do not match, we will be required to open up a suspense account to hold this difference until we can correct it.

Suspense

Detail	Amount £	Detail	Amount £
TB	100	Journal 1 (detailed below)	100
	100		**100**

A debit entry is required in the purchases account and the credit is to the suspense account.

		£	£
Dr	Purchases account	100	
Cr	Suspense account		100

Being correction of double entry for cash purchases.

Remember that normally a journal entry needs a narrative to explain what it is for – however in some assessments you are told not to provide the narratives so always read the requirements carefully.

Example

On 31 December 20X0 the trial balance of John Jones, a small manufacturer, failed to agree and the difference of £967 was entered as a debit balance on the suspense account. After the final accounts had been prepared the following errors were discovered and the difference was eliminated.

(1) A purchase of goods from A Smith for £170 had been credited in error to the account of H Smith.

(2) The purchase day book was undercast by £200.

(3) Machinery purchased for £150 had been debited to the purchases account.

(4) Discounts received of £130 had been posted to the debit of the discounts received account.

(5) Rates paid by cheque £46 had been posted to the debit of the rates account as £64.

(6) Cash drawings by the owner of £45 had been entered in the cash account correctly but not posted to the drawings account.

(7) A fixed asset balance of £1,200 had been omitted from the trial balance.

Required:

(a) Show the journal entries necessary to correct the above errors.

(b) Show the entries in the suspense account to eliminate the differences entered in the suspense account.

Note: The control accounts are part of the double-entry.

Solution

(Note that not all the errors relate to the suspense account. Part of the way of dealing with these questions is to identify which entries do not relate to the suspense account. Do not assume that they all do just because this is a question about suspense accounts.)

Journal – John Jones

		Dr £	Cr £
31 December 20X0			
1	H Smith	170	
	A Smith		170
	Being adjustment of incorrect entry for purchases from A Smith – this correction takes place in the purchases ledger (no effect on suspense account)		
2	Purchases	200	
	Purchases ledger control account		200
	Being correction of undercast of purchases day book (no effect on suspense account as control account is the double entry. However the error should have been found during the reconciliation of the control account)		
3	Machinery	150	
	Purchases		150
	Being adjustment for wrong entry for machinery purchased (no effect on suspense account)		
4	Suspense account	260	
	Discount received		260
	Being correction of discounts entered on wrong side of account		
5	Suspense account	18	
	Rates		18
	Being correction of transposition error to rates account		
6	Drawings	45	
	Suspense account		45
	Being completion of double entry for drawings		
7	Fixed asset	1,200	
	Suspense account		1,200
	Being inclusion of fixed asset balance. There is no double entry for this error in the ledger as the mistake was to omit the item from the trial balance		

Suspense account

	£		£
Difference in trial balance	967	Drawings	45
Discounts received	260	Fixed asset per trial balance	1,200
Rates	18		
	_____		_____
	1,245		1,245
	_____		_____

Make sure you realise that not all error corrections will require any entry to the suspense account.

Activity 3

GA extracted the following trial balance from his ledgers at 31 May 20X4.

	£	£
Petty cash	20	
Capital		1,596
Drawings	1,400	
Sales		20,607
Purchases	15,486	
Purchases returns		210
Stock (1 January 20X4)	2,107	
Fixtures and fittings	710	
Sales ledger control	1,819	
Purchases ledger control		2,078
Carriage on purchases	109	
Carriage on sales	184	
Rent and rates	460	
Light and heat	75	
Postage and telephone	91	
Sundry expenses	190	
Cash at bank	1,804	
	_____	_____
	24,455	24,491
	_____	_____

The trial balance did not agree. On investigation, GA discovered the following errors which had occurred during the month of May.

(1)   In extracting the debtors balance the credit side of the sales ledger control account had been overcast by £10.

(2)   An amount of £4 for carriage on sales had been posted in error to the carriage on purchases account.

(3)   A credit note for £17 received from a creditor had been entered in the purchase returns account but no entry had been made in the purchases ledger control account.

(4)   £35 charged by Builders Ltd for repairs to GA's private residence had been charged, in error, to the sundry expenses account.

(5)   A payment of a telephone bill of £21 had been entered correctly in the cash book but had been posted, in error, to the postage and telephone account as £12.

Required:

State what corrections you would make in GA's ledger accounts (using journal entries) and re-write the trial balance as it should appear after all the above corrections have been made. Show how the suspense account is cleared.

---

4 Redrafting the trial balance

Once the suspense account has been cleared, it is important to redraft the trial balance to ensure that the debit column and credit column agree.

 Example

On 30 November an initial trial balance was extracted which did not balance, and a suspense account was opened. On 1 December journal entries were prepared to correct the errors that had been found, and clear the suspense account. The list of balances and the journal entries are shown below.

Redraft the trial balance by placing the figures in the debit or credit column, after taking into account the journal entries which will clear suspense.

	Balances as at 30 November	Balances as at 1 December	
		Debit £	Credit £
Motor vehicles	10,500		
Stock	2,497		
Bank overdraft	1,495		
Petty cash	162		
Sales ledger control	6,811		
Purchases ledger control	2,104		
VAT owing to HMRC	1,329		
Capital	15,000		
Sales	47,036		
Purchases	27,914		
Purchase returns	558		
Wages	12,000		
Motor expenses	947		
Drawings	6,200		
Suspense (debit balance)	491		

Journals

Account	Debit £	Credit £
Motor expenses		9
Suspense	9	
Being to correct transposition error when recording expense		

Account	Debit £	Credit £
Drawings	500	
Suspense		500
Being to correctly analyse unknown cheque payment.		

Solution

| | Balances as at 30 November | Balances as at 1 December | |
		Debit £	Credit £
Motor vehicles	10,500	10,500	
Stock	2,497	2,497	
Bank overdraft	1,495		1,495
Petty cash	162	162	
Sales ledger control	6,811	6,811	
Purchases ledger control	2,104		2,104
VAT owing to HMRC	1,329		1,329
Capital	15,000		15,000
Sales	47,036		47,036
Purchases	27,914	27,914	
Purchase returns	558		558
Wages	12,000	12,000	
Motor expenses	947	**938**	
Drawings	6,200	**6,700**	
Suspense (debit balance)	491		
		67,522	**67,522**

The drawings and the motor expenses figures have been amended for the journals and the trial balance columns agree without the need for a suspense account.

5 Summary

Preparation of the trial balance is an important element of control over the double entry system but it will not detect all errors. The trial balance will still balance if a number of types of error are made. If the trial balance does not balance then a suspense account will be opened temporarily to make the debits equal the credits in the trial balance. The errors or omissions that have caused the difference on the trial balance must be discovered and then corrected using journal entries. Not all errors will require an entry to the suspense account. However, any that do should be put through the suspense account in order to try to eliminate the balance on the account.

Answers to chapter activities

Activity 1

Step 1

The purchases ledger control account has been debited and the purchases returns account credited but with £8,620 rather than £8,260.

Step 2

Both of the entries need to be reduced by the difference between the amount used and the correct amount (8,620 – 8,260) = £360.

Step 3

Journal entry:		£	£
Dr	Purchases returns account	360	
Cr	Purchases ledger control account		360

Being correction of misposting of purchases returns.

Alternatively, instead of reducing the incorrect amount of £8,620 down to £8,260 the incorrect journal could be reversed and the correct journal amount then accounted for. Steps 2 and 3 would then be:

Step 2

The incorrect journal amount of £8,620 should be reversed and the correct journal for purchases returns of £8,260 should then be accounted for.

Step 3

Journal entries:		£	£
Dr	Purchases returns account	8,620	
Cr	Purchases ledger control account		8,620
Dr	Purchases ledger control account	8,260	
Cr	Purchases returns account		8,260

Being correction of misposting of purchases returns.

Activity 2

As the debit balances exceed the credit balances the balance needed is a credit balance to make the two totals equal.

Suspense account

	£		£
		Opening balance	2,600

Activity 3

			Dr £	Cr £
1	Debit	Sales ledger control account	10	
	Credit	Suspense account		10
	being correction of undercast in sales ledger control account			
2	Debit	Carriage on sales	4	
	Credit	Carriage on purchases		4
	being correction of wrong posting			
3	Debit	Purchases ledger control account	17	
	Credit	Suspense account		17
	being correction of omitted entry			
4	Debit	Drawings	35	
	Credit	Sundry expenses		35
	being payment for private expenses			
5	Debit	Postage and telephone	9	
	Credit	Suspense account		9
	being correction of transposition error			

Suspense account

	£		£
Difference per trial balance (24,455 – 24,491)	36	SLCA	10
		PLCA	17
		Postage	9
	36		36

Trial balance after adjustments

	Dr £	Cr £
Petty cash	20	
Capital		1,596
Drawings	1,435	
Sales		20,607
Purchases	15,486	
Purchases returns		210
Stock at 1 January 20X4	2,107	
Fixtures and fittings	710	
Sales ledger control account	1,829	
Purchases ledger control account		2,061
Carriage on purchases	105	
Carriage on sales	188	
Rent and rates	460	
Light and heat	75	
Postage and telephone	100	
Sundry expenses	155	
Cash at bank	1,804	
	24,474	24,474

6 Test your knowledge

Workbook Activity 4

Which of the errors below are, or are not, disclosed by the trial balance? (Ignore VAT in all cases)

(a) Recording a receipt from a debtor in the bank account only.

(b) Recording bank payment of £56 for motor expenses as £65 in the expense account.

(c) Recording a credit purchase on the debit side of the purchase ledger control account and the credit side of the purchases account.

(d) Recording a payment for electricity in the insurance account.

(e) Recording a bank receipt for cash sales on the credit side of both the bank and the sales account.

(f) Incorrectly calculating the balance on the motor vehicles account.

(g) Writing off a bad debt in the bad debt expense and sales ledger control accounts only.

(h) An account with a ledger balance of £3,500 was recorded on the Trial Balance as £350.

Workbook Activity 5

Luxury Caravans Ltd's initial trial balance includes a suspense account with a balance of £2,800 as shown below:

	£
Debtors	33,440
Bank (debit balance)	2,800
Sales	401,300
Stock	24,300
Wages	88,400
Telephone	2,200
Motor car	12,000
VAT (credit balance)	5,300
Electricity	3,800
Rent	16,200
Purchases	241,180
Purchases returns	1,600
Sales returns	4,200
Office equipment	5,000
Capital	49,160
Motor expenses	5,040
Discounts allowed	4,010
Discounts received	2,410
Creditors	20,000
Drawings	40,000
Suspense (credit balance)	2,800

The following errors have been discovered:

- Rent of £200 has been debited to the motor expenses account.

- An electricity payment of £800 has been debited to both the electricity and the bank account.

- The balance on the discounts received account has been incorrectly extracted to the TB – the actual balance on the ledger account was £4,210.

- The balance on the miscellaneous expenses account of £500 was omitted from the TB.

- The purchase returns day book for 22 May was incorrectly totalled, as shown below:

Purchase returns day book					
Date	Details	Credit note number	Total £	VAT £	Net £
22 May	Todd Ltd	578	4,320	720	3,600
22 May	Fallon Ltd	579	720	120	600
22 May	Dean's Plc	580	960	160	800
	Totals		**6,000**	**1,100**	**5,000**

Required:

(a) Produce journal entries to correct all of the errors above.

(b) Redraft the trial balance using the balances above and your journal entries to show the suspense account has been cleared.

Payroll procedures

18

Introduction

In this chapter we will consider one of the most significant payments that most businesses will make either weekly or monthly – wages and salaries. Included within this topic are payments made under the Construction Industry Scheme.

1   Introduction to payroll

1.1   Introduction

The payroll system in a business is one of the most important. The payroll staff not only have a responsibility to calculate correctly the amount of pay due to each employee but they must also ensure that each employee is paid on time with the correct amount and that amounts due to external parties such as HM Revenue and Customs are correctly determined and paid on time.

There are many facets to the payroll function and each will be briefly covered as an introduction in this section and then considered in more detail in later sections of the chapter.

1.2   Calculation of gross pay

The initial calculation that must be carried out for each employee is the calculation of the employee's gross pay. Gross pay is the wage or salary due to the employee for the amount of work done in the period which may be a week or a month depending upon how frequently the employees are paid.

Gross pay may depend upon a number of factors:

- basic hours worked
- overtime hours worked
- bonus
- commission
- holiday pay
- sick pay.

1.3   Deductions

Once the gross pay for each employee has been determined then a number of deductions from this amount will be made to arrive at the net pay for the employee. Net pay is the amount that the employee will actually receive.

Some deductions are compulsory or statutory:

- Income tax in the form of PAYE
- National Insurance Contributions (NIC) which can also be referred to as social security payments.

- Other deductions are at the choice of the employer or employee and are therefore non-statutory:

- Save as you earn

- Give as you earn

- Pension contributions.

1.4 Payment of wages or salaries

Once the net pay has been determined then each employee must be paid the correct amount, by the most appropriate method at the correct time.

1.5 Payments to external agencies

As you will see later in the chapter employers deduct income tax and NIC from each employee's wages or salaries and the employer must also pay its own NIC contribution for each employee. This is done by making payment to HM Revenue and Customs on a regular basis and this is therefore another responsibility of the payroll function.

1.6 Accounting for wages and salaries

Finally once the wages and salaries for the period have been paid then the amounts involved must be correctly entered into the ledger accounts.

1.7 Accuracy and confidentiality

Whilst carrying out all of these calculations and functions it is obviously important that the calculations are made with total accuracy. Not only is the amount that each individual will be paid dependent upon these calculations but there is a statutory duty to make the correct deductions from gross pay and to pay these over to HM Revenue and Customs.

Payroll staff deal with confidential and sensitive information about individuals such as the rate of pay for an individual. It is of the utmost importance that such details are kept confidential and are not made public nor allowed to be accessed by unauthorised personnel.

2 Gross pay

2.1 Introduction

Gross pay is the total amount payable to the employee before any deductions have been made. Gross pay can be made up of many different elements, e.g.

- normal wages or salary
- overtime
- shift payments
- bonus
- commission
- holiday pay
- statutory sick pay (or SSP); and
- statutory maternity pay (or SMP).

2.2 Wages and salaries

These are fairly straightforward. Employees will have an agreed monthly, weekly or hourly rate.

The monthly and weekly rates will not need any further calculations.

However, for hourly paid employees calculations will be needed for the total earnings. The source of this information might be clock cards.

 Definition

A clock card is a card which records the hours worked by an employee.

As the employee arrives or leaves they put their card in the slot of a special clock. The mechanism inside the clock stamps the time on the card.

The payroll clerk would transfer the number of hours worked onto special calculation sheets.

2.3 Overtime and shift payments

These need to be identified so that the payroll clerk can calculate the amount payable.

Overtime is hours worked which are over and above the agreed number of weekly or monthly hours for that employee. For example, it may be agreed that an employee has a standard working week of 38 hours. If he works for 42 hours in a week then he has worked 4 hours of overtime.

Overtime or shifts worked might be recorded on:

- clock cards
- timesheets; or
- authorisation forms (signed by the employee's supervisor).

Some employees are paid at a higher rate for overtime. They might be paid at one and a half times the normal rate. This is called time and a half.

Twice the normal rate is double time.

Some employees might be paid premium rates or bonuses for working certain shifts.

2.4 Bonus and commission payments

The business may pay certain employees a bonus. This bonus may be for achieving a particular target.

Company directors often receive a bonus if the company achieves certain profits.

Companies with a large number of sales representatives may pay their sales representatives a commission as part of their salary. This commission is based on the value of the sales they make.

For instance, a salesman might be paid a basic salary of £10,000 a year plus a 1% commission on sales that he makes.

2.5 Holiday pay

Most employers pay their employees even while they are on holiday.

If the employee is paid monthly, then there is no problem. The employee is paid the usual amount at the normal time.

If the employee is paid weekly, they would prefer to be paid for the holiday period in advance. This means that if the employee is taking two weeks' holiday they will have to be paid three weeks' wages at once.

2.6 Statutory sick pay (SSP) and statutory maternity pay (SMP)

For your assessment, you will really only need to be concerned about basic wages and salaries, overtime and bonus payments.

If there is a reference to SSP or SMP you will be told how to deal with it.

3 Income tax

3.1 Introduction

Everybody in the UK has a potential liability to pay tax on their income.

Individuals pay **income tax**. The rate of tax depends on the amount of their income.

Definition

Income tax is a tax on individuals' income.

3.2 Tax-free income

Everybody is entitled to some tax-free income.

This tax-free sum is known as the personal allowance.

Definition

The personal allowance is an amount which an individual is allowed to earn tax-free.

3.3 How income tax is paid

Employees in the UK pay their income tax through the **PAYE** (or Pay As You Earn) **scheme**.

 Definition

The PAYE scheme is a national scheme whereby employers withhold tax and other deductions from their employees' wages and salaries when they are paid. The deductions are then paid over monthly to HM Revenue and Customs by the employer.

Looking at tax alone, the main advantages of this scheme are:

- employees pay the tax as they earn the income

- most people do not have to complete a tax return unless they have several different sources of income

- employers act as unpaid tax collectors (this is a serious responsibility and they can be fined for mistakes); and

- the government receives a steady stream of revenue throughout the year.

 Activity 1

Under the PAYE Scheme who pays over the income tax to the Collector of Taxes?

A   The employee

B   The employer

C   The government

D   The Inspector of Taxes

4 National Insurance contributions

4.1 What is National Insurance?

National Insurance is a state scheme which pays certain benefits including:

- retirement pensions
- widow's allowances and pensions
- jobseeker's allowance
- incapacity benefit; and
- maternity allowance.

The scheme is run by HM Revenue and Customs.

The scheme is funded by people who are currently in employment.

Most people in employment (including partners in partnerships, and sole traders) who have earnings above a certain level must pay National Insurance contributions.

4.2 Types of National Insurance contributions

Both the employer and the employee pay National Insurance contributions.

(a) Employees' National Insurance contributions

The employer deducts National Insurance contributions from an employee's weekly wage or monthly salary, and pays these to HM Revenue and Customs. Income tax and National Insurance contributions are both taxes on income, but they have different historical origins and are calculated in different ways. Employees' National Insurance is now, however, similar to income tax in many respects, and is really a form of income tax with another name.

Like income tax, employees' NI contributions are deducted from pay. The amount of the contributions an employee pays is linked to his or her earnings, and is obtained by reference to National Insurance tables supplied by HM Revenue and Customs.

You are not required to know how to use NI tables.

(b) Employer's National Insurance contributions

In addition to deducting employees' National Insurance contributions from each employee's wages or salary, an employer is required to pay the employer's National Insurance contributions for each employee. The amount payable for each employee is linked to the size of his or her earnings.

Employer's National Insurance contributions are therefore an employment tax. They are not deducted from the employee's gross pay. They are an additional cost of payroll to the employer, paid for by the employer rather than the employee.

5 Other deductions

5.1 Statutory deductions

So far we have looked at two types of deductions which the employer has to make from their employee's gross pay **by law**. These are **income tax** and **National Insurance** contributions. These are statutory deductions.

5.2 Non-statutory deductions

The employee may also choose to have further deductions made from their gross pay. These include:

- superannuation (pension) payments.

- payments under the **save as you earn scheme**; this is a strictly governed scheme offered by some employers that allows you to save a regular amount each pay day. You would use this money to buy shares in the company at a later date.

- payments under the **give as you earn scheme**; this scheme allows employees to request that their employer withhold a certain amount from their salary and pay it over to a charity, on their behalf.

- other payments, e.g. subscriptions to sports and social clubs and trade unions.

5.3 Summary of deductions and payments

It is time to summarise what deductions the employer makes from the employee's gross salary, and to whom the employer makes the various payments.

To process the payroll an employer must, **for each employee**:

- calculate the gross wage or salary for the period

- calculate the income tax payable out of these earnings

- calculate the employee's National Insurance contributions that are deductible

- calculate any non-statutory deductions

- calculate the employer's National Insurance contributions.

The employer must then:

- make the payment of net pay to each employee

- make the payments of all the non-statutory deductions from pay to the appropriate other organisations

- pay the employee's PAYE, the employee's NIC and the employer's NIC to HM Revenue and Customs for all employees.

Example

John earns £12,000 per annum. His PAYE, NIC and other deductions and the employer's NIC for the month of May 20X4 are:

	£
PAYE	125
Employee's NIC	80
Contribution to personal pension scheme	50
Employer's NIC	85

Calculate:

(a)   John's net pay

(b)   the cost to the employer of employing John

(c)   the amounts to be paid to the various organisations involved.

Solution

			Paid by employer to:
Gross pay per month		1,000	
Less: PAYE	125		HMRC
Employee's NIC	80		HMRC
Personal pension	50		Pension company
		(255)	
Net pay		745	John
Employer's NIC	85		HMRC

(a)   John's net pay is £745.

(b)   The cost of employing John is (1,000 + 85) = £1,085.

(c)   The pension company is paid £50 by the employer.

HM Revenue and Customs is paid £290 by the employer:

	£
PAYE	125
Employee's NIC	80
Employer's NIC	85
	290

Where there are many employees, the employer will pay the amounts calculated per (c) above for all employees to HM Revenue and Customs with one cheque.

6 Payroll accounting procedures

6.1 Introduction

The accounting for wages and salaries is based upon two fundamental principles:

- the accounts must reflect the full cost to the employer of employing someone (which is their gross pay plus the employer's NI contribution)

- the accounts must show the creditor for PAYE and NIC that must be paid over to HM Revenue and Customs on a regular basis, usually monthly.

We therefore need two accounts, plus a third control account.

(a) The wages expense account which shows the full cost of employing the staff.

(b) The PAYE/NIC account which shows the amount to be paid to HM Revenue and Customs.

(c) The wages and salaries control account which acts as a control over the entries in the accounts. There are different ways of writing up this control account, but we will use this account to control the gross pay and deductions from the employees, plus employers' NIC.

6.2 Double entry

The double entry reflects these two fundamentals and uses three main accounts – the wages and salaries control account, the wages expense account and the PAYE/NIC account.

1 The gross wages and salaries of the employees (i.e. wages/salaries + PAYE + employees NI) are accounted for:

Dr Wages expense account
   Cr Wages and salaries control account

The control account represents a liability that reflects the business' obligation to pay wages and related balances.

2 The net wages and salaries are paid to employees:

Dr Wages and salaries control account
   Cr Bank account

3   The employee's PAYE and NI (as calculated in step 1) are
     transferred to a PAYE/NI liability account that reflects the amount
     due to HMRC:

    Dr   Wages and salaries control account
        Cr   PAYE/NIC account

4   The employer's NI contributions are calculated and recognised in the
     appropriate HMRC liability account. This is recognised below as a
     two step process that includes the wages and salaries control
     account:

    Dr   Wages expense account
        Cr   Wages and salaries control account

    Dr   Wages and salaries control account
        Cr   PAYE/NIC account

Example

The wages and salaries information for an organisation for a week is
given as follows:

	£
Gross wages	34,000
PAYE deducted	7,400
NIC deducted	5,600
Net pay	21,000
Employer's NIC	7,800

Write up the relevant ledger accounts in the general ledger to reflect
this.

Solution

Wages and salaries control account

		£				£
2	Bank account	21,000	1	Wages expense account		34,000
			4	Wages expense account (ers NIC)		7,800
3	PAYE/NIC account (PAYE)	7,400				
3	PAYE/NIC account (ees NIC)	5,600				
4	PAYE/NIC account (ers NIC)	7,800				
		41,800				41,800

Wages expense account

	£		£
1 Wages and salaries control	34,000		
4 Wages and salaries control			
(ers NIC)	7,800	Bal c/d	41,800
	41,800		41,800

PAYE/NIC account

	£			£
		3	Wages and salaries control	7,400
		3	Wages and salaries control	5,600
Bal c/d	20,800	4	Wages and salaries control	7,800
	20,800			20,800
		Bal b/d		20,800

6.3 Commentary on the solution

(a) The wages and salaries control account controls the total gross wages plus the employer's NIC and the amounts paid to the employees and other organisations (e.g.HM Revenue and Customs for PAYE and NIC). The total gross pay is taken from the company payroll as are the deductions. Assuming that the company payroll schedule reconciles and no errors are made when posting the payroll totals to the account, the account should have a nil balance.

(b) The wages expense account shows the total cost to the employer of employing the workforce (£41,800). This is the gross wages cost plus the employer's own NIC cost.

(c) The PAYE/NIC account shows the amount due to be paid over to HM Revenue and Customs, i.e. PAYE, employee's NIC plus the employer's NIC.

Activity 2

Given below is a summary of an organisation's payroll details for a week. You are required to prepare the journals to enter the figures in the general ledger accounts and to state the balance on the control account, once the net amount has been paid to the employees.

	£
Gross wages	54,440
PAYE	11,840
Employee's NIC	8,960
Employer's NIC	12,480

7 Construction Industry Scheme

7.1 Introduction

HM Revenue and Customs introduced the Construction Industry Scheme (referred to as CIS) and it sets out the rules of how a payment to a subcontractor for construction work must be handled by a contractor in the construction industry.

7.2 Rules of the scheme

A CIS contractor needs to register with HMRC and must follow certain rules to ensure that any payment to a subcontractor within the scheme is dealt with correctly.

The CIS contractor must comply with the rules listed below:

- Verify the subcontractor with HMRC.
- Pay the subcontractor correctly – making deductions if necessary.
- Pay over deductions to HMRC.
- Provide subcontractors with deduction statements.
- Send monthly returns to HMRC.
- Keep proper records of the payments.

7.3 Verifying the subcontractor

Before an individual can be paid for work under the CIS scheme, the contractor must confirm that the individual is self-employed and not an employee and also needs to verify them with HMRC.

CIS only covers self-employed workers. The verification process simply means checking with HMRC that the subcontractor is registered with them. HMRC will then inform the contractor how the subcontractor may be paid.

7.4 Paying subcontractors and making deductions under CIS

Once a subcontractor has been verified by HMRC, they will inform the contractor how the subcontractor can be paid. This could be in one of three ways:

- Gross with no deductions from the payment.

- Net, after a deduction of tax at the standard rate of 20%.

- Net, after a deduction of tax at the higher rate of 30%.

In order to be paid gross the subcontractor must be registered with HMRC to receive gross payments.

If a subcontractor is not registered for gross payments, but can be verified by HMRC, then the standard rate deduction will apply.

If HMRC cannot verify the subcontractor then they will issue a special reference and a deduction at the higher rate will apply.

7.5 Making a deduction

The subcontractor will issue an invoice to the contractor in respect of work carried out.

To calculate any necessary deduction, the following procedures need to be adhered to.

- Start with the gross value of the invoice; and deduct any VAT charged on the invoice.

- Then deduct any of the following charged on the invoice: materials, consumables, fuel used (except travelling), plant hire, manufacturing or pre-fabricating materials: if the subcontractor is not registered for VAT, also deduct any VAT included in the price of these items.

- Apply either the standard rate (20%) or the special rate (30%) to the amount left.

- Finally keep a record of how each payment has been determined and paid.

7.6 Paying over deductions to HMRC

HMRC will set up a payment scheme as soon as a subcontractor registers with them.

If the contractor already has employees then HMRC will amend their current PAYE scheme to a PAYE/CIS scheme, and CIS deductions will be added to PAYE/NICs that are currently being paid over to HMRC.

One single payment should then be made to HMRC no later than the 19th of the month (22nd if paying electronically) following the end of the tax month.

 Example

Crescent is a contractor and often engages subcontract labour.

On January 7th 20X4 they receive an invoice from Karl Heyes, a subcontractor. On verification with HMRC, a rate of 20% applies.

They settle this invoice on January 31st 20X4.

The invoice contained the following information:

Gross amount including VAT: £720.

The VAT was therefore £720 × 20/120 = £120.

The charges before VAT were:

	£
Labour	450
Materials	50
Plant hire	100
	___
Net pay	600
	___

The CIS deduction would be:

	£
Gross	720
VAT	120
Net	600
Less: Materials	50
Less: Plant hire	100
Net	450

CIS tax deduction 20%: £450 × 20/100 = £90.

The payment made to the subcontractor by Crescent would therefore be: £720 – £90 = £630.

Double Entry procedure:

When the invoice is received from Karl Heyes, a creditor will be recognised:

Dr Subcontractor costs	£600	
Dr VAT control account	£120	
Cr Karl Hayes (purchase ledger)		£720

When Karl Heyes is paid, Crescent will pay him the value of the invoice less the CIS tax deduction:

Dr Karl Heyes (Purchase Ledger)	£720	
Cr Bank		£630
Cr PAYE/NIC/CIS Control (HMRC)		£90

Finally, Crescent will pay over the CIS tax deducted to HMRC:

| Dr PAYE/NIC/CIS Control (HMRC) | £90 | |
| Cr Bank | | £90 |

Example

On 2nd February X14 Crescent received a credit note from Ray Staniland, a subcontractor whom they often engage. Invoices from this subcontractor are subject to a CIS deduction of 20%.

The credit note contained the following information:

	£
Labour	100
VAT	20
Gross	120

The tax deduction on the original invoice against which the credit note has been issued would have been: £100 × 20% = £20.

Double Entry procedure:

Firstly, the credit note will be entered in the purchase ledger:

Dr Ray Staniland (purchase ledger)	£120	
Cr VAT control account		£20
Cr Subcontractor costs		£100

We then need to adjust for the CIS deduction made on the original invoice:

Dr PAYE/NIC/CIS Control (HMRC)	£20	
Cr Ray Staniland (Purchase Ledger)		£20

The £20 tax would then be set off against any deductions due to be paid over to HMRC for the current period.

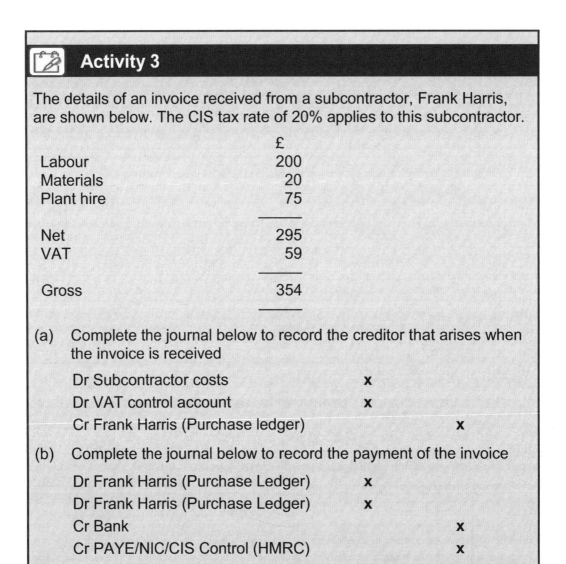

Activity 3

The details of an invoice received from a subcontractor, Frank Harris, are shown below. The CIS tax rate of 20% applies to this subcontractor.

	£
Labour	200
Materials	20
Plant hire	75
Net	295
VAT	59
Gross	354

(a) Complete the journal below to record the creditor that arises when the invoice is received

Dr Subcontractor costs	X	
Dr VAT control account	X	
Cr Frank Harris (Purchase ledger)		X

(b) Complete the journal below to record the payment of the invoice

Dr Frank Harris (Purchase Ledger)	X	
Dr Frank Harris (Purchase Ledger)	X	
Cr Bank		X
Cr PAYE/NIC/CIS Control (HMRC)		X

8 Summary

This chapter has introduced the fairly complex taxation elements that affect the payment of wages and salaries. You need to understand in principle how PAYE and NI works and be able to calculate the net pay to employees given the PAYE and NI deductions. However, you do not need to be able to use HM Revenue and Customs tables. Most importantly you do need to understand how wages and salaries are accounted for in the general ledger.

The CIS scheme is rather complex, however at this level in your studies you will only be required to deal with a subcontractor's invoice and its subsequent payment and the procedure to deal with a credit note.

Answers to chapter activities

 Activity 1

B   The employer

 Activity 2

1   Dr   Wages expense account

     Cr   Wages and salaries control account

with the gross wages of £54,440

2   Dr   Wages expense account

     Cr   Wages and salaries control account

with the employer's NI contributions of £12,480

3   Dr   Wages and salaries control account

     Cr   PAYE/NIC account

with the PAYE of £11,840, and with the employee's NIC of £8,960 and with the employer's NIC of £12,480

Once the net amount to be paid to the employee has been posted by debiting the wages and salaries control account and crediting the bank account with £33,640, the balance on the control account will be nil.

Activity 3

(a) The journal to record the creditor will be:

Dr Subcontractor costs	£295	
Dr VAT control account	£59	
Cr Frank Harris (Purchase ledger)		£354

(b) The journal to record the payment will be:

Dr Frank Harris (Purchase Ledger)	£314	
Dr Frank Harris (Purchase Ledger)	£40	
Cr Bank		£314
Cr PAYE/NICs/CIS Control (HMRC)		£40

Note that the CIS tax deduction will be calculated on the invoice value, excluding VAT, and after deducting the material and plant hire costs.

The CIS deduction will be:

	£
Gross	354
VAT	59
Net	295
Less: Materials	20
Less: Plant hire	75
Net	200

CIS tax deduction 20%: £200 × 20/100 = £40.

The payment made to the subcontractor would therefore be: £354 – £40 = £314.

9 Test your knowledge

 Workbook Activity 4

An employee has gross pay for a week of £368.70. The PAYE for the week is £46.45, the employer's NIC £30.97 and the employee's NIC £23.96.

What is the employee's net pay for the week?

 Workbook Activity 5

Given below is the wages book for the month of May 20X1 for a small business with four employees.

Wages book

Employee number	Gross pay	PAYE	Employee's NIC	Employer's NIC	Net pay
	£	£	£	£	£
001	1,200	151	78	101	971
002	1,400	176	91	118	1,133
003	900	113	58	76	729
004	1,550	195	101	130	1,254
	5,050	635	328	425	4,087

You are required to use the totals from the wages book for the month to write up journal entries to record:

- The wages expense
- The HM Revenue and Customs liability
- The net wages paid to the employees.

You can then record these entries in the ledger accounts on the following page.

Gross wages control account			
	£		£

Wages expense account			
	£		£
30 April Balance b/d	23,446		

HM Revenue and Customs account			
	£		£
19 May CPB	760	30 April Balance b/d	760

Cash based accounting

Introduction

In this chapter we will consider how small businesses can use a cash based accounting system to correctly report income and expenditure for tax purposes. We will then look at the security issues relating to bank accounts.

CONTENTS
1   The analysed cash book for small businesses
2   Writing up the analysed cash book
3   Bank security

1 The analysed cash book for small businesses

1.1 Introduction

An analysed cash book is often used by small businesses and is, other than its source documents, its principal accounting record which simply focuses on actual receipts and actual payments.

1.2 Reporting for taxation using the cash based system

In recent times the HMRC has introduced 'simpler taxation for the simplest small business' – the cash based system – whereby small businesses can report their activities based on cash received and cash paid for expenses.

Such an accounting system, based on the analysed cash book, will provide all the information on the trading activity required on the submission of a Self-Assessment tax return to HMRC.

1.3 Eligibility for the 'cash basis' scheme

HMRC has said that a move to the 'cash basis' scheme will help small businesses simplify their accounting processes and save them time and money.

Sole Traders and Partnerships with an annual income of less than £82,000 (at the date of writing) can supply details of cash received and cash paid on allowable expenses in a tax year rather than prepare accounts on the accruals basis.

Limited Companies and Limited Liability Partnerships cannot adopt the cash based system for reporting to HMRC.

The scheme is designed to suit the needs of those small businesses mainly providing services as tradesmen. This may include: taxi drivers, painters and decorators, gardeners, hairdressers, window cleaners, plumbers, electricians and photographers.

If a business enters the cash based scheme it can continue until the income reaches double the VAT threshold, currently £164,000.

The scheme allows the use of 'simplified expenses'. This will involve the use of flat rate allowances for actual business expenses for items such as: vehicle expenses (for business mileage) and the use of part of the home for business purposes.

The Federation of Small Businesses estimates that the scheme could apply to some 3 million small businesses. The Institute of Chartered Accountants in England and Wales (ICAEW) have however said that a lack of formal accounts – a Profit and Loss Account and a Balance Sheet – may make it difficult for some small businesses to access borrowing.

2 Writing up the analysed cash book

2.1 Layout

The following is an example of an analysed cash book for a sole trader operating as a joiner. The cash receipts are recorded on the left hand side of the cash book and the cash payments are recorded on the right hand side of the cash book.

Note: Here, Tools would also include consumables, and Admin includes: Telephone and Postage, Office expenses and Advertising.

CASH RECEIPTS

Date	Narrative	Details	Cash £	Bank £	Sales £	Misc £
		TOTALS				

CASH PAYMENTS

Date	Narrative	Details	Cash £	Bank £	Materials £	Motor expenses £	Tools £	Wages £	Admin £	Drawings £	Fixed assets £
		TOTALS									

Example

Nigel is a Master Joiner and his activities for the first week in January X014 were:

January 1 Cash in Hand £170.00, Bank Current Account balance £2,100.00

January 3 Received a cheque from Mrs Davenport for £450.00 for work done and banked the cheque

January 4 Paid for diesel £9.50 in cash

January 5 Purchased materials from Nobles Ltd for £750.00 paid by cheque

January 6 Paid mobile phone bill by Direct Debit £17.00

January 7 Paid the HMRC personal Income Tax £1,100.00 by cheque (Drawings)

January 7 Paid £150.00 cash into the bank

January 7 Paid £5 cash for saw blades

The entries in the analysed cash book would be:

CASH RECEIPTS						
Date	Narrative	Details	Cash £	Bank £	Sales £	Misc £
1.1.X4	Balance b/d		170.00	2,100.00		
3.1.X4	Mrs Davenport	Cheque		450.00	450.00	
7.1.X4	Cash banked	contra		150.00		
	TOTALS		170.00	2,700.00	450.00	

CASH PAYMENTS											
Date	Narrative	Details	Cash £	Bank £	Materials £	Motor expenses £	Tools £	Wages £	Admin £	Drawings £	Fixed assets £
4.1.X4	Diesel		9.50			9.50					
5.1.X4	Nobles	Chq		750.00	750.00						
6.1.X4	Mobile	DD		17.00					17.00		
7.1.X4	HMRC	Chq		1,100.00						1,100.00	
7.1.X4	Bank	contra	150.00								
7.1.X4	Blades		5.00				5.00				
		TOTALS	164.50	1,867.00	750.00	9.50	5.00		17.00	1,100.00	

Most of the entries are self-explanatory other than the contra entry when cash is transferred to the bank. It is clear that the £150.00 affects both sides of the cash book as it is shown as a cash payment and a receipt to the bank.

To calculate the closing cash and bank balances at the end of the week, total the columns for cash and bank on both sides of the analysed cash book, compare the totals and determine the difference:

Receipts side: Cash £170.00, Bank £2,700.

Payments side: Cash £164.50, Bank £1,867.00.

Closing balances:

(£170.00 – £164.50) = Cash £5.50

(£2,700.00 – £1,867.00) = Bank £833.00

At the end of each month the analysis columns would be totalled to give a full analysis of actual expenditure incurred.

The cash and bank columns would be totalled and balances determined in the same way as a ledger account would be totalled and a balance brought down in a double entry system.

3 Bank security

3.1 Introduction

It is now often the case that even a small business will use online and/or telephone banking and so it is highly important that issues relating to security are observed.

3.2 Rules for pin numbers and internet/telephone banking passwords

If passwords are used for authentication in a business for internet/ telephone banking, the safety of the access privileges will depend on their correct use and the following rules should be observed:

It must not be possible to guess the password/pin number as easily as names, motor vehicle licence numbers, birth dates or the like.

The password should consist of at least one non-letter character (special character or number) and have at least six characters. The selection of trivial passwords (BBBBBB, 123456) must be prevented.

Any preset passwords/pin numbers must be replaced by individually selected, unique passwords.

The password/pin number must be kept secret and should only be known personally to the user.

The password/pin number must be changed regularly, e.g. every 90 days. This will ensure that if an unauthorised person has obtained it, he or she will have limited use.

The password/pin number should be altered if it has, or may have, come to the knowledge of unauthorised persons.

After any alteration of the password/pin number, previous passwords/pin numbers should no longer be used.

 Activity 1

You have been asked for suggestions for a checklist of control procedures to remind authorised users about password/pin number security for online banking. What suggestions would you make?

3.3 Payment value restriction

Bank accounts should be set up with a maximum daily limit applicable to the amount of cash that can be withdrawn using a chequebook or debit card. A maximum daily limit can also be set for payments made using the Faster Payments Scheme or for online bank transfers.

These limits will all help prevent the misuse of funds that could occur as a result of one person be able to withdraw large sums of cash in one transaction.

3.4 Dual signatures

In order to prevent one person from having control over cheque payments, as well as to avoid the fraudulent use of cheques, business bank accounts should be set up so that two signatures are required on cheques.

The business will need to decide on whether all cheque payments need to be signed by two people or whether only cheques exceeding a set amount require dual signatures. For example, a charity may decide that dual signatures are required on all cheque payments to prevent misuse of funds, whereas a small business may decide that only cheques over £500 require dual signatures.

Where organisations use online banking, the online bank account can also be set up so that dual authorisation is needed for payments made online. Where this system is in place, each online signatory will have their own login details and will be able to authorise the payment separately to the other authorised signatory. This will then prevent one person from having control over the online bank account.

4 Summary

The use of an analysed cash book is often referred to as a single entry system, meaning simply that it is not part of a double entry system of accounting.

Such a system may be maintained manually using an analysed cash book but can easily be adapted to the use of a series of spreadsheets.

All organisations with a bank account with need to consider the security issues discussed in this chapter: this will help prevent the misuse of funds by individuals with access to the bank account.

5 Answers to chapter activities

Activity 1

Some of the suggestions that would be included in a checklist for password security are:

Passwords are meant to be secret and not revealed to anyone else.

Never write it down.

Change your password regularly or if you suspect someone knows it.

Do not choose an obvious password such as your name, or in the case of a PIN, your date or year of birth.

Try to avoid onlookers seeing you key in your password.

For keyboard passwords, choose keys that require both hands rather than one or two finger easy runs along a pattern of the keys.

6 Test your knowledge

Workbook Activity 2

Thomas is a painter and decorator. His business receipts and payments for March 20X4 are listed below:

March 1 Cash in Hand £100.00, Bank Current Account balance £1,450.00

March 5 Paid for petrol £20.00 in cash

March 11 Purchased paint from Deluxe Ltd for £550.00 paid by cheque

March 17 Received a cheque for £800.00 from Mrs Harrison for work decorating work

March 25 Received cash of £200.00 from Mr Clifford for painting work

March 28 Paid a cheque for £400 into his personal bank account (Drawings)

March 31 Paid £20 cash to Pens R Us for ink cartridges

Requirement:

(a) Enter the transactions for March 20X4 in Thomas's cash book shown below.

(b) Calculate the closing cash and bank balances at 31 March 20X4.

CASH RECEIPTS

Date	Narrative	Details	Cash £	Bank £	Sales £	Misc £
		TOTALS				

CASH PAYMENTS								
Date	Narrative	Details	Cash £	Bank £	Materials £	Motor £	Drawings £	Stationery £
		TOTALS						

Contract law and current legislation

Introduction

In this chapter we will consider the basic elements of a contract, the basic principles of the Data Protection Act and other current legislation relevant to the bookkeeper.

CONTENTS

1 Essential elements of a valid contract

2 Offer

3 Acceptance

4 Consideration

5 Misrepresentation

6 Performance and breaches

7 Data protection

8 What is money laundering and terrorist financing?

9 Procedures for reporting money laundering

10 Tipping off

11 Bribery

12 Health and safety in your workplace

13 Health and safety legislation and regulations

1 Essential elements of a valid contract

1.1 Introduction

 Definition

A contract is an agreement entered into voluntarily by two parties or more with the intention of creating a legal obligation.

The following elements are needed to form a valid simple contract:

- Agreement i.e. offer and acceptance
- Consideration
- Intention to create legal relations
- Capacity and legality.

1.2 Form of the contract

General rule

A simple contract can take any form. It may be written, or oral, or inferred from the conduct of the parties. Most contracts are simple contracts.

Exceptions

Some contracts must be made in a particular form (usually written). For example; contracts for the sale of land must be in writing. This is common where a lot is at stake or where the contract is set to last for a long time.

1.3 Contents of a contract

Express terms

Express terms are those specifically mentioned and agreed to by the parties at the time of contracting, either in writing or orally. They must be clear for them to be enforceable.

Implied terms

Where an issue arises upon which the parties have not made an express provision, it may be necessary for an implied term to be used to resolve the matter. These will usually be decided upon by a court.

In some instances, various statutes have provided for implied terms in certain types of contract which will apply either irrespective of the wishes of the parties or if the parties have failed to cover that particular point appropriately.

Implied terms are required to overcome omissions in contracts and give effect to the intentions of the parties involved in that contract. Such obligations will be imposed by the courts as it will be considered that the parties would have reasonably agreed to the terms, had they considered the relevant matters.

1.4 Capacity and legality

Each party to a contract must have the legal power to bind itself contractually. For example persons under the age of eighteen (minors) and persons of unsound mind or under the influence of alcohol are limited in their ability to engage in a contract.

The courts will not enforce a contract which is deemed illegal.

1.5 Intention to create legal relations

An agreement will only be recognised as a contract if the parties intended that the agreement should be legally binding. If it is not clear from the contract that the parties intended legal consequences then the law presumes the intention of the parties based on the type of agreement.

With agreements of a friendly, social or domestic nature, the law presumes that, in the absence of strong evidence to the contrary, there is no such intention. Therefore, an arrangement between friends to meet for a meal, or between husband and wife for apportioning housekeeping duties, would not be legally binding contracts.

With business agreements, on the other hand, there is a strong presumption that legal relations are intended. A business agreement would be identified where, for example: one or both contracting parties were a company or business; the agreement was clearly of a commercial nature; or the contract involved money and money was a factor of significance.

2 Offer

2.1 Introduction

 Definition

An offer is a definite and unequivocal statement of willingness to be bound on specified terms without further negotiations.

An offer can be in any form – oral, written or by conduct. However, it is not effective until it has been communicated to the offeree. For example, if a reward is offered for the return of a lost item, it cannot be claimed by someone who did not know of the reward before they returned the item.

An offer can be made to a particular person, to a class of persons or even to the whole world.

2.2 What is not an offer?

Offers must be distinguished from other actions, which may appear to be of a similar nature. The following are not binding offers:

- An invitation to treat
- A statement of selling price in response to a request for information
- A statement of intention to sell.

An invitation to treat is an indication that a person/entity is willing to enter into or continue negotiations but is not yet willing to be bound by the terms mentioned. This includes the invitation to other parties to make an offer; e.g. 'we may be prepared to sell'. Examples include:

- Most advertisements
- Shop window displays
- Goods on shop shelves

Once an offer has been established it must be communicated to the other party to become effective. Until the other party knows of the offer they cannot accept (or reject) it.

2.3 Revocation

An offer cannot continue indefinitely. It may come to an end in a number of ways so that it can no longer be accepted. An offeror may revoke or withdraw their offer at any time up to the moment of acceptance, provided that the revocation is communicated to the offeree.

Revocation may be expressly made or it may be implied by conduct which clearly shows an intention to revoke, for example, by selling goods elsewhere and the other party learning of the sale.

Communication may come directly from the seller or through some other reliable source. Revocation is possible at any time even though there has been a promise to keep the offer open for a specified period. If, however, an 'option' has been bought, that is the other party has given consideration to keep open the offer for a period of time, an early withdrawal will be a breach of this subsidiary contract.

2.4 Rejection

The offeree may reject the offer, again provided that the rejection is communicated to the offeror, since this only becomes effective when the offeror learns of it.

Rejection may take the form of a counteroffer or by attempting to introduce new terms into the agreement.

2.5 Lapse

An offer will lapse if a time limit is fixed for acceptance and this is not adhered to by the offeree. If no time limit is expressly fixed, the offer will lapse after a reasonable time which will depend upon the circumstances.

3 Acceptance

3.1 Introduction

Definition

Acceptance is the unqualified and unconditional assent to the terms of the offer.

Acceptance can be oral, written or by conduct. The offeror can stipulate a mode of acceptance. However, if he merely requests a mode, the offeree is not limited to that mode.

3.2 Communication

As a general rule, acceptance is not effective until it is communicated to the offeror. The **postal rule** is the exception to this rule that acceptance must be communicated. The postal rule states that acceptance is effective as soon as a letter expressing acceptance is posted. There must be evidence of the posting for this rule to be effective.

The postal rule does not apply to almost instantaneous methods of communication, such as email, fax, telephone or telex, where acceptance is only effective when and where it reaches the other party.

4 Consideration

4.1 The basic rule

Every simple contract must be supported by consideration from each party.

 Definition

Consideration is an act or forbearance (or the promise of it) on the part of one party to a contract as the price of the promise made to him by the other party to the contract.

Thus, a contract must be a two-sided affair, each side providing or promising to provide some consideration in exchange for what the other is to provide. This may take the form of an act, a forbearance to act, or a promise.

4.2 Types of consideration

Executory consideration is given where there is an exchange of promises to do something in the future.

Executed consideration means that the consideration is in the form of an act carried out at the time the contract is made.

Consideration must be sufficient but need not be adequate.

Past consideration has no value and therefore is not valid consideration. One party will have provided a benefit (which was in the past). This will then be identified as consideration for a subsequent promise made by another. If a promise is made for work already done, the work cannot constitute consideration for the promise, as its benefit has already been received.

On the other hand, if work is requested or authorised and it is the type of work which is normally paid for, then it may be implied that everyone concerned intended from the outset that the work would be paid for this time. The buyer, in effect, is taken to promise at the outset that he will pay the bill – so long as it is reasonable – in due course.

5 Misrepresentation

5.1 Introduction

During the negotiations preceding a contract, statements may be made with a view to inducing the other party to enter into a contract. For example; when buying a car, statements are often made about the reliability or performance of said vehicle. If any such statement is false and the other party is misled about the true state of affairs, the contract may be void due to misrepresentation.

 Definition

Misrepresentation can be defined as a false statement of fact made by one person to the other before the contract is agreed, made with the view of inducing the other to enter into it.

5.2 Consequences of misrepresentation

If misrepresentation is proved the deceived party may sue for breach of contract. Damages will not be paid if the person liable for misrepresentation can prove that they reasonably believed their statements to be truthful at the time.

In all cases of misrepresentation the contract is said to be voidable at the option of the deceived party. In such cases the contract may be rescinded or ended and the parties restored to their original positions, pre-contract.

A claim for damages is the other possible remedy. This is particularly likely if the claimant can prove that the misrepresentation was made deliberately and fraudulently.

6 Performance and breaches

6.1 Introduction

Performance is the most common way of bringing an end to a contract. Each party must perform precisely what they agreed to do. Anything else would constitute a breach of contract.

6.2 Valid reasons for non-performance

Various valid reasons can be used by a party to justify non-performance of their contractual obligations. These include:

- A new agreement replaces the existing one.

- Frustration of the existing agreement occurs because an event beyond the control of the parties renders the contract meaningless or ridiculous.

- Serious breach by one party where there are valid reasons for refusing to perform obligations.

6.3 Types of breach

There are many ways in which a contract can be broken:

- One party rejects the contract in such a way that it can no longer be performed (e.g. by destroying the object of the contract, i.e. the item for sale).

- One party refuses to proceed with the agreement. The other party can either press for performance of the contract or agree to terminate it.

- Defective performance of the contract (e.g. supplying goods of unsatisfactory quality). The victim in this event can either claim damages or treat the contract as ended.

6.4 Remedies for breach of contract

A breach of contract can either result in that contract being terminated or in monetary awards being made to any victims of that breach. In some instances monetary awards will be inadequate so a court can order the carrying out of specific performances or contractual obligations. If the order is not obeyed then the courts can take further punitive measures against the offender.

A final, equitable method of resolving a breach is an injunction. This is a court order, directed at a specific person, not to break the terms of a specified contract. The injunction can be used as a valid restraint preventing any further breaches of the contract.

 Activity 1

In relation to the law of contract, distinguish between and explain:

(a)   a term and a mere representation

(b)   express and implied terms.

 Activity 2

Briefly explain the meaning of the following terms in the law of contract:

(a)   an invitation to treat, compared with an offer for sale

(b)   revocation of an offer

(c)   the postal rule for acceptance of an offer.

---

7   Data protection

7.1   Introduction

The Data Protection Act 1998 regulates the use of 'personal data' in the United Kingdom.

7.2   Key principles

We will briefly review over the key principles of the Act.

- Data may only be used for specific purposes for which it was collected.

- Data must not be disclosed to other parties without the consent of the individual whom the information is about, unless there is legislation or another overriding legitimate reason to share the information. An example is the prevention or the detection of criminal activity. It is an offence for other parties to obtain this personal data without having authorisation.

- Individuals have a right of access to the information that is held about them, although this is subject to certain exceptions such as the prevention or the detection of criminal activity.

- Personal information may be kept for no longer than is deemed necessary. In addition, the information must be kept up to date.

- Personal information may not be sent outside the EEA (European Economic Area) unless the individual whom the information is about has consented or there is adequate protection in place such as a prescribed form of contract to govern the transmission of the data.

- Subject to some exceptions for organisations that only do very simple processing, and for domestic use, all entities that process personal information must register with the Information Commissioner's Office.

- The departments of a company that are holding personal information are required to have adequate security measures in place. These measures may be technical, for example using firewalls, and organisational for example staff training.

- Subjects have the right to have factually incorrect information corrected. It must be noted that this does not extend to matters of opinion.

8 What is money laundering and terrorist financing?

8.1 Money laundering

> ### 🔍 Definitions
>
> **Money laundering** is the process by which criminally obtained money or other assets (criminal property) are exchanged for 'clean' money or other assets with no obvious link to their criminal origins. It also covers money, however come by, which is used to fund terrorism.
>
> **Criminal property** is property which was obtained as a result of criminal conduct and the person knows or suspects that it was obtained from such conduct. It may take any form, including money or money's worth, securities, tangible property and intangible property.

In simple terms:

- Criminals make money through illegal actions.

- This money can be traced by the police so criminals try and stop it being tracked by buying and selling valuable items.

- The proceeds are constantly being re-invested in something else and it becomes very difficult to trace the money.

- 'Dirty cash' becomes a nice clean cheque.

There are three acknowledged phases to money laundering:

- **Placement**

  Cash generated from crime is placed in the financial system, for example paid into a bank account. This is the point when proceeds of crime are most apparent and at risk of detection.

- **Layering**

  Once proceeds of crime are in the financial system, layering obscures their origins by passing the money through complex transactions. These often involve different entities like companies and trusts and can take place in multiple jurisdictions.

- **Integration**

  Once the origin of the funds has been obscured, the criminal is able to make the funds reappear as legitimate funds or assets. They will invest funds in legitimate businesses or other forms of investment such as property.

Activities related to money laundering include:

- Acquiring, using or possessing criminal property.

- Handling the proceeds of crimes such as theft, fraud and tax evasion.

- Being knowingly involved in any way with criminal or terrorist property.

- Entering into arrangements to facilitate laundering criminal or terrorist property.

- Investing the proceeds of crimes in other financial products.

- Investing the proceeds of crimes through the acquisition of property/assets.

- Transferring criminal property.

8.2 Terrorist financing

 Definitions

Terrorism is the use or threat of action designed to influence government, or to intimidate any section of the public, or to advance a political, religious or ideological cause where the action would involve violence, threats to health and safety, damage to property or disruption of electronic systems.

Terrorist financing is fund raising, possessing or dealing with property or facilitating someone else to do so, when intending, knowing or suspecting or having reasonable cause to suspect that it is intended for the purposes of terrorism.

Terrorist property is money or property likely to be used for terrorist purposes or the proceeds of commissioning or carrying out terrorist acts.

The definition of 'terrorist property' means that all dealings with funds or property which are likely to be used for the purposes of terrorism, even if the funds are 'clean' in origin, is a terrorist financing offence.

Money laundering involves the proceeds of crime whereas terrorist financing may involve both legitimate property and the proceeds of crime.

8.3 What are the money laundering and terrorist financing offences?

Anyone can commit a money laundering offence.

However, the Proceeds Of Crime Act (POCA) and the Terrorism Act (TA) include additional offences which can be committed by **individuals working in the regulated sector,** that is by people providing specified professional services such as accountancy.

This means that an **accountant** (i.e. an ICB member in practice) will be personally liable for breaching POCA and/or TA if he or she provides accountancy services while turning a 'blind eye' to a client's suspect dealings.

The Money Laundering Regulation (MLR) imposes duties on 'relevant persons' (sole traders and firms (not employees) operating within the regulated sector) to establish and maintain practice, policies and procedures to detect and deter activities relating to money laundering and terrorist financing. It is the sole trader or firm which will be liable therefore for any breach of the MLR.

The practice, policies and procedures required by the MLR of accountants include:

- Customer Due Diligence on clients

- reporting money laundering/terrorist financing

- record keeping.

Materiality or **de minimis** exceptions are not available in relation to either money laundering or terrorist financing offences – meaning no amount is too small not to bother about.

 Definition

'**de minimis**' means '**considered trivial**'.

In this context it means that all potential offences must be reported as no amount is too small to be of consequence.

A person commits a money laundering offence if he/she:

- Conceals, disguises, converts or transfers criminal property, or removes criminal property from England and Wales, or from Scotland or from Northern Ireland.

- Enters into or becomes concerned in an arrangement which he knows or suspects facilitates (by whatever means) the acquisition, retention, use or control of criminal property.

- Acquires, uses or has possession of criminal property except where adequate consideration was given for the property.

Conviction of any of these offences is punishable by up to 14 years imprisonment and/or an unlimited fine.

8.4   Money laundering regulation

UK anti-money laundering regime requirements are set out in the:

- Proceeds of Crime Act 2002 (POCA)

- The Money Laundering Regulations 2007 (2007 Regulations)

- The Terrorism Act 2000 (TA 2000) and the Terrorism Act 2006 (TA 2006).

The UK legislation on money laundering and terrorist financing applies to the proceeds of conduct that is a criminal offence in the UK and also to most conduct occurring elsewhere that would have been an offence if it had taken place in the UK.

9 Procedure for reporting money laundering

9.1 Summary of key points

- **Suspicious activity reports (SARs)** submitted by the regulated sector are an important source of information used by **NCA** (National Crime Agency) in meeting its harm reduction agenda, and by law enforcement more generally.

- Businesses are required to have procedures which provide for the nomination of a person, this person is called a **Money Laundering Reporting Officer (MRLO)** to receive disclosures (internal reports) and requires that everyone in the business complies with the Proceeds of Crime Act (POCA) in terms of reporting knowledge, suspicion or reasonable grounds for knowledge or suspicion of money laundering.

- Without the presence within an organisation of an MLRO an individual MUST report directly to the National Crime Agency (NCA).

- An individual other than the MLRO fulfils his reporting obligations by making an internal report to his MLRO.

- The MLRO is responsible for assessing internal reports, making further inquiries if need be (either within the business or using public domain information), and, if appropriate, filing SARs with NCA.

- When reports are properly made they are 'protected' under POCA in that nothing in them shall be taken to breach confidentiality.

- A person who considers he may have engaged or is about to engage in money laundering, should make an 'authorised' disclosure. Such a disclosure, provided it is made before the act is carried out, or is made as soon as possible on the initiative of that person after the act is done and with good reason being shown for the delay, may provide a defence against charges of money laundering. When properly made such reports shall not be taken to breach confidentiality.

9.2   An accountant's duty to report

POCA and TA impose an obligation on accountants (individuals within the regulated sector, including those involved in providing accountancy services to clients i.e. ICB members in practice), to submit in defined circumstances:

- An internal report to a Money Laundering Reporting Officer (MLRO), by those employed in a group practice.

- A Suspicious Activity Report (SAR) to the National Crime Agency (NCA), by sole practitioners and MLROs.

There are two circumstances when a required disclosure in an internal report or a SAR, collectively referred to below as a report, must be made by an accountant:

1   When the accountant wishes to provide services in relation to property which it is actually known or suspected relates to money laundering or terrorist financing. In such circumstances, the reporter must indicate in the report that consent is required to provide such services, and must refrain from doing so until consent is received.

2   When the accountant actually knows or suspects, or there are reasonable (objective) grounds for knowing or suspecting, that another person is engaged in money laundering or terrorist financing, whether or not he or she wishes to act for such person. The person in question could be a client, a colleague or a third party.

9.3   Required disclosure

The required disclosure which must be included in a suspicious activity report (SAR) is as follows:

- The identity of the suspect (if known).

- The information or other matter on which the knowledge or suspicion of money laundering (or reasonable grounds for such) is based.

- The whereabouts of the laundered property (if known) is passed as soon as is practicable to the MLRO.

- Additional information held by the individual that identifies other parties involved in or connected to the matter should also be given to the MLRO.

9.4 Failure to disclose

An offence is committed if an individual fails to make a report comprising the required disclosure as soon as is practicable either in the form of an:

- Internal report to his MLRO or

- a SAR to a person authorised by the National Crime Agency (NCA) to receive disclosures.

- The obligation to make the required disclosure arises when: a person knows or suspects, or has reasonable grounds for knowing or suspecting that another person is engaged in money laundering.

An MLRO is obliged to report to the NCA if he is satisfied that the information received in an internal report is serious in nature.

An MLRO may commit an offence if he fails to pass on reportable information in internal reports that he has received, as soon as is practicable, to NCA.

The maximum penalty doe failure to disclose is 5 year imprisonment and/or an unlimited fine.

9.5 Exceptions to the duty to report

The obligation of an accountant to report does NOT apply if:

- the information which forms the basis of knowledge or suspicion or the reasonable grounds to know or suspect was obtained other than in the course of the accountant's business, for example, on a social occasion

- the information came about in privileged circumstances, that is in order for the accountant to provide legal advice, such as explaining a client's tax liability (except when it is judged that the advice has been sought to enable the client to commit a criminal offence or avoid detection) or expert opinion or services in relation to actual or contemplated legal proceedings

- there is a reasonable excuse for not reporting, in which case the report must be made as soon as reasonable in the circumstances.

9.6 Protected and authorised disclosures

Protected disclosure

Any report providing the required disclosure which is made by **any** person, not just an accountant, forming a money laundering suspicion, at work or when carrying out professional activities (whether or not providing accountancy services to clients), is a protected disclosure. This means the person is protected against allegations of breach of confidentiality; however the restriction on disclosure of information was imposed.

Authorised disclosure

Any person who realises they may have engaged in or be about to engage in money laundering should make what is known as an authorised disclosure to the appropriate authority. This may provide a defence against charges of money laundering provided it is made before the act is carried out (and NCA's consent to the act is obtained), or it is made as soon as possible on the initiative of that person after the act is done and with good reason being shown for the delay.

If NCA's consent is refused within seven working days, law enforcement has a further 31 calendar days (the 'moratorium period') to further the investigation into the reported matter and take further action e.g. restrain or seize funds.

If consent, or a refusal, is not received by the member within 7 working days, starting on the first working day after the consent request was made, consent is deemed.

If a refusal is received within that 7 working days, then the member may continue with the client relationship or transaction after a further 31 days has elapsed, starting with the day on which the member received notice of the refusal, unless a restraining order is obtained to prohibit this.

There is no deemed consent in relation to suspicions of terrorist financing.

 Activity 3

Tony is an accountant working for McIntosh Ltd.

Recently Megavac plc, a customer of McIntosh Ltd, sent in a cheque for £100,000 in payment of an invoice for £20,000. When Tony queried this, the client said it was a mistake and asked for a cheque for the difference of £80,000 to be written to Omnivac plc, a sister company of Megavac plc.

Advise Tony.

Activity 4

Emma is an accountant in practice working on the audit of Ghest Ltd.

During the audit Emma discovered that some customers of Ghest Ltd have overpaid their invoices and some have paid twice. On further investigation Emma discovers that the Ghest Ltd has a policy of retaining all overpayments by customers and crediting them to the profit and loss account if they are not claimed within a year.

Advise Emma.

10 Tipping off

10.1 The offence of tipping off

 Definition

Tipping off is the legal term meaning

- to tell the potential offender of money laundering that the necessary authorities have been informed, or

- to disclose anything that might prejudice an investigation.

The criminal offence of tipping off arises where a person in the regulated sector (e.g. accountants) discloses either:

- that a disclosure has been made by a person of information to an MLRO or to NCA or to the police or HMRC and the disclosure is likely to prejudice any investigation that might be conducted following the disclosure referred to; **or**

- that an investigation into allegations that a money laundering offence has been committed, is being contemplated or is being carried out and the disclosure is likely to prejudice that investigation and the information disclosed came to the person in the course of a business in the regulated sector.

The penalty for this offence is a maximum of 5 years imprisonment, or an unlimited fine, or both.

Tipping off is a serious criminal offence. You commit the offence if you make any disclosure likely to prejudice an investigation. An example might be if you tell the client that a SAR is or is about to be filed in respect of them. You don't have to speak to commit the offence. You can even tip off by failing to respond where an answer is expected.

There are exceptions that apply in certain circumstances, including those where a person does not know or suspect that the disclosure would prejudice a money laundering investigation, and where the disclosure is made in a valid attempt to persuade a client not to commit a money laundering offence.

Considerable care is required in carrying out any communications with clients or third parties following a report. Before any disclosure is made relating to matters referred to in an internal report or SAR, it is important to consider carefully whether or not it is likely to constitute offences of tipping off or prejudicing an investigation.

It is suggested that businesses keep records of these deliberations and the conclusions reached.

However, individuals and businesses in the regulated sector will frequently need to continue to deliver their professional services and a way needs to be found to achieve this without falling foul of the tipping off offence.

10.2 Prejudicing an investigation

'Prejudicing an investigation' is a potential offence for all persons. An offence may be committed where **any** person (not just an accountant):

- knows or suspects that a money laundering investigation is being conducted or is about to be conducted; and

- makes a disclosure which is likely to prejudice the investigation; or falsifies, conceals or destroys documents relevant to the investigation, or causes that to happen.

The person making the disclosure does not have to intend to prejudice an investigation for this offence to apply.

However, there is a defence available if the person making the disclosure did not know or suspect the disclosure would be prejudicial, did not know or suspect the documents were relevant, or did not intend to conceal any facts from the person carrying out the investigation.

10.3 Record keeping

Under the MLR, records should be maintained to assist any future law enforcement investigation relating to clients, and to demonstrate that the accountant has complied with statutory obligations. Such records should include:

- copies of or reference to the Customer Due Diligence identification evidence (see below). These records must be kept for 5 years starting with the date on which the accountant's relationship with the client ends

- copies or originals of documents relating to transactions that have been subject to Customer Due Diligence measures or ongoing monitoring. These must be kept for 5 years starting with the date on which the accountant completed the client's instructions.

 Activity 5

What is the maximum prison term for tipping off?

11 Bribery

11.1 Bribery

As well as ensuring they are not involved in bribery personally, accountants should be vigilant to identify situations when their firm (or clients) are involved in or exposed to bribery.

 Example 1 – Bribery

Bribery is now recognized to be one of the world's greatest challenges.

For example, KPMG surveyed FTSE 100 companies in August 2009 and found that two thirds said it was not possible to do business in some countries without being involved in bribery, yet only 35 per cent had stopped doing business there.

 Activity 6

Give some reasons why businesses should not be engaged in bribery.

Accountants need to very careful when deciding whether to accept gifts, hospitality and inducements, especially if 'excessive', as these may be perceived to be bribes.

Bribery can be viewed as a threat to objectivity and also compromises the fundamental principles of integrity and professional behaviour.

11.2 The Bribery Act (2010)

The Bribery Act (2010) creates the following offences:

1   Bribing a person to induce or reward them to perform a relevant function improperly (active bribery).

2   Requesting, accepting or receiving a bribe as a reward for performing a relevant function improperly (passive bribery).

3   Using a bribe to influence a foreign official to gain a business advantage.

4   Failing to prevent bribery on behalf of a commercial organisation.

 Example 2 – Hospitality or bribery?

Firms are allowed to provide hospitality.

For example, to provide tickets to sporting events, take clients to dinner or offer gifts to clients as a reflection of good relations.

However where hospitality may be a cover for bribing someone, the authorities would look at such things as the level of hospitality offered, the way in which it was provided and the level of influence the person receiving it had on the business decision in question.

 Example 3 – Facilitation payments

Facilitation payments are additional payments to induce officials to perform routine functions they are otherwise obliged to perform.

For example, additional payments to customs officials so they prioritise processing the import of your goods.

The UK Act criminalises facilitation payments abroad. Other countries, such as the United States, do not prohibit such payments abroad.

Note: You can pay for legally required administrative fees or 'fast-track' services. These are not facilitation payments.

11.3 Penalty and culpability

Under the Bribery Act (2010), the penalty for an offence is imprisonment for up to ten years with unlimited fine.

Companies can be liable for bribery committed for their benefit by their employees or other associated persons.

A company or corporate entity is culpable for board-level complicity in bribery, including bribery through intermediaries. There is also personal liability for senior company officers that turn a blind eye to such board-level bribery.

In addition, a company or corporate entity is culpable for bribes given to a third party with the intention of obtaining or retaining business for the organisation or obtaining or retaining an advantage useful to the conduct of the business by their employees and associated persons, even if they had no knowledge of those actions.

11.4 Defences

The Act is unusual in that a business can be guilty of an offence if an employee or associate commits an offence even if the management are not aware of, or condoned, the unlawful behaviour.

Because of this KPMG have described the Act as "one of the most draconian pieces of anti-bribery and corruption (AB&C) legislation in the world".

If prosecuted under the act, then the company can invoke in its defence only that it 'had in place **adequate** procedures designed to prevent persons associated [with the company] from undertaking such conduct'.

11.5 Jurisdiction and application

The scope of the law is extra-territorial. Under the Bribery Act, a relevant person or company can be prosecuted for the above crimes if the crimes are committed abroad.

The Bribery Act applies to UK citizens, residents and companies established under UK law. In addition, non-UK companies can be held liable for a failure to prevent bribery if they do business in the UK.

 Activity 7

A UK client company is considering expanding its business into a new country.

Describe some preliminary steps the company could undertake to assess the risks of bribery and corruption in the country.

12 Health and safety in your workplace

12.1 The importance of health and safety at work

Of course, health and safety not only relates to computer screen equipment but to the workplace in general. The maintenance of safe working conditions and the prevention of accidents are most important. Top of your list of importance is obviously to protect yourself and others from dangers that might cause injury or sickness.

Health and safety is as important in an office as in a factory. Constant absenteeism through poor working conditions or accidents is costly for any organisation, and people do not work as productively if they are ill, tired or in an unsatisfactory environment. It is therefore in the organisation's interests, as well as the employees', that health and safety procedures are observed. The costs of not having adequate measures to ensure health and safety include the following:

Cash, cheques, equipment, machinery and stock (i.e. company assets) may be destroyed, lost or damaged. If the losses are serious the organisation may have to close down for a time. It may not be possible to complete orders on time, leading to a loss of customers and the consequent effect on profits and jobs.

There may be serious injury to employees, customers and/or the general public, which could lead to claims for compensation and damage to the reputation of the organisation.

Confidential records (e.g. correspondence and information on creditors, debtors and stock) may no longer be available.

Because health and safety at work is so important, there are regulations that require all of us not to put others or ourselves in danger. The regulations are also there to protect the employees from workplace danger.

13 Health and safety legislation and regulations

13.1 The basic requirements

Health and safety in the workplace is mainly a matter of common sense but, of course, none of us is entirely sensible all the time. This means that we need to have policies, procedures and rules about making our workplaces safe and healthy so that we are not put at risk whilst working.

The basis of British health and safety law is the **Health and Safety at Work Act 1974**, which is enforceable by law. It provides the legal framework to promote, stimulate and encourage high standards. The Health and Safety Executive and Environmental Health Officers check to make sure that all the regulations currently in force are being complied with by employers and the self-employed, **so far as is reasonably practicable.**

The Act sets out the general duties that employers have towards employees and members of the public, and also the responsibilities that employees have for themselves and to each other.

The provisions of the Act place a duty on the employer to take all reasonable and practicable steps and precautions, to provide a working environment that is safe and free from health hazards. Such steps and provisions should include information regarding the employee's work procedures, operations and general environment, and the provision of instruction, training and supervision. The employer has an obligation to ensure that an employee follows recognised safety codes of practice and is not endangering himself/herself and/or other employees.

Your employer has a duty to provide the following:

safe ways in and out of the place of work

a safe working environment

safe equipment and procedures

arrangements for the safe use, handling, storage and transport of articles and substances

adequate information, instruction, training and supervision

adequate investigation of accidents.

Failure to do so could result in a criminal prosecution in the Magistrates Court or a Crown Court. Failure to ensure safe working practises could also lead to an employee suing for personal injury, or in some cases the employer being prosecuted for corporate manslaughter.

Your employer must also take out Employer's Liability Insurance and display the insurance certificate on the premises. This insurance will cover the employer for any accidents you might have at work.

But it is not only the employer who has a responsibility to make the workplace safe, the employee also has a responsibility to follow the safety rules and to protect both themselves and their colleagues from getting hurt. In some circumstances employers and employees can be prosecuted if they cause an accident by not following the health and safety regulations.

You as an employee (or a self-employed person) must:

take care of your own health and safety in the workplace and not endanger the people you work with

co-operate with anyone carrying out duties under the Act (including the employer)

make sure you know what the health and safety rules of your employer are and keep to these rules

correctly use work items provided by your employer including personal protective equipment (PPE) in accordance with training or instructions

never interfere with or misuse anything provided for your health, safety or welfare.

As you can see, your employer has a duty to provide a safe working environment but you, the employee, have a duty to look after yourself and other people within that environment.

14 Summary

This chapter has focused on key areas of current legislation of which you need to have a knowledge both for your ICB assessment and for your future career as a bookkeeper. These also influence organisational procedures as a **business must adhere to the various legislation that has an effect upon the workplace** and those engaged in the business activity.

Answers to chapter activities

 Activity 1

(a) A term is a statement that will be considered part of the contract.

A representation is a pre-contractual statement which is not considered to be part of the contract. They include statements that induce contracts but do not become a term of the contract.

(b) Express terms are statements actually made by one of the parties with the intention that they become part of the contract and thus binding and enforceable through court action if necessary.

Express statements may be made by word of mouth or in writing as long as they are sufficiently clear for them to be enforceable.

Implied terms are not actually stated or expressly included in contracts, but are introduced into the contract by implication. In other words the exact meaning and thus the terms of the contract are inferred from its context. Implied terms can be divided into various types.

Terms implied by statute

In this instance a particular piece of legislation may state that certain terms have to be taken as constituting part of an agreement, even where it is not considered in the contractual agreement between the various parties.

Terms implied by custom or usage

An agreement may be subject to terms that are customarily found in such contracts within a particular market, trade or locality.

Terms implied by a court

Generally, it is a matter for the parties concerned to decide the terms of a contract, but on occasion a court may presume that the parties intended to include a term which is not expressly stated. They will do so where it is necessary to give business efficacy to the contract.

Alternatively courts will imply certain terms into contracts where the parties have not reduced the general agreement into specific details.

Activity 2

(a) An invitation to treat is an indication that a person is willing to enter into or continue negotiations but is not yet willing to be bound by the terms mentioned.

They are statements or actions which precede an offer. They are not capable of being accepted and have no contractual significance.

An offer, on the other hand, is a definite statement of willingness to be bound on specified terms. It is capable of maturing, through acceptance, into a legally binding contract.

(b) A revocation is a rebuttal or refusal of an offer.

The general rule is that an offeror is free to revoke an offer at any time until it is accepted, although the revocation needs to be communicated to the offeree: a revocation is only effective when it has been communicated.

(c) The postal rule states that acceptance of an offer is effective as soon as a letter expressing acceptance is posted.

There must be evidence of the posting for this rule to be effective and this rule only applies when the use of the postal service is reasonable in the sense that the post would be within contemplation of the parties.

 Activity 3

The overpayment and request to pay a third party are grounds for suspicion of money laundering (see note below).

Any overpayment by a customer should be thoroughly investigated by a senior member of finance function staff and only repaid to the customer once it has been established that it is right/legal to do so.

Similarly the request to pay a third party should be scrutinised before any payment is agreed to. Without further information the transaction does not make commercial sense.

Unless investigations satisfy any concerns raised, then

- Tony should report the matter to the firm's MRLO.

- McIntosh Ltd should refuse the payment.

- The MRLO should fill in a Suspicious Activity Report (SAR) to be sent to NCA.

Tutorial note: It seems highly unlikely a customer would overpay by £80,000 by accident! Also, why doesn't the client, Megavac plc, simply want McIntosh Ltd to repay them and then it up to them whether they want to pay anything to Omnivac plc? Is it to make funds difficult to trace, so 'dirty' cash becomes a nice 'clean' cheque from a reputable accounting firm?

 Activity 4

Emma should consider whether the retention of the overpayments might amount to theft by Ghest Ltd from its customers. If so, the client will be in possession of the proceeds of its crime, a money laundering offence.

In the case of minor irregularities where there is nothing to suggest dishonest behaviour, (for example where Ghest Ltd attempted to return the overpayments to its customers, or if the overpayments were mistakenly overlooked), Emma may be satisfied that no criminal property is involved and therefore a report is not required.

If there are no such indications that Ghest Ltd has acted honestly, Emma should conclude that Ghest Ltd may have acted dishonestly.

Emma must thus make a report to her firm's MLRO.

 Activity 5

The maximum prison term for tipping off is 5 years.

Activity 6

Why bribery is wrong – the ethical argument

- It is a misuse of power and position and has a disproportionate impact on the poor and disadvantaged.

- It undermines the integrity of all involved and damages the fabric of the organizations to which they belong.

Why bribery is wrong – the business argument

- Legal risks – bribery may be illegal

- Reputational risks if found out

- Financial costs – fines and the cost of bribes

- Pressure to repeat offend/exposure to blackmail

- Impact on staff – trust and confidence eroded.

 Activity 7

- Use simple internet searches to find out about the levels of bribery in the particular country you propose to do business in.

- Consult the Foreign Office for advice.

- Consult business representative bodies here and in the relevant country for up to date local knowledge.

- UK firms can use the Government sponsored Business Anti Corruption Portal aimed at small and medium sized businesses involved in overseas trade.

15 Test your knowledge

Workbook Activity 8

(a) If you suspect money laundering is occurring, you should

A   Talk it through with the people involved, to confirm that you have understood the situation fully.

B   Report the problem to your line manager.

C   Disclose the issue to your MLRO.

(b) If you are involved in money laundering, you face

A   Life imprisonment.

B   A £500 fine.

C   14 years imprisonment, and/or an unlimited fine.

Professional Ethics

Introduction

In this chapter we will consider professional ethics and how the bookkeeper should apply the principles of professional ethics in their work.

CONTENTS
1   The need for professional ethics
2   Applying the fundamental principles
3   Worked example

1 The need for professional ethics

1.1 Introduction

In recent years we have experienced an adverse effect on global markets with the high profile Enron corporate scandal, the collapse of a major bank in the US and, most recently, the Polly Peck scandal.

The response to such unethical business activity has been global recognition of the need for a more transparent and open approach to corporate governance. Legislation was introduced in the US in the form of the Sabanes-Oxley Act 2002, and there have been various EU directives, and legislation in the UK, focussing on fraud, bribery and money laundering.

The International Federation of Accountants (IFAC) published a Code of Ethics as a benchmark and guide for all within the Accountancy Profession. Bookkeepers, and indeed Members of the Institute of Certified Bookkeepers, are an integral part of this global profession.

1.2 Fundamental principles

The most recent revision of the National Occupational Standards for Accountancy and Finance includes a unit on Professional Ethics. It covers the essential aspects of working in an ethical manner in the accounting environment and lists three main reasons for this:

- The level of confidence that the public has in accounting and finance practices and functions.

- Your organisation's probity and reputation.

- Your own professional reputation and legal liability.

It clearly involves:

- Acting with honesty and integrity.

- Exercising objectivity, fairness and due care.

- Respecting confidentiality.

- Adhering to professional values and codes of practice and behaving professionally.

- Maintaining professional and technical competence.

Many major professional bodies have these fundamental principles listed above embedded in their Ethical Guidelines.

2 Applying the fundamental principles

2.1 Introduction

For your ICB studies you will need to know how the fundamental principles of ethical behaviour can be applied to the work and actions of the Certified Bookkeeper.

2.2 Integrity

Bookkeepers should behave with integrity, that is fair dealing and honesty in all business, professional and personal financial relationships.

2.3 Objectivity

Bookkeepers should strive for objectivity and thus avoid bias and prejudice so as to be fair in all their professional work.

2.4 Professional and technical competence

Bookkeepers should not accept or perform work which they are not competent to undertake. They have a duty to maintain and develop professional knowledge by undertaking Continuing Professional Development (CPD) which will benefit the client, the employer and the public at large.

2.5 Due care

Bookkeepers should carry out their work with due skill, care and diligence, also adhering to professional standards.

2.6 Confidentiality

Bookkeepers should treat all information obtained in the scope of their work in a confidential manner. Disclosure of such information needs specific authority from the client or the employer, other than where there is a right or duty to disclose something by law.

2.7 Professional behaviour

Bookkeepers should act in a manner consistent with being a member of a profession and avoid conduct that may compromise this.

2.8 Compliance with Professional and Technical Standards

Bookkeepers have a duty to adhere to the regulatory framework which influences their professional work. They must maintain an up-to-date knowledge of changes to codes of practice, regulation or legislation that affect their role and functions in the profession.

In conclusion it can be said that we all have a duty to ourselves, our employers, clients and the public at large to maintain the highest professional standards.

3 Worked example

3.1 Introduction

The fundamental principles we have looked at in this chapter are: Integrity, Objectivity, Professional and Technical Competence, Due Care, Confidentiality, Professional Behaviour and Compliance with Professional and Technical Standards.

You should now work through the mini case study below to check your understanding of these principles.

Note that this mini case study formed part of an article on Professional Ethics by Dr Philip E Dunn, previously published in an ICB Newsletter.

 Activity 1: Mini case study

You are a Certified Bookkeeper and are employed as Assistant to the Practice Manager in a large doctors' surgery. Your principal responsibility is both the bookkeeping and the preparation of the financial statements.

For each of the situations that follow you need to identify which fundamental principle would apply.

(a) Your Practice Manager is on leave and a sales representative from a large pharmaceutical company calls to promote a new drug. In the course of the conversation he offers you a leather briefcase as a gift, asking you to recommend his firm favourably to the practice. You refuse to accept his offer, otherwise this would be a breach of your ....?

(b) You have recently met with your senior partner responsible for staffing to agree salary rises for all staff excluding the doctors. Over lunch the following day you are in conversation with the staff member responsible for the pharmacy based at the surgery who asks you what the current salary level is for a receptionist, as one of his friends plans to apply for a post shortly. You refuse to divulge this information as it would be a breach of............?

(c) Again, whilst your Practice Manager is on leave, one of the staff approaches you with questions on various clauses in her contract of employment. She is aware that you are studying the CIPD Qualification that includes elements of employment law. You point out to her that you have not yet covered contracts of employment and she should await the return of your boss. Had you given the advice it would have been out of the scope of your.......................?

(d) You are working on the budgets for the following year and your Practice Manager has brought forward the meeting with the Partners by two weeks. You stress to her that you will be 'hard pushed' to complete the budget reports within this time scale and this is of great concern to you as the figures need to be accurate and justifiable. If you are forced to work to this deadline, the work may be carried out without.......................?

(e) Recently the driveway at the surgery has been re-surfaced by a local contractor. There was some material left over and the contractor asks you if you would like your home driveway re-surfaced for £75 using the spare material. You refuse this offer as it would be a breach of your..............?

(f) One of your responsibilities is the maintenance of payroll and the relationship with HMRC. You are fully aware that in April 2013 RTI became operational. To cope with this change you have undertaken CPD. By undertaking this CPD, you are adhering to compliance with what.......................?

(g) One of the receptionists is constantly late for work each morning and your boss asks you to deal with this. You mention this to the member of staff in front of two other colleagues, and, unfortunately, the conversation becomes heated and you 'dress down' the staff member. This situation may be a compromise of your...................?

4 Summary

This session has reviewed the need for professional ethics and the fundamental principles of ethical behaviour which a bookkeeper should comply with. You have also learnt how to apply these fundamental principles to real-life scenarios.

Answers to chapter activities

 Activity 1: Mini case study

(a) Objectivity

Bookkeepers should not allow the undue influence of others to override their professional judgement.

(b) Confidentiality

Bookkeepers should not disclose information obtained as a result of professional and business relationships to a third party without proper and specific authority.

(c) Professional and Technical Competence

Bookkeepers should not accept or perform work which they are not competent to undertake.

(d) Due Care

Bookkeepers should carry out their work with due skill, care and diligence, all of which may be compromised when working under severe pressure.

(e) Integrity/Honesty

Bookkeepers should act with integrity and honesty in all professional and business relationships.

(f) Compliance with Professional and Technical Standards

Bookkeepers must maintain an up-to-date knowledge of changes to codes of practice, regulation or legislation that affect their role and functions in the profession.

(g) Professional Behaviour

Bookkeepers should avoid any action that discredits their profession.

Workbook Activities Answers

1 Types of business units

Workbook Activity 1

D

A private company cannot invite the public to subscribe for its shares. This is the key difference between a public and a private company.

Workbook Activity 2

The term 'partnership' is defined in **the Partnership Act 1890.**

People can form such organisations informally or formally and they **do not need** written agreements.

The definition of a partnership is **the relationship which subsists between persons carrying on a business in common with a view to profit.**

Workbook Activity 3

A public limited company must have a minimum allotted share capital of £50,000 and a trading certificate.

2 **Double entry bookkeeping – introduction**

Workbook Activity 1

(a) (i)   Asset

(ii)   Liability

(iii)   Asset

(iv)   Asset

(v)   Asset

(vi)   Asset

(b)   Any 3 from the choice of:

- Shareholders (investors)
- Potential investors
- HMRC
- Banks
- Customers
- Suppliers
- Employees (of the business)
- Government

(c)   1   Dual effect – each transaction has two financial effects.

2   Separate entity – the owner of the business and the business are seen as two separate entities. All transactions are recorded in the point of view of the business.

3   Accounting equation –
Assets – Liabilities = Capital + Profit – Drawings

Workbook Activity 2

Answer 1

	Assets £		Capital £
Cash	10,000	Capital introduced	10,000

Answer 2

Dual effect

Increase stock	£2,500	($\uparrow$ asset)
Decrease cash	£2,500	($\downarrow$ asset)

	Assets £		Capital £
Stock	2,500	Capital introduced	10,000
Cash	7,500		
	10,000		10,000

Answer 3

Dual effect

Increase stock	£2,000	($\uparrow$ asset)
Increase creditor	£2,000	($\uparrow$ liability)

	Net assets £		Capital £
Stock	4,500	Capital introduced	10,000
Cash	7,500		
	12,000		
Less: Creditors	(2,000)		
	10,000		10,000

Answer 4

Dual effect

Increase fixed asset	£1,000	(↑ asset)
Decrease cash	£1,000	(↓ asset)

	Net assets £		Capital £
Fixed asset	1,000	Capital introduced	10,000
Stock	4,500		
Cash	6,500		
	————		
	12,000		
Less: Creditors	(2,000)		
	————		————
	10,000		10,000
	————		————

Answer 5

Dual effect

Increase cash	£3,000	(↑ asset)
Decrease stock	£2,000	(↓ asset)
Increase profit	£1,000	(↑ profit)

	Net assets £		Capital £
Fixed asset	1,000	Capital introduced	10,000
Stock	2,500	Profit	1,000
Cash	9,500		
	————		
	13,000		
Less: Creditors	(2,000)		
	————		————
	11,000		11,000
	————		————

Answer 6

Dual effect

Increase debtors	£5,000	(↑ asset)
Decrease stock	£2,000	(↓. asset)
Increase profit	£3,000	(↑ profit)

	Net assets £		Capital £
Fixed asset	1,000	Capital introduced	10,000
Stock	500	Profit	4,000
Debtors	5,000		
Cash	9,500		
	———		
	16,000		
Less: Creditors	(2,000)		
	———		———
	14,000		14,000
	———		———

Answer 7

Dual effect

Decrease cash	£500	(↓ asset)
Decrease profit	£500	(↓ profit)

	Net assets £		Capital £
Fixed asset	1,000	Capital introduced	10,000
Stock	500	Profit	3,500
Debtors	5,000		
Cash	9,000		
	———		
	15,500		
Less: Creditors	(2,000)		
	———		———
	13,500		13,500
	———		———

Answer 8

Dual effect

Increase cash	£2,000	(↑ asset)
Increase creditors	£2,000	(↑ liability)

	Net assets £		Capital £
Fixed asset	1,000	Capital introduced	10,000
Stock	500	Profit	3,500
Debtors	5,000		
Cash	11,000		
	17,500		
Less: Creditors	(2,000)		
Loan	(2,000)		
	13,500		13,500

The loan will be shown separately from creditors for purchases, which are known as trade creditors.

Answer 9

Dual effect

Decrease cash	£1,500	(↓ asset)
Decrease creditors	£1,500	(↓ liability)

	Net assets £		Capital £
Fixed asset	1,000	Capital introduced	10,000
Stock	500	Profit	3,500
Debtors	5,000		
Cash	9,500		
	16,000		
Less: Creditors	(500)		
Loan	(2,000)		
	13,500		13,500

Answer 10

Dual effect

Decrease debtors	£3,000	(↓ asset)
Increase cash	£3,000	(↑ asset)

	Net assets £		Capital £
Fixed asset	1,000	Capital introduced	10,000
Stock	500	Profit	3,500
Debtors	2,000		
Cash	12,500		
	16,000		
Less: Creditors	(500)		
Loan	(2,000)		
	13,500		13,500

Answer 11

Dual effect

Decrease cash	£750	(↓ asset)
Increase drawings	£750	(↓ capital)

	Net assets £		Capital £
Fixed asset	1,000	Capital introduced	10,000
Stock	500	Profit	3,500
Debtors	2,000		
Cash	11,750		
	15,250		13,500
Less: Creditors	(500)	Less: Drawings	(750)
Loan	(2,000)		
	12,750		12,750

We do not simply deduct drawings from profit as we want to show separately the profit or loss for the period before any drawings were made.

Workbook Activity 3

(a) Opening capital

		£		£
Assets	Cash	5,000	Capital	5,000

(b) Cash purchase

		£		£
Assets	Stock	500	Capital	5,000
	Cash (5,000 – 500)	4,500		
		5,000		5,000

(c) Credit purchase

		£		£
Assets	Stock (500 + (5 × 200))	1,500	Capital	5,000
	Cash	4,500		
		6,000		
Liabilities	Creditors	(1,000)		
		5,000		5,000

(d) Cash sale

		£		£
Assets	Stock (1,500 – 500)	1,000	Capital	5,000
	Cash (4,500 + 750)	5,250	Profit (750 – 500)	250
		6,250		
Liabilities	Creditors	(1,000)		
		5,250		5,250

(e) Cash sale

		£		£
Assets	Stock (1,000 – 800)	200	Capital	5,000
	Debtors	1,200	Profit (250 + 1,200 – 800)	650
	Cash	5,250		
		6,650		
Liabilities	Creditors	(1,000)		
		5,650		5,650

(f)   Paid rent

		£		£
Assets	Stock	200	Capital	5,000
	Debtors	1,200	Profit (650 – 250)	400
	Cash (5,250 – 250)	5,000		
		6,400		
Liabilities	Creditors	(1,000)		
		5,400		5,400

(g)   Drawings

		£		£
Assets	Stock	200	Capital	5,000
	Debtors	1,200	Profit	400
	Cash (5,000 – 100)	4,900		
		6,300	Drawings	(100)
Liabilities	Creditors	(1,000)		
		5,300		5,300

(h)   Sundry income

		£		£
Assets	Stock	200	Capital	5,000
	Debtors (1,200 + 50)	1,250	Profit (400 + 50)	450
	Cash	4,900		
		6,350	Drawings	(100)
Liabilities	Creditors	(1,000)		
		5,350		5,350

(i)   Payment to creditor

		£		£
Assets	Stock	200	Capital	5,000
	Debtors	1,250	Profit	450
	Cash (4,900 – 500)	4,400		
		5,850	Drawings	(100)
Liabilities	Creditors (1,000 – 500)	(500)		
		5,350		5,350

(j) Receipt from Debtor

		£		£
Assets	Stock	200	Capital	5,000
	Debtors (1,250 – 1,200)	50	Profit	450
	Cash (4,400 + 1,200)	5,600		
		5,850	Drawings	(100)
Liabilities	Creditors	(500)		
		5,350		5,350

(k) Purchase of van

		£		£
Assets	Van	4,000	Capital	5,000
	Stock	200	Profit	450
	Debtors	50		5,450
	Cash (5,600 – 4,000)	1,600		
			Drawings	(100)
		5,850		
Liabilities	Creditors	(500)		
		5,350		5,350

(l) Telephone bill

		£		£
Assets	Van	4,000	Capital	5,000
	Stock	200	Profit (450 – 150)	300
	Debtors	50		5,300
	Cash	1,600		
			Drawings	(100)
		5,850		
Liabilities Creditors (500 + 150)		(650)		
		5,200		5,200

KAPLAN PUBLISHING

3 Ledger accounting

Workbook Activity 3

Bank

		£			£
(a)	Capital	4,000	(b)	Computer	1,000
(d)	Sales	800	(c)	Rent	400

Capital

		£			£
			(a)	Bank	4,000

Rent

		£			£
(c)	Bank	400			

Sales

		£			£
			(d)	Bank	800

Computers

		£			£
(b)	Bank	1,000			

Workbook Activity 4

Capital

	£			£
		(a)	Bank	4,000

Purchases

		£		£
(b)	Bank	700		
(g)	Bank	1,200		

Entertainment

		£		£
(c)	Bank	300		

Computers

		£		£
(d)	Bank	3,000		

Sales

	£			£
		(e)	Bank	1,500

Drawings

		£		£
(f)	Bank	500		

Telephone

		£			£
(h)	Bank	600	(i)	Bank	200

Stationery

		£		£
(j)	Bank	157		

Bank

		£				£
(a)	Capital	4,000	(b)	Purchases		700
(e)	Sales	1,500	(c)	Entertainment		300
(i)	Telephone	200	(d)	Computers		3,000
			(f)	Drawings		500
			(g)	Purchases		1,200
			(h)	Telephone		600
			(j)	Stationery		157

Workbook Activity 5

Sales

	£		£
		B	1,000
		C	90

B Debtor

	£		£
Sales	1,000	Bank	500

C Debtor

	£		£
Sales	90	Bank	90

Bank

	£		£
B	500		
C	90		

4 Drafting an initial trial balance

Workbook Activity 3

Bank

	£		£
Capital	10,000	Computer	1,000
Sales	2,000	Telephone	567
Sales	3,000	Rent	1,500
Sales	2,000	Rates	125
		Stationery	247
		Petrol	49
		Purchases	2,500
		Drawings	500
		Petrol	42
Sub-total	17,000	Sub-total	6,530
		Balance c/d	10,470
	17,000		17,000
Balance b/d	10,470		

Workbook Activity 4

Bank

	£		£
Capital	5,000	Purchases	850
Sales	1,000	Fixtures	560
Sales	876	Van	1,500
Rent rebate	560	Rent	1,300
Sales	1,370	Rates	360
		Telephone	220
		Stationery	120
		Petrol	48
		Car repairs	167
Sub-total	8,806	Sub-total	5,125
		Balance c/d	3,681
	8,806		8,806
Balance b/d	3,681		

Workbook Activity 5

Bank

	£		£
Balance b/f	23,700	Drawings	4,000
Sales	2,300	Rent	570
Sales	1,700	Purchases	6,000
Debtors	4,700	Rates	500
		Salaries	3,600
		Car expenses	460
		Petrol	49
		Petrol	38
		Electricity	210
		Stationery	89
Sub-total	32,400	Sub-total	15,516
		Balance c/d	16,884
	32,400		32,400
Balance b/d	16,884		

Workbook Activity 6

Trial balance of XYZ at 31 August 20X9

	Dr £	Cr £
Sales		41,770
Purchases	34,680	
Debtors	6,790	
Creditors		5,650
General expenses	12,760	
Loan		10,000
Plant and machinery at cost	5,000	
Motor van at cost	6,000	
Drawings	2,000	
Rent and rates	6,700	
Insurance	4,000	
Bank overdraft		510
Capital		20,000
	77,930	77,930

Workbook Activity 7

Purchases

		£		£
(a)	Creditors	1,000		
(j)	Bank	400	Balance c/d	1,400
		1,400		1,400
	Balance b/d	1,400		

Creditors

		£			£
(g)	Bank	300	(a)	Purchases	1,000
	Balance c/d	700			
		1,000			1,000
				Balance b/d	700

Rent

	£		£
(b) Bank	500	Balance c/d	500
	500		500
Balance b/d	500		

Sales

	£		£
		(c) Debtors	1,500
Balance c/d	3,500	(k) Bank	2,000
	3,500		3,500
		Balance b/d	3,500

Debtors

	£		£
(c) Sales	1,500	(f) Bank	400
		Balance c/d	1,100
	1,500		1,500
Balance b/d	1,100		

Computers

	£		£
(d) Bank	900	Balance c/d	900
	900		900
Balance b/d	900		

Wages

	£		£
(e) Bank	1,000	Balance c/d	1,000
	1,000		1,000
Balance b/d	1,000		

Telephone

	£			£
(h) Bank	200	(i) Bank		50
		Balance c/d		150
	200			200
Balance b/d	150			

Bank

	£			£
(f) Debtors	400	(b) Rent		500
(i) Telephone	50	(d) Computer		900
(k) Sales	2,000	(e) Wages		1,000
		(g) Creditors		300
		(h) Telephone		200
		(j) Purchases		400
Balance c/d	850			
	3,300			3,300
		Balance b/d		850

Trial Balance as at 31 July 20X9:

	Dr £	Cr £
Purchases	1,400	
Creditors		700
Rent	500	
Sales		3,500
Debtors	1,100	
Computers	900	
Wages	1,000	
Telephone	150	
Bank overdraft		850
	5,050	5,050

5 Business documents

Workbook Activity 2

(i) Has the correct pricing been used on the invoice?

Yes – the price quoted on the purchase order was £40 per 100 which is equal to £0.40 for each item.

(ii) Has the correct discount been applied?

No – the trade discount agreed on the purchase order was 10%, not the 20% charged on the invoice.

(iii) What should the correct amount of VAT charged be?

The VAT should have been charged on the correct discounted amount of £160 less 10% discount, therefore a net amount of £144.

VAT should have been £144 × 20% = £28.80.

(iv) What should the correct total amount payable be?

The correct amount payable be the correct discounted amount of £144 plus the correct VAT of £28.80, so the total amount payable should be £172.80.

Workbook Activity 3

(a) To allow for expansion of the number of accounts in the general (main) ledger

(b) Any three from:

- Customer account codes
- Supplier account codes
- Product codes
- Stock codes
- VAT codes
- Department codes

(c)

	TRUE/FALSE
General ledger codes help when barcoding an item of stock	FALSE
General ledger codes help when filing a financial document	FALSE
General ledger codes help trace relevant accounts quickly and easily	TRUE
General ledger codes help find the total amount owing to a supplier	FALSE

 ## Workbook Activity 4

Credit note from J M Bond & Co

The trade discount deducted should have been £6.17. This error then impacts on the VAT amount and the total amount of credit.

 ## Workbook Activity 5

Invoice from A J Broom & Company Ltd

Seven joist hangers were invoiced and delivered but only five were ordered.

Invoice from Jenson Ltd

The incorrect settlement discount has been applied. The settlement discount of 3% should be applied as follows:

Net (585.40 × 97/100)	567.84
VAT	113.56
Gross	681.40

Invoice from Haddow Bros

12 sheets were invoiced and ordered but only 10 were delivered.

Workbook Activity 6

Invoice from:	Supplier account code	General ledger code
Haddow Bros	HAD29	GL112
Jenson Ltd	JEN32	GL140
AJ Broom & Company Ltd	AJB14	GL110
JM Bond & Co	JMB33	GL110

6 Credit sales – discounts and VAT

 Workbook Activity 3

(a) VAT = £140.00 × 20%   =   £28.00

(b) VAT = £560.00 × 20%   = £112.00

(c) VAT = £780.00 × 20%   = £130.00

(d) VAT = £1,020.00 × 20%   = £170.00

Workbook Activity 4

(a) VAT = £(280.00 – (2% × 280.00)) × 20% = £54.88

(b) VAT = £(480.00 – (3% × 480.00)) × 20% = £93.12

(c) VAT = £800.00 × $\frac{20}{120}$ =   £160.00

(d) VAT = £650.00 × $\frac{20}{120}$ =   £130.00

Workbook Activity 5

(a) B takes the settlement discount:

	£
Net price	600.00
Settlement discount	(18.00)
Net Invoice value	582.00
VAT	116.40
Amount paid	698.40

(b) B does not take the settlement discount:

	£
Net price	600.00
VAT	120.00
Invoice value	720.00

If B does not take the settlement discount, B will pay the full £720.00.

7 The sales day book – general and subsidiary ledgers

Workbook Activity 3

Sales day book						
Date	Invoice no	Customer name	Code	Total £	VAT £	Net £
20X1						
1/5	03466	Fraser & Co	SL14	154.41	25.73	128.68
	03467	Letterhead Ltd	SL03	309.48	51.58	257.90
2/5	03468	Jeliteen Traders	SL15	115.89	19.31	96.58
	CN0746	Garner & Co	SL12	(82.44)	(13.74)	(68.70)
3/5	03469	Harper Bros	SL22	321.78	53.63	268.15
	03470	Juniper Ltd	SL17	126.45	21.07	105.38
4/5	03471	H G Frank	SL30	353.60	58.93	294.67
	CN0747	Hill Traders	SL26	(141.21)	(23.53)	(117.68)
5/5	03472	Keller Assocs	SL07	132.69	22.11	110.58
				1,290.65	215.09	1,075.56

Workbook Activity 4

				Sales day book					
Date	Invoice no	Customer name	Code	Total £	VAT £	01 £	02 £	03 £	04 £
18/4/X1	06116	B Z S Music		1,463.04	243.84		432.00		787.20
18/4/X1	06117	M T Retail		642.00	107.00	210.00			325.00
18/4/X1	06118	Harmer & Co		1042.80	173.80		575.00	294.00	
				3,147.84	524.64	210.00	1,007.00	294.00	1,112.20

Note that when a trade discount has been deducted on the invoice in total it must be deducted from each type of sale when entering the figures in the analysed sales day book.

Settlement discounts are not deducted from the invoice value until customers have paid the invoice and the discount has been taken up.

 Workbook Activity 5

				Sales day book			
Date	Invoice no	Customer name	Code	Total £	VAT £	Maintenance £	Decorating £
01/5/X1	07891	Portman & Co	P2	166.80	27.80	139.00	
03/5/X1	07892	Stanton Assocs	S3	1,320.00	220.00		1,100.00
05/5/X1	07893	Boreham Bros	B7	283.20	47.20	106.00	130.00
				1,770.00	295.00	245.00	1,230.00

8 Checking receipts

Workbook Activity 4

The following problems exist on the cheques received:

Cheque from K T Lopez – not signed

Cheque from L Garry – post dated

Cheque from L Barrett – made out to wrong name

Cheque from P Ibbott – more than six months old

Cheque from J Lovell – discrepancy between words and figures.

Workbook Activity 5

Cheque from BZS Music – settlement discount has been taken correctly as the cheque is received within 10 days of the invoice date.

Cheque from Musicolor Ltd – settlement discount of £22.00 has been taken – but is not valid as the cheque has been received after 10 days from the invoice date. However, in the interest of good customer relations, perhaps the discount should be granted but the customer should be informed and reminded of the settlement discount terms.

Cheque from Harmer & Co – settlement discount has been taken correctly as the cheque is received within 10 days of the invoice date.

Cheque from Newford Music – settlement discount has been taken – this is not valid as the receipt is too late to claim the discount. Again the discount might be granted in the interest of good customer relations but the customer should be informed and reminded of the settlement discount terms.

Cheque from Trent Music – settlement discount has been taken – but the cheque has been incorrectly written out for £430.98. Customer should be informed of the error.

9 The analysed cash receipts book

 Workbook Activity 1

Step 1

Write up the sales day book.

SALES DAY BOOK

Date	Customer	Total £	VAT £	Sales £
	A	960.00	160.00	800.00
	B	3,840.00	640.00	3,200.00
		4,800.00	800.00	4,000.00

Step 2

Write up the cash receipts book.

CASH RECEIPTS BOOK

Date	Narrative	Total £	VAT £	SLCA £	Cash sales £	Discount allowed £	VAT adjustment £
	A (W)	912.00		912.00		40.00	8.00
	B	2,000.00		2,000.00			
	C	360.00	60.00		300.00		
		3,272.00	60.00	2,912.00	300.00	40.00	8.00

Working:

	£
Settlement discount (800.00 × 5%)	40.00
VAT adjustment (160.00 – 152.00)	8.00

Step 4

Post the totals to the general ledger.

Sales				VAT			
	£		£		£		£
		SDB	4,000.00	CRB	8.00	SDB	800.00
		CRB	300.00			CRB	60.00

SLCA				Discount allowed			
	£		£		£		£
SDB	4,800.00	CRB	2,912.00	SDB	40.00		
		CRB	40.00				
		CRB	8.00				

Step 4

Post individual amounts for the SDB and CRB to the sales ledger.

A				B			
	£		£		£		£
SDB	960.00	CRB	912.00	SDB	4,000.00		2,000.00
		CRB	40.00				
		CRB	8.00				

Workbook Activity 2

The entries in the sales ledger will be:

Account name	Amount £	Dr ✓	Cr ✓
G Heilbron	108.45		✓
L Tessa	110.57		✓
L Tessa	3.31		✓
L Tessa	0.66		✓
J Dent	210.98		✓
J Dent	6.32		✓
J Dent	1.26		✓
F Trainer	97.60		✓
A Winter	105.60		✓
A Winter	3.16		✓
A Winter	0.63		✓

The entries in the general ledger will be:

Account name	Amount £	Dr ✓	Cr ✓
Discounts allowed	12.79 ✓	✓	
Sales ledger control account	12.79		✓
Sales ledger control account	633.20 ✓		✓
Sales	225.60		✓
VAT	45.12		✓
VAT	2.55 ✓	✓	
Sales ledger control account	2.55		✓

 Workbook Activity 3

The entries in the sales ledger will be:

Account name	Amount £	Dr ✓	Cr ✓
McCaul & Partners	147.56		✓
McCaul & Partners	2.95		✓
McCaul & Partners	0.59		✓
P Martin	264.08		✓
F Little	167.45		✓
D Raine	265.89		✓
D Raine	7.97		✓
D Raine	1.59		✓

Show what the entries in the general ledger will be:

Account name	Amount £	Dr ✓	Cr ✓
Discounts allowed	10.92	✓	
Sales ledger control account	10.92		✓
VAT	2.18	✓	
Sales ledger control account	2.18		✓
Sales ledger control account	844.98		✓

10 Debtors' statements

 Workbook Activity 3

225 School Lane
Weymouth
Dorset
WE36 5NR
Tel: 0261 480444
Fax: 0261 480555
Date: 30 April 20X1

To: Grant & Co

STATEMENT

Date	Transaction	Debit £	Credit £	Balance £
1 April	Opening balance			337.69
4 April	Inv 32656	150.58		488.27
12 April	Credit 0335		38.70	449.57
18 April	Inv 32671	179.52		629.09
20 April	Payment		330.94	298.15
20 April	Discount		6.75	291.40
20 April	VAT adjustment		1.35	290.05
24 April	Credit 0346		17.65	272.40
25 April	Inv 32689	94.36		366.76

May we remind you that our credit terms are 30 days

F A R M H O U S E
PICKLES
LTD

To: Mitchell Partners

225 School Lane
Weymouth
Dorset
WE36 5NR
Tel: 0261 480444
Fax: 0261 480555
Date: 30 April 20X1

STATEMENT

Date	Transaction	Debit £	Credit £	Balance £
1 April	Opening balance			180.46
7 April	Inv 32662	441.57		622.03
12 April	Credit 0344		66.89	555.14
20 April	Inv 32669	274.57		829.71
21 April	Payment		613.58	216.13
21 April	Discount		8.45	207.68
21 April	VAT adjustment		1.69	205.99

May we remind you that our credit terms are 30 days

Workbook Activity 4

Ryan's Toy Shop LTD
125 Finchley Way Bristol BS1 4PL Tel: 01272 200299
STATEMENT OF ACCOUNT

Customer name Arnold's Toys Ltd
Customer address 14 High Street, Bristol, BS2 5FL

Statement date 1st December		Amount		Balance	
Date	Transaction	£	p	£	p
19/11	Invoice 2195	118	08	118	08
20/11	Invoice 2198	2201	95	2,320	03
20/11	Credit note 2198	323	60	1,996	43
22/11	Cheque	118	08	1,878	35
				1,878	35

11   Credit purchases – discounts and VAT

Workbook Activity 1

(a)   VAT = £400.00 × 20%   =   £80.00

(b)   VAT = £650.00 × 20%   =   £130.00

(c)   VAT = £528.00 × $\frac{20}{120}$ =   £88.00

(d)   VAT = £120.00 × $\frac{20}{120}$ =   £20.00

Workbook Activity 2

(a)   When the invoice is first received, VAT is recorded of 20% × £850 = £170

When the settlement discount is subsequently taken, the VAT on the invoice will be reduced to 20% × (850.00 – (3% × 850.00)) = £164.90

A VAT adjustment of £170.00 – £164.90 = £5.10 will be required to correct the Input VAT claimed in respect of the invoice.

(b)   When the invoice is first received, VAT is recorded of 20% × £600.00 = £120.00

When the settlement discount is subsequently taken, the VAT on the invoice will be reduced to 20% × (600.00 – (5% × 600.00)) = £114.00

A VAT adjustment of £120.00 – £114.00 = £6.00 will be required to correct the Input VAT claimed in respect of the invoice.

(c)   VAT = £325.00 × 20%   =   £65.00

(d)   VAT = £57.00 × 20%   =   £11.40

Workbook Activity 3

Calculate the initial invoice value which will be entered in the accounts when the invoice is received.

	£
Net price	600.00
VAT £600.00 × 20%	120.00
Invoice value	720.00

Calculate the invoice value, net of the discount, which Z pays A on 10.10.X5.

Net price less settlement discount	582.00
(£600.00 – (600.00 × 3%))	
VAT £582.00 × 20%	116.40
Invoice value	698.40

Calculate the VAT adjustment required as a result of the settlement discount being taken: £120.00 – £116.40 = £3.60

Purchases

	£		£
PLCA	600.00		

PLCA

	£		£
Bank	698.40	Purchases + VAT	720.00
Discount	18.00		
VAT	3.60		
	720.00		720.00

Bank

	£		£
		PLCA	698.40

VAT

	£		£
PLCA	120.00	PLCA	3.60

Discounts received

	£		£
		PLCA	18.00

12 The purchases day book – general and subsidiary ledgers

Workbook Activity 3

Purchases day book								
Date	Invoice no	Code	Supplier	Total	VAT	Fabric	Header tape	Other
07/4/X1	06738	PL03	Fabric Supplies Ltd	1,123.92	187.32	798.00	138.60	
07/4/X1	0328	PL04	Lillian Fisher	110.04	18.34			91.70
07/4/X1	CN0477	PL05	Headstream & Co	(81.60)	(13.60)	(51.40)	(16.60)	
08/4/X1	07359	PL01	Mainstream Fabrics	337.82	56.3	281.52		
				1,490.18	248.36	1,028.12	122.00	91.70

Workbook Activity 4

Purchases day book

Date	Invoice no	Code	Supplier	Total	VAT	Wood	Bricks/ Cement	Consum- ables
1/5/X1	077401	PL16	Magnum Supplies	505.92	84.32		421.60	
1/5/X1	046193	PL08	JR Ryan & Co	120.99	20.16	85.08		15.75
1/5/X1	47823	PL13	HT Todd Plc	444.96	74.16	284.80	86.00	
				1,071.87	178.64	369.88	507.60	15.75

Workbook Activity 5

Purchases returns day book

Date	Credit note no	Code	Supplier	Total	VAT	Wood	Bricks/ Cement	Consum- ables
28/4/X1	CN06113	PL13	HT Todd Plc	30.69	4.98	25.71		
28/4/X1	06132	PL03	BL Lukey Ltd	42.57	6.97	35.60		
30/4/X1	C4163	PL16	Magnum Supplies	46.76	7.66		39.10	
				120.02	19.61	61.31	39.10	–

13 Making payments

Workbook Activity 4

REMITTANCE ADVICE

To:

Building Contract Supplies
Unit 15 Royal Estate
Manchester
M13 2EF

Nethan Builders
Brecon House
Stamford House
Manchester
M16 4PL

Tel:	0161 521 6411
Fax:	0161 530 6412
VAT reg:	471 3860 42
Date:	18 May 20X1

Date	Invoice no	Amount £	Discount taken (including VAT adj) £	Paid £
18 May 20X1	07742	204.18	3.06	201.12

Total paid	£201.12
Cheque no	200550

REMITTANCE ADVICE

To:	**Nethan Builders**
Jenson Ltd	Brecon House
30 Longfield Park	Stamford House
Kingsway	Manchester
M45 2TP	M16 4PL

Tel:	0161 521 6411
Fax:	0161 530 6412
VAT reg:	471 3860 42
Date:	18 May 20X1

Date	Invoice no	Amount £	Discount taken (including VAT adj) £	Paid £
18 May 20X1	47811	185.13	5.55	179.58

Total paid	£179.58
Cheque no	200551

REMITTANCE ADVICE

To:	**Nethan Builders**
Magnum Supplies	Brecon House
140/150 Park Estate	Stamford House
Manchester	Manchester
M20 6EG	M16 4PL

Tel:	0161 521 6411
Fax:	0161 530 6412
VAT reg:	471 3860 42
Date:	18 May 20X1

Date	Invoice no	Amount £	Discount taken (including VAT adj) £	Paid £
18 May 20X1	077422	758.88	15.18	743.70

Total paid	£743.70
Cheque no	200552

REMITTANCE ADVICE

To: Haddow Bros The White House Standing Way Manchester M13 6FH	**Nethan Builders** Brecon House Stamford House Manchester M16 4PL

Tel:	0161 521 6411
Fax:	0161 530 6412
VAT reg:	471 3860 42
Date:	18 May 20X1

Date	Invoice no	Amount £	Discount taken (including VAT adj) £	Paid £
18 May 20X1	G33940	512.64	–	512.64

Total paid	£512.64
Cheque no	200553

14 The analysed cash payments book

Workbook Activity 2

The entries in the purchases ledger will be:

Account name	Amount £	Dr ✓	Cr ✓
Homer Ltd	168.70	✓	
Homer Ltd	5.06	✓	
Homer Ltd	1.01	✓	
Forker & Co	179.45	✓	
Forker & Co	5.38	✓	
Forker & Co	1.07	✓	
Print Ass.	190.45	✓	
ABG Ltd	220.67	✓	
ABG Ltd	6.62	✓	
ABG Ltd	1.32	✓	
G Greg	67.89	✓	

The entries in the general ledger will be:

Account name	Amount £	Dr ✓	Cr ✓
Discounts received	17.06		✓
Purchases ledger control account	17.06	✓	
Purchases ledger control account	827.16	✓	
VAT	3.40		✓
Purchases ledger control account	3.40	✓	
Purchases	450.00	✓	
VAT	90.00	✓	

 ## Workbook Activity 3

The entries in the purchases ledger will be:

Account name	Amount £	Dr ✓	Cr ✓
J M Bond	247.56	✓	
Magnum Supplies	662.36	✓	
Magnum Supplies	13.25	✓	
Magnum Supplies	2.65	✓	
A J Broom	153.57	✓	
Jenson Ltd	336.57	✓	
Jenson Ltd	6.73	✓	
Jenson Ltd	1.34	✓	
KKL Traders	442.78	✓	
KKL Traders	8.85	✓	
KKL Traders	1.77	✓	

The entries in the general ledger will be:

Account name	Amount £	Dr ✓	Cr ✓
Discounts received	28.83		✓
Purchases ledger control account	28.83	✓	
Purchases ledger control account	1,842.84	✓	
VAT	5.76		✓
Purchases ledger control account	5.76	✓	
Purchases	92.48	✓	
VAT	18.49	✓	

KAPLAN PUBLISHING

15 Petty cash

Workbook Activity 5

The entries in the general ledger will be:

Account name	Amount £	Dr ✓	Cr ✓
Postage	26.25	✓	
Staff welfare	31.40	✓	
Stationery	19.40	✓	
Travel expenses	33.01	✓	
VAT	9.12	✓	

Workbook Activity 6

Postage

	£		£
Balance b/f	231.67		
PCB	20.01		

Staff welfare

	£		£
Balance b/f	334.78		
PCB	4.68		

Tea and coffee

	£		£
Balance b/f	53.36		
PCB	12.03		

Travel expenses

	£		£
Balance b/f	579.03		
PCB	20.17		

VAT account

	£		£
PCB	4.94	Balance b/f	967.44

16 VAT and EU issues

 Workbook Activity 2

(a) Output VAT

Output VAT on UK sales:

(£60,500.00 + £89,510.00 + £70,400.00) × 20%	44,082.00
	44,082.00

Note that both the exports made outside of the EU, and the exports made within the EU to VAT registered customers are zero rated sales.

(b) Input VAT

Input VAT on UK purchases:

(£34,600.00 + £31,590.00 + £33,670.00) × 20%	19,972.00
Bad debts (£6,000 × 20/120)	1,000.00
	20,972.00

 Workbook Activity 3

Output VAT on acquisitions from EU registered businesses:

20% × £7,650 =1,530.00

This figure will entered on the VAT return (in Box 2) as Output VAT payable but will not be entered in the VAT control account.

Input VAT reclaimed on the VAT return:

20% × (£31,250 + £7,650 + £15,850) = £10,950.00

This figure will be entered on the VAT return as Input VAT reclaimable.

Note that the Input VAT on the purchases from EU registered businesses is not entered in the VAT control account – see below.

Input VAT entered in the VAT control account:

20% × (£31,250 + £15,850) = £9,420.00

Workbook Activity 4

(a) Output VAT   £

External sales   916,000
Less: Exports to EU countries (zero rated)   (65,000)

Standard rated sales   851,000

Output VAT (£851,000 × 20%)   170,200.00

Note that the exports made outside of the EU are zero rated sales.

(b) Input VAT

                                                                            £

VAT on standard rated purchases   62,000.00
(£310,000 × 20%)

17 Suspense accounts and errors

Workbook Activity 4

(a) Error disclosed by the trial balance – a single entry

(b) Error disclosed by the trial balance – a transposition error

(c) Error NOT disclosed by the trial balance – a reversal of entries

(d) Error NOT disclosed by the trial balance – an error of commission

(e) Error disclosed by the trial balance – two entries on one side

(f) Error disclosed by the trial balance – a casting error

(g) Error NOT disclosed by the trial balance – double entry is correct, it is only the subsidiary sales ledger that hasn't been updated

(h) Error disclosed by the trial balance – an extraction error

Workbook Activity 5

Account name	Amount £	Dr ✓	Cr ✓
Rent	200	✓	
Motor expenses	200		✓

Account name	Amount £	Dr ✓	Cr ✓
Bank	1,600		✓
Suspense	1,600	✓	

Account name	Amount £	Dr ✓	Cr ✓
Discounts received	1,800		✓
Suspense	1,800	✓	

Account name	Amount £	Dr ✓	Cr ✓
Miscellaneous expenses	500	✓	
Suspense	500		✓

Account name	Amount £	Dr ✓	Cr ✓
VAT	100	✓	
Suspense	100		✓

Re-drafted trial balance

	£	£
Debtors	33,440	
Bank	1,200	
Sales		401,300
Stock	24,300	
Wages	88,400	
Telephone	2,200	
Motor car	12,000	
VAT		5,200
Electricity	3,800	
Rent	16,400	
Purchases	241,180	
Purchases returns		1,600
Sales returns	4,200	
Office equipment	5,000	
Capital		49,160
Motor expenses	4,840	
Discounts allowed	4,010	
Discounts received		4,210
Creditors		20,000
Drawings	40,000	
Miscellaneous expenses	500	
	481,470	481,470

18 Payroll procedures

Workbook Activity 4

	£
Gross pay	368.70
Less: PAYE	(46.45)
NIC	(23.96)
Net pay	298.29

Workbook Activity 5

Account name	Amount £	Dr ✓	Cr ✓
Wages expense	5,475	✓	
Wages control	5,475		✓

Account name	Amount £	Dr ✓	Cr ✓
HM Revenue and Customs	1,388		✓
Wages control	1,388	✓	

Account name	Amount £	Dr ✓	Cr ✓
Bank	4,087		✓
Wages control	4,087	✓	

Gross wages control account

		£			£
31 May	Net pay – Bank	4,087	31 May	Gross – wages expense	5,050
	PAYE – HMRC	635	31 May	Emp'ers NIC – wages exp	425
	Emp'ees NIC – HMRC	328			
	Empl'ers NIC – HMRC	425			
		5,475			5,475

Wages expense account

		£			£
30 Apr	Balance b/d	23,446			
31 May	Gross – wages control	5,050			
	Emp'ers NIC – control	425	31 May	Balance c/d	28,921
		28,921			28,921
31 May	Balance b/d	28,921			

HM Revenue and Customs account

		£			£
19 May	CPB	760	30 Apr	Balance b/d	760
			31 May	PAYE – wages control	635
				Emp'ees NIC – control	328
31 May	Balance c/d	1,388		Emp'ers NIC – control	425
		2,148			2,148
			31 May	Balance b/d	1,388

19 Cash based accounting

Workbook Activity 2

(a)

CASH RECEIPTS

Date	Narrative	Details	Cash £	Bank £	Sales £	Misc £
1.3.X4	Bal b/d		100.00	1,450.00		
17.3.X4	Mrs Harrison	chq		800.00	800.00	
25.3.X4	Mr Clifford		200.00		200.00	
		TOTALS	300.00	2,250.00	10,00.00	

CASH PAYMENTS

Date	Narrative	Details	Cash £	Bank £	Materials £	Motor £	Drawings £	Stationery £
5.3.X4	Petrol		20.00			20.00		
11.3.X4	Paint	chq		550.00	550.00			
5.3.X4	Drawings	chq		400.00			400.00	
31.3.X4	Ink carts	cash	20.00					20.00
		TOTALS	40.00	950.00	550.00	20.00	400.00	20.00

(b)   Closing cash balance: £300.00 – £40.00 = £260.00

Closing bank balance: £2,250.00 – £950.00 = £1,300.00

20 Contract law and current legislation

 Workbook Activity 8

(a)   **C** – If you suspect money laundering is occurring, you should disclose the issue to your MLRO.

(b)   **C** – If you are involved in money laundering, you face 14 years imprisonment, and/or an unlimited fine.

KAPLAN PUBLISHING

INDEX